# SAUNDARANANDA KAVYA

OF

# ARYA BHADANTA ASVAGHOSA

Owing to the antiquity and rarity of this book, certain pages are regrettably absent, and readability is compromised due to the blurring of the original text. If you possess any insights regarding the availability of these missing sections, kindly inform us. Your assistance is crucial in ensuring the completion of this significant work for the benefit of future generations.

# SAUNDARANANDA KAVYA

OF

## ARYA BHADANTA ASVAGHOSA

EDITED BY

**MAHAMAHOPADHYAYA
HARAPRASAD SHASTRI**

GYAN

*Published by*

Gyan Publishing House
5, Ansari Road
Daryaganj, New Delhi-110002
Phone: 011-47034999, 9811692060
E-mail: books@gyanbooks.com

*Distribution Network*
gyanbooks.com
India, USA, Canada, UK, Australia



ISBN: 978-93-6780-305-9 (HB)

First Published, 1939

2nd Impression 2024

*Printed at:* Gyan Press, Delhi.



**SAUNDARANANDA KAVYA OF ARYA BHADANTA ASVAGHOSA**
Editor: MAHAMAHOPADHYAYA HARAPRASAD SHASTRI

BIBLIOTHECA INDICA

WORK No. 192

---

# SAUNDARANANDA KĀVYA

SANSKRIT TEXT

# SAUNDARANANDA KĀVYA

OF

# ĀRYA BHADANTA AŚVAGHOṢA

EDITED BY

MAHAMAHOPADHYAYA HARAPRASAD SHASTRI,
C.I.E., M.A., D.Litt., F.A.S.B.

*RE-ISSUE*

*With additions by*

*CHINTAHARAN CHAKRAVARTI*

PRINTED AT THE BAPTIST MISSION PRESS

PUBLISHED BY THE ROYAL ASIATIC SOCIETY OF BENGAL

CALCUTTA

1939

## CONTENTS

| | Page |
|---|---|
| Preliminary Note | 7* |
| Bibliography | 11* |
| Abbreviations | 15* |
| Errata | 17* |
| उत्सर्गपत्रम् | 19* |
| Preface to the First edition | i |
| Text | १ |
| Appendix: Textual notes | 127 |
| Emendations | 139 |

# PRELIMINARY NOTE

In 1910 the late Mahamahopadhyaya Hara Prasad Shastri published the *editio princeps* of the *Saundarananda Kāvya* in the *Bibliotheca Indica.* In his preface he explained how in 1898 he discovered the existence of this important poem in Nepal.

The venerable editor was well aware of the imperfections inherent in his work and modestly admitted: 'My future critics may find fault with me, might point out errors of judgment, but I have a satisfaction of having done my best for three or four months which I passed in company with Aśvaghoṣa'.

In a conversation on this subject shortly before his death he maintained this modest attitude, giving full recognition to the brilliant emendations of his labours made by other scholars. Perfect or imperfect, the edition evoked the greatest interest on the part of a select circle of students of Buddhism, and soon an appreciable literature grew up around the work to which some of the most perspicacious Sanskritists added their contributions.

The Shastri, an Indian scholar of the old type, steeped in his Sanskrit knowledge, was somewhat disdainful of the rigid observance of the minor methods and graces of critical scholarship such as unity in transliteration, precision in quotation, method in abbreviation and reference, and so on. Besides, his main life-work had become more and more centred in his bibliographical work, the continuation of Rajendralal Mitra's *Notices*, and the preparation of the Catalogue of the Sanskrit Manuscripts of the Asiatic Society of Bengal. Nevertheless, simultaneous with the performance of the larger task he was amazingly active as a writer in the Bengali vernacular as well as in English. His various publications of smaller Sanskrit texts were, as it were, by-products of his tireless energy. In the *Bibliotheca Indica* he published four smaller and two larger

Sanskrit texts, to which he added the edition of two further small Sanskrit texts in the Asiatic Society's *Memoirs*.

The material response to these publications shown by the world of scholarship in general has been somewhat restricted. The *Six Buddhist Nyāya Tracts*, *Saundarananda Kāvya*, *Catuḥśatikā*, and *Rāmacarita* were all of outstanding importance, but the works only sold very slowly. Only when the Shastri had become an old man the editions had nearly all become disposed of. The undersigned discussed with the Shastri the plan of preparing revised and up-to-date editions of at least the four above-mentioned texts and he welcomed the plan very warmly. Unhappily his death in 1932 prevented its execution.

The Council of the Society has since considered the situation and decided that it would be advisable to prepare new editions of these four texts in some form or other, both in order to make them once more available in response to a persistent and slowly growing demand and as a tribute to the memory of the late scholar.

It seemed advisable to make a beginning with the *Saundarananda*, probably the most important and immediately needed of the four texts. The question arose how to arrange the task. As said, a considerable literature had grown up around the *editio princeps*, most important amongst which are the critical edition and English translation by E. H. Johnston, prepared for the Punjab University (Punjab University Oriental Publications).

Prof. A. C. Woolner, C.I.E., Vice-Chancellor of the Punjab University was consulted and generously gave his blessing to the undertaking. In this connection our acknowledgments are due to Prof. Woolner and the Punjab University. In order to prevent the possibility that the reprint should in any way be regarded as a rival of the Lahore edition the text is made into a re-issue only and not into a new edition. What on the contrary was very necessary was to bring together in an appendix all the critical material available to date, the whole apparatus of suggestions, corrections, emendations, embodied in no less than 15 separate publications, the majority of which are only accessible with great difficulty, especially to students residing in India. The work of seeing through the press a faithful reprint of the text was entrusted to the late Mahamahopadhyaya Kamal Kṛṣṇa Smṛtitirtha, himself a devoted and capable contributor of long standing to the *Bibliotheca Indica.* The final proofs so obtained were then checked off by Mr. Chintaharan Chakravarti to introduce certain formal, but no textual, changes in the text as follows :—

(1) All the errata to the old edition noted by the Shastri himself in the first edition were transferred from the separate list of errata and corrected in the reprinted text itself.

(2) Typographical errors not corrected by the Shastri in his list of errata to the first edition have been left in the reprinted text, as the various emendators have drawn attention to these and so the corrected forms are included in the list of emendations.

(3) The inconsistent use of व and ब in the first edition, so prevalent in Bengal, has been silently remedied throughout.

(4) The Bengali usage of ड़ has throughout been changed into that of ड.

(5) The typographical peculiarities of the Shastri's edition have not been changed in the re-issue. Especially the Shastri's practice of generally not joining the words by sandhi between two feet in a verse has not been disturbed. The instances of this practice, though corrected by Johnston in his critical edition, have not generally been included in the list of variants as too obvious.

(6) The orthographical peculiarities of Johnston's edition (e.g., *gautama* for *gotama*, *vaiḍūrya* for *vaidūrya*, the use of *anusvāra* instead of the usual *m* at the end of each complete half of a śloka, the non-duplication of consonants occurring after *r*, etc.), where they differ from those of the Shastri, have similarly not been included in the list of variants.

(7) The *virāma* has been taken out in the page headings.

Concerning the reprint of the Preface, of which Mr. Chakravarti took exclusive charge, the following remarks are to be noted :—

1. Misprints have been corrected.
2. Diacritical marks have been equalised.
3. The long Pali quotations from the commentary on the *Dhammapada* have been compared with and corrected according to the Pali Text Society's edition, which appeared partly after the publication of the first issue of the *Saundarananda*.
4. Various references have been verified and where necessary corrected, or newly added between square brackets.
5. A few new headings have been introduced, also between square brackets.

New additions to this re-issue, by Mr. Chintaharan Chakravarti, are the following :—

1. An amalgamated list of all emendations, etc., found in the various publications dealing with the *Saundarananda*.
2. A bibliography of the *Saundarananda*, together with a list of abbreviations used in the summary of emendations.

It is hoped that the re-issue in this new and handy, as well as inexpensive, form will be helpful to the students of Sanskrit and of Buddhism, will serve as a tribute to the several scholars who have laboured on the difficult text (and whose work was so fully recognized by the Shastri himself), and will serve as a monument to the memory of the scholar who first brought the important text to light and first published it.

CALCUTTA,
1, Park Street,
*May*, 1939.

JOHAN VAN MANEN,
*General Secretary*,
*Royal Asiatic Society of Bengal*.

# BIBLIOGRAPHY

1905. H. P. Shastri .. A Catalogue of Palm-leaf and selected Paper MSS. belonging to the Durbar Library, Nepal, p. XXXIII, 74.

Notice of a fragmentary MS.

1909. H. P. Shastri .. *The recovery of a Lost Epic by Aśvaghoṣa.* JPASB, (Vol. V, pp. 165-6).

A brief account of the work.

1910. H. P. Shastri .. A critical edition of the work in the *Bibliotheca Indica* Series.

1911. F. W. Thomas .. *Saundaranandakāvya, VIII, 35.* JRAS (1911, pp. 1125-6).

Discussion of the authorship of VIII, 35.

1912. M. A. Baston .. *Le Saundaranandakāvya d'Açvaghoṣa.* Journal Asiatique (Tome XIX, 1912, pp. 79–100).

Translation of cantos I and II with incidental textual criticism.

1914. J. S. Speyer .. *Some notes on the text of Saundarananda the poem of Açvaghoṣa.* Verslagen en Mededeelingen der Koninklijke Akademie van Wetenschappen (Twaalfde Deel, pp. 125–39).

Textual criticism followed by a list of new words which occur in the work but are not registered in the St. Petersburg Dictionary.

1914. Vidhushekara Bhattacharya *The Saundarananda of Aśvaghoṣa.* JRAS (1914, pp. 747-8).

Reference to the mention of Śūnyavāda in the work.

1915. H. P. Shastri .. A Catalogue of Palm-leaf and selected Paper MSS. belonging to the Durbar Library, Nepal (Vol. II, p. XVII, 98).

Notice of a dilapidated palm-leaf MS.

1918. E. Hultzsch .. *Zu Aśvaghosha's Saundarananda.* ZDMG (Band 72, 1918, pp. 111–144).

Textual criticism.

1918. L. de laVallée Poussin *Critical Notes to Saundaranandakāvya.* Bulletin of the School of Oriental Studies, London (Vol. I, Pt. II, pp. 133–40).

Textual criticism.

1919. A. Gawroński .. *Studies about the Sanskrit Buddhist Lit.* Prace Komisji Orjentalistycnej Polskiej, Akademji Umiejętności (Nr. 2, pp. 1–80).

The last two sections of the paper (pp. 49–80) refer to the influence of the poems of Aśvaghoṣa on the *Divyāvadāna* and give critical notes on the text of the *Saundarananda*.

1919. E. Hultzsch .. *Zu Aśvaghosha's Saundarananda.* ZDMG (Band 73, 1919, pp. 229–32).

Textual criticism and reference to traces of influence of Aśvaghoṣa in Subandhu, Bāṇa and Daṇḍin.

1919. H. Jacobi .. ZDMG (Band 73, 1919, p. 232).

Textual criticism (in a letter published as an addendum to the above paper).

1920. E Hultzsch .. *Zu Aśvaghosha's Saundarananda Nr. III.* ZDMG (Band 74, 1920, pp. 293–5).

Textual criticism.

1920. M. Winternitz .. Geschichte der Indischen Littoratur, Zweiter Band (pp. 206–8).

A critical account.

1922. A. Gawroński .. *Notes on the Saundarananda—critical and explanatory—Second Series.* *Op. cit.* Nr. 6 (pp. 1–38).

1922. 1923. B. C. Law .. Saundaranandakāvya (2 editions).

Bengali translation.

1923. G. Tucci .. .. *Note sul Saundarananda Kāvya di Açvaghoṣa.* Rivista degli Studi Orientali (Vol. X pp. 145–9).

Reference to traces of influence of Aśvaghoṣa on Vasubandhu and Hemacandra.

1923, 1927, 1932, 1936. A. B. Keith .. Classical Sanskrit Literature, (pp. 24-5). (Four editions.)

Critical account.

1928. A. Gawroński .. *Notes on the Saundarananda—critical and explanatory—Third Series.* Rocznik Orjentalistyczny (Tom IV, 1926, str. 219–29).

1928. C. W. Gurner .. *Notes on the text of Aśvaghoṣa's Saundarananda.* JRAS (1928, pp. 131-2).

Textual criticism.

1928. E. H. Johnston

Critical Edition with notes.

1928. A. B. Keith .. A History of Sanskrit Literature (pp. 56–58, 59ff.).

Critical account of the work, its style and language.

1929. E. J. Thomas .. JRAS (1929, pp. 352-3).

Review of Johnston's edition.

1930. C. W. Gurner .. *The Psychological Simile in Aśvaghoṣa*—JPASB (Vol. XXVI, pp. 175–80).

Reference to psychological similes in the work.

1930. Sukumar Sen .. *The language of Aśvaghoṣa's Saundarananda-kāvya.* JPASB (XXVI, pp. 181–206).

Study of the linguistic peculiarities of the work.

1932. E. H. Johnston

English translation with an appendix, noting ' addenda and corrigenda to the Sanskrit text '.

1933. E. J. Thomas .. JRAS (1933, pp. 165-6).

Review of Johnston's English translation.

1933. M. Winternitz .. A History of Indian Literature (English translation). (Vol. II, pp. 262–4),

A critical account.

## ABBREVIATIONS USED IN THE LIST OF EMENDATIONS

| | | |
|---|---|---|
| B | .. .. | Baston, 1912.[1] |
| G | .. .. | Gawroński, 1919 |
| G2 | .. .. | Gawroński, 1922. |
| G3 | .. .. | Gawroński, 1928. |
| Gu | .. .. | Gurner, 1928. |
| H | .. .. | Hultzsch, 1918. |
| H2 | .. .. | Hultzsch, 1920. |
| Happ | .. .. | Haraprasad Shastri, 1910—<br>Appendix to *Bibliotheca Indica* edition. |
| J | .. .. | Johnston, edition, 1928. |
| Ja | .. .. | Jacobi, 1919. |
| Japp | .. .. | Johnston, 1932—<br>Appendix to translation. |
| Jmp | .. .. | Misprints in Johnston's edition 1928. |
| Jn | .. .. | Johnston, 1928—<br>Notes in the edition. |
| P | .. .. | de la Vallée Poussin, 1918. |
| S | .. .. | Speyer, 1914. |
| T1 | .. .. | Thomas, 1929. |
| T2 | .. .. | Thomas, 1933. |

---

[1] The year of publication enables the reader to identify the publication from the *Bibliography*, given above.

## ERRATA TO THE REPRINTED TEXT

The following errata have been noticed in the reprint. The errata given in the first edition have been corrected in the reprinted text and are therefore not separately repeated here.

| | | |
|---|---|---|
| I. | 6d | *Read* °बभौ *for* वभौ |
| III. | 27c | *Read* °मधिगम्यमुनेः *for* °मधिगम्य मुनेः |
| IV. | 29c | *Read* पुरतोविवत्तुः *for* पुरतो विवत्तुः |
| V. | 30a | *Read* बधान *for* वधान |
| V. | 30b | *Read* °बाणाः *for* °वाणाः |
| V. | 52d | *Read* °बभासे *for* °वभासे |
| XIII. | 22a | *Read* °निषत् सौम्य *for* °निष सौम्यत् |
| XVI. | 14d | *Read* °प्यवैहि *for* °प्यथैहि |

# उत्सर्गपत्रम्

स्वस्ति । श्रीमदतिप्रचण्डभुजदण्डेत्यादि-विविध-विरुदावलि-विराजित-मानोन्नत-श्रीश्रीश्रीमहाराज मेजर जनरल सर चन्द्र-शम्सेर जङ्ग बाहादुर राणा जि, सि, बि, जि, सि, एस, आइ एण्ड डि, सि, एल अनररि कर्णेल फोर्थ गोर्खाज् खोङ् लिन् पिम्भा कोकाङ् वाङ् स्यान प्राइम मिनिष्टार एण्ड मार्शेल, नेपाल करकमलेषु ।

यदश्वघोषः प्रवरः कवीनां
चकार काव्यं रसभावपूर्णम् ।
प्रमाश्रयं लोकहितं गभीरं
बभूव तत् कालवशाद्विलुप्तम् ॥

तवाश्रयाद् भारतरत्नकोषा-
दुद्धृत्य यन्मुद्रितमेतदद्य ।
गुणानुसन्धाननिविष्टबुद्धे
गुणज्ञतायास्तव सोऽनुभावः ॥

यथाश्वघोषस्य गुरोः प्रसादात्
सुविस्तृतं राज्यमभूत् कणर्कैः ।
तत्काव्यमुज्जीवयतस्तथा ते
राज्यं समृद्धञ्च सुभिक्षमस्तु ॥

# PREFACE

In 1898 I examined very hastily a Palm-leaf MS, greatly dilapidated, of Saundaranandaṃ Kāvyaṃ at the Durbar Library, Nepal. It was so dilapidated that I did not venture to turn the leaves over. I mentioned the existence of the manuscript in p. 74 of my Nepal Catalogue published in 1905. When again in Nepal in 1907 one of my first objects was to examine this manuscript very carefully. It proved to be a poem by Aśvaghoṣa. But as it was impossible to make a copy from that ruined manuscript, I expressed my regret that such an important work should be obtained in such a ruined condition. The ever kind and courteous Librarian, Subba Viṣṇuprasāda Rāja-Bhaṇḍārī, brought a complete paper manuscript of the work for my inspection. It was written in the 18th century Newari hand and full of mistakes. But it delighted me to have a complete copy of one of Aśvaghoṣa's great epics; and I at once asked for a copy of the MS. Coming to Calcutta, I began to copy this manuscript for the press, but found the task very difficult. For modern scribes of Nepal do not know Sanskrit and change च and छ at pleasure. [The three sibilants and the two nasals are not carefully distinguished.] The final त is in most cases dropped; and they often make strange combinations according to their fancy. The 18th century MS was thus full of inaccuracies, and the modern copy made for me simply added to these.

When my MS copy for the press was ready, I found it impossible to go to press with that copy, and I wondered how Prof. E. B. Cowell prepared his MS for the press, of the Buddhacarita with two 19th century MSS only. I knew that the Mahārāja of Nepal was very unwilling to lend Palm-leaf MSS to anybody. So I did not venture for a long time to ask him for a loan of the MS. But at last I took courage and explained to him the circumstance under which I could not do without the loan, and that a good work of a great man would be lost without it. He was graciously pleased to lend me both the dilapidated Palm-leaf and the Paper manuscripts for three months, and I set to work at once.

The Palm-leaf MS, which I indicate with the letters P.L.M., is complete. It has thirty-five leaves of six lines each. But the first two lines of the reverse side and the last two lines of the obverse side of every leaf are almost gone. Sometimes the lacuna invades the third and even the fourth line. There are some worm-eaten places besides. But the MS is of great use. It is written in the 12th century Newari character. The writing agrees with that of Professor Bendall's No. 1693, dated 1165; and it is uniformly correct. I have, wherever possible, followed the readings of P.L.M.

Where that aid was not available, I had to follow the Paper manuscript indicated by P.M., and my difficulties were great. I had to restore letters, sometimes words; I had to slightly alter the text, which I have indicated by the letter T in the notes. Sometimes I had to carefully observe the remnants of letters in P.L.M., sometimes the top or end of a vertical stroke, sometimes a dot, sometimes the remnants of a curve to ascertain what might have been the word in that manuscript. This has necessitated the inclusion of notes on reading at the end of the work. My future critics may find fault with me, might point out errors of judgment; but I have the satisfaction of having done my best for three or four months which I passed in company with Aśvaghoṣa.

It may not be out of place to mention here that I do not think that P.M. is a transcript of P.L.M. There are remarks in the 'notes' which will show the readers that the original from which P.M. has been copied is a different MS from our P.L.M. For P.M. sometimes gives a better reading; sometimes it supplies omissions in P.L.M.

[AUTHORSHIP]

Now the question is: Is the work really by Aśvaghoṣa? And my answer is in the affirmative. My reasons are as follow:—

(i) The last colophon of Saundarananda in both P.L.M. and P.M. describes Aśvaghoṣa as Sāketaka, Suvarṇākṣīputra, as Bhadanta, Ārya and Ācārya—the same colophon in fact that is given in the Tibetan version of Aśvaghoṣa's Buddhacarita (see Thomas' paper on Matṛiceṭa and Mahārājakanikalekha—Ind. Ant., 1903, September, p. 350).

(ii) The two works Saundarananda and Buddhacarita supplement each other in giving information about Buddha's life. His departure from the palace and his studies and meditations are given in detail in the Buddhacarita, but very briefly in Saundarananda. The establishment of Kapilavāstu as a capital is given in detail in Saundarananda, but very briefly in Buddhacarita. Buddhacarita touches only on the conversion of Nanda, but it is expanded into a whole poem in Saundarananda.

(iii) The Vedic and the Paurāṇika allusions are almost identical in the two works. The failings of Parāśara are mentioned in B.C. IV. 76 and in S. VII. 29. Vaśiṣṭha's failings are described in B.C. IV. 77 and S. VII. 28. The failings of Pāṇḍu are given in B.C. IV. 79 and in S. VII. 45. The troubles of Vyāsa with a woman of ill-fame at Benares are described in B.C. IV. 16 and S. VII. 30. The failings of Ṛṣyaśṛaṅga, Gautama, Viśvāmitra and others are similarly described in both the works. A deep knowledge of Brahminic lore is perceptible in both the works.

(iv) The words तर्ष, घर्म्मन्, पुष्पवर्ष, प्रविद्ध uncommon in classical Sanskrit are common in both these works. The incorrect form of गृह्य is used in both the works. The collocation प्रासादसोपानतलप्रणादं and बहुविविधमार्गगामिनं are common to both. उप + पद in the sense of birth, परि + गम in the sense of spending time, and स्था in the sense of standing still, are peculiar to both. Instances may be multiplied, but I need not increase the bulk of the Preface with them.

(v) Peculiarities of style are the same in both. Both the works are fine examples of the Vaidarbhī rīti and Prasāda guṇa (or the perspicuity of style), with this difference, that the style of the Buddhacarita compared to the beautiful style of the Saundarananda, appears to be a little ruder. This may be owing to the want of good materials on which Cowell worked, or perhaps it was the earlier work. Deviations from Classical Sanskrit are numerically less in the Saundarananda than in the Buddhacarita. The easiness and flow are greater in the Saundarananda, and the poetry deeper and more attractive.

[THE STYLE OF THE SAUNDARANANDA]

But for want of art the Saundarananda would have been equal to any of the best poems in Sanskrit. I would not venture to brand either the poetry or the language of Saundarananda as artificial. The language is popular and the poetry fascinating.

To an ordinary critic Kālidāsa's fame rests on similes. If so, Aśvaghoṣa certainly excels him. Nothing can be simpler than the following :—

तां सुन्दरीं चेन्न लभेत नन्दः
सा वा निषेवेत न तं नतभ्रूः ।
द्वन्द्वं ध्रुवं तद् विकलं न शोभे-
तान्योन्यहीनाविव रात्रिचन्द्रौ ॥ [IV. 7.]

Compared to this—

परस्परेण स्पृहणीयशोभं
न चेदिदं द्वन्द्वमयोजयिष्यत् ।

अस्मिन् द्वये रूपविधानयत्नः
पत्युः प्रजानां वितथोऽभविष्यत् ॥
[*Kumārasambhava* VII. 66.]

vould appear to be stale and insipid.

Compare also—

तं गौरवं बुद्धगतं चकर्ष
भार्य्यानुरागः पुनराचकर्ष ।
सोऽनिश्चयान्नापि ययौ न तस्थौ
तरंस्तरङ्गेष्विव राजहंसः ॥ [IV. 42.]

and

मार्गाचलव्यतिकराकुलितेव सिन्धुः ।
शैलाधिराजतनया न ययौ न तस्थौ ॥
[*Kumārasambhava* V. 85.]

In the Buddhacarita are to be found all sorts of Buddhist technical terms. But in the Saundarananda the most abstruse ideas of the Buddhist philosophy are expressed in the simplest language and with the help of the most homely netaphors, as an instance :—

दीपो यथा निर्वृतिमभ्युपेतो
नैवावनिं गच्छति नान्तरिक्षम् ।
दिशं न काञ्चिद् विदिशं न काञ्चित्
स्नेहक्षयात् केवलमेति शान्तिम् ।
तथा कृती निर्वृतिमभ्युपेतो
नैवावनिं गच्छति नान्तरिक्षम् ।
दिशं न काञ्चित् विदिशं न काञ्चित्
क्लेशक्षयात् केवलमेति शान्तिम् ॥ XVI. 28, 29.

The four noble truths are expressed in the following terms :—

बाधात्मकं दुःखमिदं प्रसक्तं
दुःखस्य हेतुः प्रभवात्मकोऽयं

दुःखक्षयो निःसरणात्मकोऽयं
त्यागात्मकोऽयं प्रशमाय मार्गः ॥ XVI. 4.

जरादयो नैकविधाः प्रजानां
सत्यां प्रवृत्तौ प्रभवन्त्यनर्थाः ।
प्रवात्सु घोरेष्वपि मारुतेषु
न ह्यप्रसूतास्तरवश्चलन्ति ॥ XVI. 10.

तज्जन्मनो नैकविधस्य सौम्य
तृष्णादयो हेतव इत्यवेत्य
तांश्छिन्धि दुःखाद् यदि निर्म्मुमुक्षा
कार्य्यक्षयः कारणसंक्षयाद्धि ॥ XVI. 25.

The turning of the wheel of law is expressed in the following terms:—

अथ धर्म्मचक्रमृतनाभि धृतिमतिसमाधिनेमिमत् ।
तत्र विनयनियमारमृषिर्जगतो हिताय परिषद्यवर्त्तयत् ॥
III. 11.

[SUMMARY OF THE STORY]

Kapila, belonging to the Gautama gotra, practised austerities like the Gautama Kakṣīvān. He was second to Dīrghatapas and third to Kāvya and Aṅgirāh. His hermitage was on the slopes of the Himavat.

Some Ikṣvāku Princes came to that hermitage, banished by their father at the instigation of their step-mother. Kapila became their Upādhyāya, and from the gotra of their Guru they became Gautamas though they were Kautsas before this. The sons of one father may have different gotras from accepting different Gurus, just as Rāma was Gārgya and Vāsubhadra was Gautama. These Ikṣāku Princes were called Śākyas, because they lived at a spot covered by Śāka trees. One day the Ṛṣi rose to the sky with a pitcher of water and asked them to follow him in their conveyances and told them to mark the line of water falling from the inexhaustible pitcher. Then he asked them to raise a city on the ground marked out by the water-line after his death—which happened in proper time. The Princes became unrestrained and the Ṛṣis left the place for the Himālayas. The Princes in their roamings obtained much hoarded treasure, and with that built a splendid city, which, as it was built at the Vāstu or residence of Kapila, was named Kapilavāstu.

In ancient India several hermitages were converted into cities; the most notable of them is Kauśāmbī, from the hermitage Kuśāmba. As they never imposed taxes on people against the rule of the Śāstras, this city soon became rich and populous. But a kingdom without a king is a prey to anarchy. So the Princes raised their eldest brother to the throne.

After some generations Śuddhodana became the king of the Śākyas. He was a good king and an ideal man.

Just at this time the gods of the Śuddhāvāsa heaven were on a tour of inspection on earth with the view to find a family in which Buddha, falling from the Tuṣita heaven, may be born; and they selected the Śākya family. The Queen Māyā saw in a dream that a white elephant with six tusks was entering into her womb. The dream was interpreted very favourably, and a short time after Buddha was born. A younger queen gave birth to another boy named Nanda, the handsomeness of whose person earned for him the surname Sundara. Between these two sons the king shone like the Madhyadeśa between Himavat and Pāripātra. Of these Nanda sought for pleasure, while Buddha was always grave and serious.

He left Kapilavāstu for the purpose of practising austerities. He first went to Arāḍa, the preacher of emancipation, and then to Udraka, the lover of spiritual peace. But he left them as their ways did not appear to be the proper ways. Anxious to know what is the highest bliss in this world, he practised severe penances, but he left that too, as it was not the proper way. Austerities he thought lead to disease, and so he ate rice and determined to know the immortal. He went under a fig tree and began to meditate. He conquered the armies of Māra and obtained the imperishable truth, and in order to preach that truth he went to the city surrounded by Varaṇā and Asā. There he revolved for the first time the wheel of law. Having instructed many people in Gayā, in Kāśi and at Girivraja, he went to instruct his own people at Kapilavastu. The meeting of the father and the son was extremely pathetic, but Buddha was not moved at all. He preached and induced many people to enter the monastic order, and those who could not enter the order owing to serious family responsibilities, practised the rules of the order at home. The king, finding that his son was a much greater being, fell at his feet and received his instructions.

Though the whole city was under commotion, Nanda lived in his palace, immersed in pleasures in the company of his wife, a famous beauty. The husband and the wife were very fond of each other. One day the wife asked her husband to hold a mirror before her to enable her to paint and decorate her face. She looked at the beard of her husband and began to paint her cheek in imitation of a beard. The husband playfully bedewed the mirror and she was non-plussed. She felt annoyed but was at last appeased, and she finished her painting, when an old maid-servant informed the Prince that Buddha came to his house for begging his food, but as no one was there to give him anything he went away. Ashamed at his conduct Nanda left the palace in spite of the protestations of his wife who, however, extorted a promise from him to come before the paint in her cheek was dry, and went in search of the *Muni*. He found Buddha surrounded by a large concourse of men and so could not approach him. He waited and waited and very late Nanda prostrated himself before Buddha and urged him to accept his hospitality. But Buddha hinted that he did not require it. He placed his alms-bowl in Nanda's hand, but Nanda was so anxious to return to his wife before the paint was dry that he wished to go back with the bowl in hand. Buddha saw this and spiritually attracted him. But Nanda's mind was bent on home. Buddha asked him to follow him to the Vihāra, which Nanda had to do. There Buddha instructed him. But it had no effect. Then Vaideha Muni came to the place, and was ordered by Buddha to initiate Nanda. But Nanda positively refused to renounce the world. Vaideha Muni reported the matter to Buddha who appealed to the good sense of Nanda. "I am your elder brother. I have renounced the world. Many of the Śākyas have done the same, others are leading an ascetic life though at home. All great Rājās renounce the world and why should you not do the same?" Nanda gave a reluctant consent and he was immediately shaved. Nanda wept bitterly, but in vain.

Sundarī was greatly affected at the news. Her lamentations take up the whole of the 6th Canto. The next canto is devoted to the sorrows of Nanda who finds no pleasure in a mendicant life and thinks of failings of great Ṛṣis and great kings and at last resolves to fly away from mendicant life as soon as Buddha goes out the next day for begging.

The next canto begins with Maitreya, a Bhikṣu, asking Nanda how he felt. They go to a retired spot where they argue out the question in full, in two cantos, the 8th and 9th. The 8th condemns the company of females and the 9th is directed against pride in general. Nanda was inexorable, and so Maitreya reported the affairs to Buddha who sent for Nanda, and finding him unshaken in his determination, took his hand and went up to heaven. They passed like birds through the Himalayan regions, which are described with great power and fancy. Then Buddha saw a she-monkey with one eye only, and asked if Nanda's wife was better than that blind creature. Nanda said 'infinitely better.' Then they passed to heaven, where the Apsaras caught the fancy of Nanda, who thought the distance between those and his wife was as great as that between her and the one-eyed monkey. He was anxious to get those, but Buddha told him that they could be had only by the practice of austerities, and Nanda consented to practise them for the sake of heavenly damsels, Buddha standing guarantee for his success.

Nanda got weak and emaciated by his penances. He was austere but his heart was all for the heavenly damsels. Ánanda came to him, congratulated him for his change of front and asked him if it was true that he was practising austerities for the sake of Apsaras. Being replied in the affirmative, he began a tirade against the enjoyments of the world and even those in heaven, all of which he declared to be transitory. The tirade had the desired effect. It produced a sense of shame. Nanda forgot his wife for the Apsaras and he now forgot the Apsaras for immortality. He became bold enough to approach Buddha and tell him that he was no longer anxious for the heavenly damsels. Glad to hear this from Nanda, Buddha lectured to him for nearly five cantos and then asked him to meditate on peace and spiritual advancement. At the beginning of the 17th Canto Nanda retires to a forest for deep meditation. He is successful. He gets to the door of Nirvāṇa. He practises the four meditations, understands the evanescent character of the world, and becomes an Arhat. Grateful for what Buddha had done for him, he comes and takes the feet of the great preacher who orders him not to be satisfied with his own emancipation but to emancipate others also. Herein comes the distinctive creed of Mahāyāna. He goes out, sees his wife and relations, but quite a different Nanda. With this the book comes to an end, worthy of a great poet and of a great preacher.

> इत्यर्हतः परमकारुणिकस्य शास्तुः
> मूर्ध्ना वचश्च चरणौ च समं गृहीत्वा ।
> स्वस्थः प्रशान्तहृदयो विनिवृत्तकार्य्यः
> पार्श्वान्मुनेः प्रतिययौ विमदः करीव ॥
> भिक्षार्थं समये विवेश च पुरं दृष्टीर्जनस्याक्षिपन् ।
> लाभालाभसुखासुखादिषु समः स्वस्थेन्द्रियो निःस्पृहः ॥
> निर्मोक्षाय चकार तत्र च कथाः काले जनायार्थिने ।
> नैवोन्मार्गगतान् जनान् परिभवन्नात्मानमुत्कर्षयन् ॥

There are two more verses in which the poet explains the object of the poem. They are :—

> इत्येषा व्युपशान्तये न रतये मोक्षार्थगर्भाकृतिः
> श्रोतॄणां ग्रहणार्थमन्यमनसां काव्योपचारात् कृता ।
> यन्मोक्षात् कृतमन्यदत्र हि मया तत् काव्यधर्म्मात् कृतम्
> पातुं तिक्तमिवौषधं मधुयुतं हृद्यं कथं स्यादिति ॥
> प्रायेणालोक्य लोकं विषयरतिपरं मोक्षात् प्रतिहतं
> काव्यव्याजेन तत्त्वं कथितमिह मया मोक्षपरमिति ॥
> तद् बुद्ध्वा शामिकं यत् तदवहितमितो न ललितम्
> पांसुभ्यो धातुजेभ्यो नियतमुपकरं चामीकरमिति ॥

This shows that the poet wrote other works not of a poetical nature. This work he wrote काव्यधर्म्मात् ; other works he wrote मोक्षात् (that is, for liberation, emancipation, philosophy). By this Aśvaghoṣa certainly alludes to his philosophical works, many of which are mentioned in Nanjio's Catalogue of the Chinese Tripiṭaka, and one of which has been translated from Japanese into English.

Nāgārjuna is the founder of the Mādhyamaka theory of the Mahāyāna school. He is often called the founder of the Mahāyāna itself. This is wrong, for the word Mahāyāna was known before him. Aśvaghoṣa has a book named Mahāyānaśraddhotpāda Śāstra; and even before him there were works of the Mahāyāna school, for instance, the Laṅkāvatāra Sūtra and the Śrīmālasūtra are known as Māhāyāna Sūtras. So Nāgārjuna was the founder of one of the sects of the Māhāyāna school. The Madhyamaka theory did not exist before him. The theory of Śūnyatā is the essence of the Mādhyamaka theory. But in Śaundarananda the idea—even the word Śūnyatā—does not occur. So Aśvaghoṣa seems to have belonged to some earlier school of the Māhāyāna, and that school, I believe, was Yogācāra. He often speaks of the practice of Yoga and uses the word Yogācāra twice. (See XIV, 19, and XV, 68.) The Vibhāṣā commentary is said to have been composed in the third council of Kaniṣka, and the Vaibhāṣika school of philosophy had its origin at that time. So Yogācāra comes between the Vaibhāṣika and the Mādhyamaka.

### NANDA LEGEND FROM SANSKRIT SOURCES

[The Chinese Version of the] Buddhacarita, SBE, Vol. 19, Chapter XIX:—

"The princes, too, of the Śākya tribe, their minds enlightened to perceive the perfect fruit of righteousness, 1583.

"Entirely satiated with glittering joys of the world, forsaking home, rejoiced to join his company (become hermits). Ānanda, Nanda, Kin-pi (Kimbila), Anuruddha, 1584.

"Nandupananda, with Cuṇḍadana, all these principal nobles and others of the Śākya family, 1585.

1586 "From the teaching of Buddha became disciples and accepted the law."

Kern's *Manual of Indian Buddhism*, page 27, note 7

refers to the 35th legend of the Bhadra Kalpāvadāna in which Sundara and Sundarananda appear synonymous with Nanda. But unfortunately the Asiatic Society's copy of the Bhadra Kālpāvadāna contains 34 legends only.

### The Story of Nanda in the Pāli Literature

In the Dhammapada the following verses (Dhp. Nos. 13 and 14) are said to have been uttered by Buddha referring to Nanda :—

Yathā agāraṁ ducchannaṁ vuṭṭhī samativijjhati
Evaṁ abhāvitaṁ cittaṁ rāgo samativijjhati,
Yathā agāraṁ succhannaṁ vuṭṭhī na samativijjhati
Evaṁ Subhāvitaṁ cittaṁ rāgo na samativijjhati.

The first verse was said with reference to Nanda's state of mind before conversion, and the second with reference to his state of mind after the attainment of *sambodhi*. The commentary on these verses gives in full the story of his conversion. It runs thus [1] :—* * * * * * tato dutiyadivase Nanda-kumārassa abhisekagehappavesana-vivāha-maṅgalesu vattamānesu (satthā), piṇḍāya pavisitvā Nanda-kumārassa hatthe pattaṁ datvā maṅgalaṁ vatvā uṭṭhāyāsanā pakkamanto kumārassa hatthato pattaṁ na gaṇhi. So pi Tathāgate gāravena 'pattaṁ vo bhante gaṇhathā' ti vattuṁ nāsakkhi; evaṁ pana cintesi: 'sopānasīse pattaṁ gaṇhissatīti'; Satthā tasmiṁ pi ṭhāne na gaṇhi. Itaro 'sopānapādamūle gaṇhissatīti' cintesi; Satthā tatthāpi na gaṇhi. Itaro 'rājaṅgane gaṇhissatīti' cintesi; Satthā tatthāpi na gaṇhi. Kumāro nivattitukāmo aruciyā gacchanto Satthu gāravena 'pattaṁ gaṇhathā' ti vattuṁ na sakkoti; 'idha gaṇhissati, ettha ettha gaṇhissatīti' cintento gacchati.

---

1 [*The Commentary on the Dhammapada*, H. C. Norman, Pali Text Society, London (1906–1915), Vol. I, pp. 115–122.]

Tasmiṁ khaṇe Janapadakalyāṇiyā ācikkhiṁsu: 'ayye Bhagavā Nandarājānaṁ gahetvā gato, tumhehi taṁ vinākarissatīti'. Sā udakabindūhi paggharanteh'eva aḍḍhullikhitehi kesehi vegena gantvā: 'tuvaṭaṁ kho ayyaputta āgaccheyyāsīti' āha. Taṁ tassā vacanaṁ tassa hadaye tiriyaṁ patitvā viya ṭhitaṁ; Satthāpi tassa hatthato pattaṁ agaṇhitvā va taṁ vihāraṁ netvā: 'pabbajissasi Nandāti' āha. So Buddhagāravena 'na pabbajissāmīti' avatvā 'āma pabbajissāmīti' āha. Satthā: 'tena hi Nandaṁ pabbājethāti' āha. Satthā Kapilapuraṁ gantvā tatiyadivase Nandaṁ pabbājesi * * *

* * * * * * * * *

Evaṁ satthari Jetavane viharante āyasmā Nando ukkaṇṭhitvā bhikkhūnaṁ etaṁ atthaṁ ārocesi: 'anabhirato ahaṁ āvuso, brahmacariyaṁ carāmi, na sakkomi brahmacariyaṁ santānetuṁ, sikkhaṁ paccakkhāya hīnāyāvattissāmīti'. Bhagavā taṁ pavattiṁ sutvā āyasmantaṁ Nandaṁ pakkosāpetvā etad avoca: 'saccaṁ kira tvaṁ Nanda sambahulānaṁ bhikkhūnaṁ evaṁ ārocesi: "anabhirato ahaṁ . . . . . hīnāyāvattissāmīti."' 'Evaṁ bhanteti.' 'Kīssa pana tvaṁ Nanda anabhirato brahmacariyaṁ carasi, na sakkosi brahmacariyaṁ santānetuṁ sikkhaṁ paccakkhāya hīnāyāvattissasīti.' 'Sākiyānī maṁ bhante Janapadakalyānī gharā nikkhamantassa aḍḍhullikhitehi kesehi apaloketvā etad avoca—"tuvaṭaṁ kho ayyaputta āgaccheyyāsīti," so kho ahaṁ bhante tad anussaramāno anabhirato brahmacariyaṁ carāmi . . . . . . . . . . . . . . . . . . . . hīnāyāvattissāmīti.' Atha kho Bhagavā āyasmantaṁ Nandaṁ bāhāya gahetvā iddhibalena tāvatiṁsa-devalokaṁ nento antarāmagge ekasmiṁ jhāmakkhette jhāmakhānuke nisinnaṁ chinna-kaṇṇa-nāsā-naṅguṭṭhaṁ ekaṁ paluṭṭhamakkaṭiṁ dassetvā tāvatiṁsabhavane Sakkassa devaraññọ upaṭṭhānaṁ āgatāni kakuṭapādāni pañca accharāsatāni dassesi. 'Kakuṭapādānīti' rattavaṇṇatāya pārāpatapāda

-sadisāni pādāni. Dassetvā ca pan 'āha: 'tvaṁ kiṁ maññasi Nanda katamā nu kho abhirūpatarā vā dassanīyatarā vā pāsādikatarā vā sākiyānī vā Janapadakalyāṇī imāni vā pañca accharāsatāni kakuṭapādānīti.' 'Seyyathā pi sā bhante chinna-kaṇṇanāsā-naṅguṭṭha-paluṭṭha-makkaṭī, evaṁ eva kho bhante Sākiyānī Janapadakalyāṇī imesaṁ pañcannaṁ accharāsatānaṁ upanidhāya saṅkhaṁ pi na upeti, kalaṁ pi na upeti, kalabhāgaṁ pi na upeti; atha kho imān'eva pañca accharā-satāni abhirūpatarāni c'eva dassanīyatarāni ca pāsādikatarāni cā ti.' 'Abhirama Nanda ahaṁ te pāṭibhogo pañcannaṁ accharāsatānaṁ paṭilābhāya kakuṭapādīnaṁ ti.' 'Sace me bhante Bhagavā pāṭibhogo ................ abhiramissām'ahaṁ bhante bhagavati brahmacariyeti.' Atha kho Bhagavā āyasmantaṁ Nandaṁ gahetvā tattha antarahito Jetavane yeva pāturahosi. Assosuṁ kho bhikkhū: 'āyasmā kira Nando Bhagavato bhātā matucchāputto accharānaṁ hetu brahmacariyaṁ carati, Bhagavā kir'assa pāṭibhogo pañcannaṁ accharāsatānaṁ paṭilābhāya kakuṭapādīnaṁ ti.' Atha kho āysmato Nandassa sahāyakā bhikkhū āyasmantaṁ Nandaṁ bhatakavādena ca upakkitakavādena ca samudācaranti: 'bhatako kirāyasmā Nando, upakkitako kirāyasmā Nando, accharānaṁ hetu .......... kakuṭapādīnaṁti'. Atha kho āyasmā Ānando sahāyakānaṁ bhikkhūnaṁ bhatakavādena ca upakkitakavādena ca aṭṭiyamāno harāyamāno jigucchamāno eko vūpakaṭṭho appamatto ātāpī pahitatto viharanto, no cirass'eva yass' atthāya kulaputtā sammad eva agārasmā anagāriyaṁ pabbajanti tad anuttaraṁ brahmacariyapariyosānaṁ diṭṭhe va dhamme sayaṁ abhiññā sacchikatva, 'khīṇā jāti, vusitaṁ brahmacariyaṁ, kataṁ karaṇīyaṁ nāparaṁ itthattāyā'ti abhiññāsi; aññataro ca kho pan' āyasmā arahataṁ ahosi.

Ath' ekā devatā rattibhāge sakalaṁ Jetavanaṁ obhāsetvā Satthāraṁ upasaṅkamitvā vanditvā ārocesi: 'āyasmā bhante Nando Bhagavato mātucchāputto āsavānaṁ khayā..............upasampajja viharatīti'. Bhagavato pi kho ñānaṁ udapādi, 'Nando āsavānaṁ khayā.......... upasampajja viharatīti.

So p'āyasmā tassā rattiyā accayena Bhagavantaṁ upasaṁkamitvā vanditva etad avoca: 'yaṁ me bhante Bhagavā pāṭibhogo pañcannaṁ accharāsatānaṁ paṭilābhāya kakuṭapādīnaṁ, muñcām'ahaṁ bhante Bhagavantaṁ etasmā patissavāti'. 'Mayā pi kho Nanda cetasā ceto paticca vidito. "Nando āsavānaṁ khayā.......... viharatīti"; ' devatā pi me etaṁ atthaṁ ārocesi, 'āyasmā Nando......viharatīti; yad eva kho te Nanda anupādaya āsavehi cittaṁ vimuttaṁ, athāhaṁ mutto etasmā patissavā ti'. * * * * * *

In the Theragāthā we find the following two significant verses put into the mouth of Nanda:—

Ayonisomanasīkārā maṇḍanaṁ anuyuñjisaṁ,
Uddhato capalo cāsiṁ kāmarāgena aṭṭito.
Upāyakusalenāhaṁ buddhenādiccabandhunā
Yoniso paṭipajjitvā bhave cittaṁ udabbahinti.

(Theragāthā verses 157, 158.)

These verses were said by Nanda after he became an arhat.

Of Nanda's wife we have the following references in Pāli literature. The following verse in the Dhammapada was said by the Buddha with reference to her:—

Aṭṭhīnaṁ nagaraṁ katvā maṁsalohitalepanaṁ,
Yattha jarā ca maccu ca, māno makkho ca ohito.

(Dhp. verse 150.)

On account of her beauty she used to be called Rūpanandā, Sundarīnandā and Janapadakalyāṇī. The commentary on the above verse contains the following story relating to her [1]:—

[1] [Norman—*op. cit.*, Vol. III, pp. 113–117.]

* * * sā kira ekadivasaṁ cintesi: 'mayhaṁ jeṭṭhabhātiko pi rajjasiriṁ pahāya pabbajitvā loke aggapuggalo Buddho jāto, putto pi'ssa Rāhulakumāro pabbajito, bhattāpi me pabbajito, mātāpi me pabbajitā, aham pi ettake ñātijane pabbajite gehe kiṁ karissāmi, aham pi pabbajissāmīti' bhikkhunīupassayaṁ gantvā pabbaji ñātisinehen'eva no saddhāya; abhirūpatāya pana Rūpānandā ti paññāyi. Sā 'Satthā kira rūpaṁ aniccaṁ...... vadetī' ti sutvā, 'so evaṁ dassanīye pasādike mama pi rūpe dosaṁ katheyyā'ti satthu sammukhibhāvaṁ na gacchati. * * * * * * * * Rūpanandā bhikkhunīnañc'eva upāsikānaṁ ca santikā Tathāgatassa guṇakathanaṁ sutvā cintesi: ativiya me bhātikassa vaṇṇaṁ kathenti, ekadivasaṁ me rūpe dosaṁ kathento kittakaṁ kathessati, yannūnāhaṁ bhikkhunīhi saddhiṁ gantvā attānaṁ adassetvā va Tathāgataṁ passitvā dhammaṁ sunitvā āgaccheyyan' ti, sā 'ahaṁ ajja dhammasavaṇaṁ gamissāmī'ti bhikkhunīnaṁ ārocesi. Bhikkhuniyo 'cirassaṁ vata Rūpanandāya satthu upaṭṭhānaṁ gantukāmatā uppannā, ajja satthā imaṁ nissāya vicittadhammadesanaṁ desissatī' ti tuṭṭhamānasā taṁ adāya nikkhamiṁsu. Sā nikkhantakālato paṭṭhāya, 'ahaṁ attānaṁ n'eva dassessāmīti' cintesi. Satthā 'ajja Rūpanandā mayhaṁ upaṭṭhānaṁ āgamissati, kīdisi nu kho tassā dhammadesanā sappāyā' ti cintetvā, rūpagarukā esā, attabhāve balavasinehā, kaṇṭakena kaṇṭakuddharaṇaṁ viya, rūpen'ev' assā rūpanimmadanaṁ sappāyaṁ' ti sanniṭṭhānaṁ katvā tassā vihāraṁ pavisanasamaye ekaṁ abhirūpaṁ itthiṁ soḷasavassuddesikaṁ rattavatthanivatthaṁ sabbābharaṇapaṭimaṇḍitaṁ vījaniṁ gahetvā attano santike ṭhatvā vījamānaṁ iddhibalena abhinimmi. Taṁ kho pana itthiṁ satthā c'eva passati Rūpanandā ca. Sā bhikkkunīhi saddhiṁ pavisitvā bhikkhunīnaṁ piṭṭhipasse ṭhatvā pañcapatiṭṭhitena Sathāraṁ vanditvā bhikkhunīnaṁ antare nisinnā pādantarato paṭṭhāya satthāraṁ

olokentī lakkhaṇavicittaṁ anubyañjanasamujjalaṁ byāmappabhāparikkhittaṁ Satthu sarīraṁ disvā puṇṇa-candasassirikaṁ mukhaṁ olokentī samīpe ṭhitaṁ itthirūpaṁ addasa. Sā taṁ oloketvā attabhāvaṁ olokentī, suvaṇṇa-rājahaṁsiyā purato kākasadisaṁ attānaṁ amaññi, iddhi-mayarūpaṁ diṭṭhakālato paṭṭhāy' eva hi'ssā akkhīni bhamiṁsu. Sā 'aho imissā kesā sobhanā aho nalāṭā sobhanā'ti sabbesaṁ sarīrappadesānaṁ rūpasiriyā samāka-ḍḍhitacittatāya tasmiṁ rūpe balavasinehā ahosi. Satthā tassā tattha abhiratiṁ ñatvā dhammaṁ desento va taṁ rūpaṁ soḷasavassuddesikabhāvaṁ atikkamitvā vīsativassu-ddesikabhāvaṁ katvā dassesi. Rūpanandā oloketvā 'na vata idaṁ rūpaṁ purimasadisaṁ ti' thokaṁ virattacittā ahosi. Satthā anukkamen'eva tassā itthiyā sakiṁvijātavaṇṇaṁ majjhīmitthīvaṇṇaṁ jarājiṇṇamahallikitthīvaṇṇaṁ ti dassesi. Sāpi anupubbeneva 'idaṁ antarahitaṁ idaṁ pi antarhitaṁ' ti jarājiṇṇakāle taṁ virajjamānā khaṇḍadantaṁ phalitasiraṁ obhaggaṁ gopānasīvaṅkaṁ daṇḍaparāyaṇaṁ pavedhamānaṁ disvā ativiya virajji. Atha satthā taṁ vyādhinā abhi-bhūtaṁ katvā dassesi, sā taṁ khaṇaṁ yeva daṇḍaṁ ca tālavantaṁ ca chaḍḍetvā mahāviravaṁ viravamānā bhūmiyaṁ patitvā sake muttakarīse nimuggā aparāparaṁ vaddhī. Rūpanandā taṁ pi disvā ativiya virajji. Satthāpi tassā itthiyā maraṇaṁ dassesi. Sā taṁ khaṇaṁ yeva uddhumātakabhāvaṁ āpajji, navahi vaṇamukhehi pubbavaṭṭiyo c'eva puḷavā ca paggharimsu kākādayo sannipatitvā vilumpiṁsu. Rūpanandā oloketvā 'ayaṁ itthī imasmiṁ yeva ṭhāne jaraṁ pattā, vyādhiṁ pattā, maraṇaṁ pattā, imissāpi attabhāvassa evaṁ evaṁ jarāvyādhi-maraṇāni āgamissantī'ti attabhāvaṁ aniccato passi, anic-cato diṭṭhattā evaṁ pana dukkhato anattato diṭṭhā yeva hoti. Ath'assā tayo bhavā ādittā viya gehā, gīvāya baddhakunapaṁ viya ca upaṭṭhahiṁsu, kammaṭṭhānābhi-mukhaṁ cittaṁ pakkhandi. Satthā tāya aniccato diṭṭha-bhāvaṁ ñatvā, 'sakkhissati nu kho sayam eva attano patiṭṭhaṁ kātuṁ' ti olokento 'na sakkhissati, bahiddhā paccayaṁ laddhuṁ vaṭṭatī' ti cintetvā tassā sappāyavasena dhammaṁ desento āha :

Āturaṁ asuciṁ pūtiṁ passa Nande samussayaṁ
Uggharantaṁ paggharantaṁ bālānaṁ abhipatthitaṁ
Yathā idaṁ tathā etaṁ, yathā etaṁ tathā idaṁ,
dhātuto suññato passa mā lokaṁ punar āgami,
bhave chandaṁ virājetvā upasantā carissasī

* * * * * *

Nandā desanānusārena ñānaṁ pesetvā sotāpattiphalaṁ pāpuṇi. * * * * *

In the Therīgāthā the following verses have been attributed to Nandā :—

Āturaṁ asuciṁ pūtiṁ passa Nande samussayaṁ
Asubhāya cittaṁ bhāvehi ekaggaṁ susamāhitaṁ.
Yathā īdaṁ tathā etaṁ yathā etaṁ tathā idaṁ
Duggandhaṁ pūtikaṁ vāti bālānaṁ abhinanditaṁ.
Evaṁ etaṁ avekkhantī rattindivaṁ atanditā
Tato sakāya paññāya abhinibbijja dakkhisaṁ.
Tassā me appamattāya vicinantiyā yoniso
Yathābhūtaṁ ayaṁ kāyo diṭṭho santara-bāhiro.
Atha nibbind'ahaṁ kāye ajjhattañ ca virajj'ahaṁ,
Appamattā visaṁyuttā upasanta mhi nibbutā.

(Therīgāthā, verses 82-86.)

In the Paramatthadīpanī, in the commentary on these verses, we find a short story which is substantially the same as that given in the commentary on the 150th verse of the Dhammapada, quoted above, with this difference, that the verses put into the mouth of the Buddha, are a little different there and agree with the Therīgāthā verses 82—84 quoted above. The commentary says that of the five verses attributed to Nandā in the Therīgāthā, the first three verses are the words of the Buddha and quoted only by Nandā, and the last two are her own sayings. The Apadānas also contain substantially the same stories in verse.

## Difference between the Pali and the Sanskrit Version

In Saundarananda Buddha entered the house when Nanda and his wife were both immersed in pleasure, in the Pāli version Buddha entered the palace where arrangements were complete for the marriage and coronation of Nanda. The placing of the almsbowl in Nanda's hand is given in both the versions. But in Pāli Nanda is represented as anxious to return the bowl, now at the head of the staircase, now at the foot of it, now in the courtyard, and so on. In the Sanskrit, he was anxious to return with the bowl in his hand. In the Sanskrit version Nandā extorts a promise from her husband to return before the paint on her cheek was dry, but in the Pāli, she cried out to her husband to return quickly. In Pāli it is not stated who converted Nanda, but in Sanskrit he is converted by Vaideha muni (Ānanda). He made several attempts to return home in Sanskrit. But in Pāli he simply said that he was practising austerities against his own will. The she-monkey in Sanskrit is one-eyed, but in Pāli she is without nose, ears and tail. When Nanda was practising austerities for the sake of the heavenly damsels, Ānanda only upbraided him in the Sanskrit version, but in Pāli he is made the butt of ridicule of all the bhikṣus.

For the quotations from Pāli I am indebted to my friend Professor Nīlamaṇi Cakravartī, M.A., of the Presidency College, Calcutta, who has throughout the printing of Saundarananda evinced a genuine interest in the work.

## [Popularity in Bengal]

It has been said that Saundarananda is not known either in China or in Tibet. But there is ample evidence to shew that the work was known and studied in Bengal in the beginning of the 15th century of the Christian Era. Sarvvānanda Banerji, who wrote a commentary on the Amarakoṣa, cites Saundarananda as an authority. Paṇḍita Śeṣagiri Śastrī thinks that the commentary was written between 1417 and 1431.[1] In the latter year another commentary on the Amarakoṣa was written by Bṛhaspati with the title of Rāyamukuṭa. In that commentary, too, Saundarananda has been cited as an authority.[2] This shows the popularity of the work in Bengal at that time.

## [Aśvaghoṣa]

The author Aśvaghoṣa has been described as the son of Suvarṇākṣī, an inhabitant of Sāketa, Arya, Bhadanta, Mahāpaṇḍita and Mahāvādin. All this points him out as a great Buddhist preacher and writer. Nanjio attributes seven works to him and Suzuki enumerates eight works as composed by him. *The awakening of faith in the Mahāyāna* translated by Suzuki into English belongs undoubtedly to the Mahāyāna school. But the doctrine of Śūnyavāda or spiritual nihilism of Nāgārjuna has not yet been developed, while the idea of saving others and not being contented with the saving of one's own soul differentiates Aśvaghoṣa's doctrines from the older Śrāvakayāna, which remains content with one's own salvation only. There is an Indian tradition preserved in China that Aśvaghoṣa was the spiritual preceptor of Kaniṣka, the great Indo-Scythian monarch of Peshawar. In the list of patriarchs of Buddhism his place is third in the descending line from that of Pārśva, who presided at the great council of Kaniṣka, and third in the ascending line from Nāgārjuna, the founder of Śūnyavāda. All this shows that he must have flourished about the end of the 1st century A.D. Because Nāgārjuna's date is very nearly fixed by the in-

---

1 Report on a search of Sanskrit and Tamil Manuscripts for the years 1893-94, pp. 24 and 32. [The work has since been published in the *Trivandrum Sanskrit Series*.]

2 Z.D.M.G., [Vol. 28], p. 117.

scription of his *praśiṣya* in the Jaggayyapeta Stūpa.[1] That inscription is written in the third century Kusan Brahmi (and not in later Gupta as Burgess seems to suppose in putting it down at 600 A.D.), so Nāgārjuna must have flourished two successions before him, *i.e.*, about the end of the 2nd century A.D., and Aśvaghoṣa two successions previous to Nāgārjuna, and so he must have flourished about the end of the 1st century.

It may be suggested here that the inscription[2] in the Aśoka pillar at Sāranātha recording something of Rājā Aśvaghoṣa in the 40th year (of Kaniṣka) (?), may be referred to our author, as powerful monks even in our days have the appellation of Rājā and Mahārāja given to them. Thus there is a chain of evidence to connect our author with the early period of Indo-Scythian dominion in India.

As to the place of his birth Suzuki cites several Indian traditions known in China and concludes that he may have been born anywhere in India but in the north. But the tradition embodied in the colophon of the palm-leaf manuscript of Nepal written undoubtedly in the 12th century is much more reliable than echoes of Indian traditions from China; and according to that tradition he was an inhabitant of Sāketa, a city in the modern province of Oudh. That he was a Brahmin by birth is evident from his intimate knowledge of the Vedic lore displayed both in Saundarananda and Buddhacarita.

Besides the works attributed to him by Nanjio and Suzuki there is another work known in India alone which has undergone a peculiar transformation in the hands of the followers of Śaṁkara. This work is entitled Vajrasūcī or the diamond-needle. It is a polemical work written with great power against the caste-system. Professor Bendall describes it in his Cambridge Catalogue. Rev. Mr. Williamson got a copy of the work at Elichpur, in the

[1] [*Buddhist Stūpas of Amaravati and Jaggayyapeta*]—Arch. Surv., South Ind., [Vol. I], Burgess, p. 112.

[2] Epi. Ind., Vol. VIII, pp. 171, 172.

Berars, published it in 1839 with a refutation by a Brāhmaṇa, entitled Vajrasūcīṭanka. A MS of the work is to be found in our Library. But in our Library there are other copies of the Vajrasūcī written almost in the same words but regarded as Upaniṣads and attributed to Śaṁkarācārya. It shows how deeply the Advaitamata is indebted to the great writers of the Mahāyāna school.

The Kavīndravacanasamuccaya, an anthology discovered by me in Nepal quotes Aśvaghoṣa.[1] It would be exceedingly interesting to compare the verses attributed to Aśvaghoṣa in that work with those in Buddhacarita and Saundarananda. But the work is not in India. It has been borrowed by Mr. Thomas of the India Office Library, who is editing it and who will undoubtedly make the comparison, which I am not in a position to do. But one thing is certain. The MS is written in the 10th century character and the latest poets mentioned are Bhavabhūti, Murāri and Rājaśekhara, who flourished in the 8th, 9th and 10th centuries, respectively. The work may be safely put down in the 10th century, shewing that at that time Aśvaghoṣa was counted among the great poets of India. So popular was Aśvaghoṣa in ancient and mediæval India that many other poets have been confounded with him. Just as in Bengali common tradition, any pretty story or any smart saying is attributed to Kālidāsa, so the works of many minor poets used in ancient India to be attributed to *the* great poet of Buddhism. Mr. Thomas has ably dealt with these,—what he, following Tāranātha, calls different names of Aśvaghoṣa—in his article in the Album Kern and in his paper on Mātriceṭa and Mahārājakanikalekha in the Indian Antiquary, September, 1903, so that I need not discuss the question here at all.

---

1 My *Rep. Search of Sans. MSS.—1895 to 1900*, pp. 21 and 22. [The work has since been published in the *Bibliotheca Indica.*]

# सौन्दरनन्दम् काव्यम्

## प्रथमः सर्गः

ॐ नमो बुद्धाय

गोतमः कपिलो नाम मुनिर्धर्म्मभृतां वरः ।
बभूव तपसि श्रान्तः काक्षीवानिव गोतमः ॥१॥
अशिश्रियत् यस्य ततं दीप्तं काश्यपवत्तपः ।
सुश्रियाय च तद्बुद्धौ सिद्धिं काश्यपवत् पराम् ॥२॥
हविषे यश्च स्वात्मार्थं गामधुक्षत् वशिष्ठवत् ।
तपःशिष्टेषु शिष्येषु गामधु(धो)क्षत् वशिष्ठवत् ॥३॥
माहात्म्यात् दीर्घतपसो यो द्वितीय इवाभवत् ।
तृतीय इव यश्चाभूत् काव्याङ्गिरसयो र्द्धिया ॥४॥
तस्य[1] विस्तीर्णतपसः पार्श्वे हिमवतः शुभे ।
क्षेत्रं चायतनञ्चैव तपसामाश्रयो[2]ऽभवत् ॥५॥
[3]चारुवीरुत्तरुवनः प्रस्निग्धमृदुशाद्वलः ।
हविर्धूमवितानेन यस्सदाभ्र इवावभौ ॥६॥
मृदुभिः सैकतैः[4] स्निग्धैः केसरास्तरपाण्डुभिः[5] ।
भूमिभागैरसंकीर्णैः साङ्गराग[6] इवाभवत् ॥७॥

---

१ P. M. तस्या T.
२ P. M. आश्रियो T.
३ P. M. चरु० T.
४ P. M. सैकटैः T.
५ P. M. केसरास्तरणपाण्डुभिः ।
६ P. M. साङ्गराग ।

शुचिभिस्तीर्थसंख्यातैः पावनैर्भावनैरपि ।
बन्धुमानिव यस्तस्थौ सरोभिः ससरोरुहैः ॥८॥
पर्य्याप्तफलपुष्पाभिः सर्व्वतो वनराजिभिः ।
शुशुभे ववृधे चैव नरः साधनवानिव ॥९॥
नीवारफलसन्तुष्टैः स्वस्थैः[१] शान्तैरनुत्सुकैः ।
आकीर्णोऽपि तपोभृद्भिः शून्यशून्य इवाभवत् ॥१०॥
अग्नीनाम् हूयमानानाम् शिखिनाम् कूजतामपि ।
तीर्थानाञ्चाभिषेकेषु शुश्रुवे तत्र निस्वनः ॥११॥
विरेजुः हरिणा यत्र सुप्ता मेध्यासु[२] वेदिषु ।
सलाजैर्माधवीपुष्पैरुपहाराः कृता इव ॥१२॥
अपि क्षुद्रमृगा यत्र शान्तास्चेरुः समं मृगैः ।
शरण्येभ्यस्तपस्विभ्यो विनयं शिक्षिता इव ॥१३॥
सन्दिग्धेऽपि पुनर्भावे विरुद्धेष्वागमेष्वपि ।
प्रत्यक्षिण[३] इवाकुर्व्वंस्तपो यत्र तपोधनाः ॥१४॥
यत्र स्म मीयते[४] ब्रह्म कैश्चित् कैश्चित् न मीयते[४] ।
काले निमीयते[५] सोमो[६] न चाकाले प्रमीयते[७] ॥१५॥
निरपेक्षा[ः]शरीरेषु धर्म्मे यत्र स्वबुद्धयः ।
संहृष्टा इव यत्नेन[८] तापसास्तेपिरे तपः ॥१६॥

---

१ P. M. सुस्थैः । २ P. M. सुप्तमध्यासु ।
३ P. M. प्रदक्षिणा । ४ P. M. लीयते ।
५ P. M. निलीयते । ६ P. M. भूमौ ।
७ P. M. प्रलीयते । ८ P. M. यत्तेन ।

श्राम्यन्तो मुनयो यत्र स्वर्गायोद्युक्तचेतसः ।
तपोरागेण धर्म्मस्य विलोपमिव चक्रिरे ॥१७॥

अथ तेजस्विसद्नं[1] तपःक्षेत्रं[2] तमाश्रमम् ।
केचिदिक्ष्वाकवो जग्मू राजपुत्रा विवत्सवः[3] ॥१८॥

सुवर्णस्तम्भवर्म्माणः सिंहोरस्का महाभुजाः ।
पात्रं शब्दस्य महतः[4] श्रियाश्च[5] विनयस्य च ॥१९॥

अर्हरूपा ह्यनर्हस्य[6] महात्मानश्चलात्मनः ।
प्राज्ञाः प्रज्ञाविमुक्तस्य भ्रातृव्यस्य यवीयसः ॥२०॥

मातृशुल्कादुपगतां ते श्रियं न विषेहिरे ।
ररक्षुश्च[7] पितुः सत्यं यस्माच्छिश्रियिरे वनम् ॥२१॥

तेषां मुनिरुपाध्यायो गोतमः कपिलोऽभवत् ।
गुरोर्गोत्रादतः कौत्सास्ते भवन्ति स्म गौतमाः ॥२२॥

एकपित्रोर्यथा भ्रात्रोः पृथग्गुरुपरिग्रहात् ।
राम एवाभवत् गार्ग्यो[8] वासुभद्रोऽपि गोतमः ॥२३॥

शाकवृक्षप्रतिच्छन्नं[9] वासं यस्माच्च चक्रिरे ।
तस्मादिक्ष्वाकुवंश्यास्ते भुवि शाक्या इति स्मृताः ॥२४॥

---

१ P. M. तेजाखसदने ।
२ P. M. ०च्चत्रं ।
३ P. M. विवस्वभूः ।
४ P. M. मेदतः ।
५ P. M. श्रिया च ।
६ P. M. ह्यनेहस्य ।
७ P. M. सरक्षुश्च ।
८ P. M. गर्ग्यो ।
९ P. M. पोकवक्षप्रतिच्छन्नं ।

स तेषां गोतमश्चक्रे स्ववंशसदृशीः[१] क्रियाः ।
मुनिरूर्ध्वः[२] कुमारस्य सगरस्येव भार्गवः ॥२५॥
कण्वः शाकुन्तलस्येव भरतस्य तरस्विनः ।
वाल्मीकिरिव धीमांश्च धीमतोः मैथिलेययोः ॥२६॥
तद्वनं मुनिना तेन तैश्च क्षत्रियपुङ्गवैः ।
शान्तां गुप्तां च युगपत् ब्रह्मक्षत्रश्रियं दधे ॥२७॥
अथोदकलसं गृह्य तेषां वृद्धिचिकीर्षया ।
मुनिः स वियदुत्पत्य तानुवाच नृपात्मजान् ॥२८॥
आपतेत्कलशादस्मात् अक्षय्यसलिलात् महीम् ।
धारा तामनतिक्रम्य मामन्वे(न्व)त यथाक्रमम् ॥२९॥
ततः परममित्युक्त्वा शिरोभिः प्रणिपत्य च ।
रथानारुरुहुः सर्व्वे शीघ्रवाहनलङ्कृतान् ॥३०॥
ततः स तैरनुगतः स्यन्दनस्थैर्नभोगतः ।
तदाश्रममहीं[ ] यां तु परिचिक्षेप वारिणा ॥३१॥
अष्टापदमिवालिख्य निमित्तैः सुरभीकृत[ा]म् ।
तामुवाच मुनिः स्थित्वा भूमिपालसुतानिदम् ॥३२॥
अस्मिन् धारापरिक्षिप्ते नेमिचिह्नितलक्षणे ।
[३]निर्म्मिमीध्वं पुरं यूयं मयि याते त्रिविष्टपम् ॥३३॥
ततः कदाचित् ते वीराः तस्मिन् प्रतिगते मुनौ ।

---

१ P. M. सदृशाः क्रियाः । २ P. M. मनिबद्धं ।
३ P. M. निर्म्मिताध्वं T.

बभ्रमु[:] [१]यौवनोद्दामा गजा इव निरङ्कुशाः ॥२४॥
[२]बद्धाङ्गुष्ठाङ्गुलित्राणा [३]हस्ताधिष्ठितकार्म्मुका[:] ।
शराध्मातं महातूणं व्यायता विद्धवाससः ॥२५॥
जिज्ञासमाना नागेषु कौशलं श्वापदेषु च ।
अ[नु]चक्रुर्वनस्थस्य दौष्मन्तेर्दैवकर्म्मणः ॥२६॥
तान्[४] दृष्ट्वा प्रकृतिं यातान् वृद्धा[न्] व्याघ्रशिशूनिव ।
तापसास्तत् वनं हित्वा हिमवन्तं सिषेविरे ॥२७॥

ततस्तदाश्रमस्थानं शून्यं तैः शून्यचेतसः ।
पश्यन्तो मन्युना तप्ता व्याला[५] इव निशश्वसुः ॥२८॥
अथ ते पुण्यकर्म्माणः प्रत्युपस्थितवृद्धयः ।
तत्र तज्ज्ञैरुपाख्यातान् अवापुर्महतो निधीन् ॥२९॥
अलं धर्म्मार्थकामानां निखिलानामवाप्तये ।
निधयो नैकविधयो भूरयस्ते गतारयः ॥४०॥
ततस्तत्प्रतिलम्भाच्च परिणामाच्च कर्म्मणः ।
तस्मिन् वास्तुनि वास्तुज्ञाः पुरं श्रीमन्न्यवेशयन् ॥४१॥
सरिद्विस्तीर्णपरिखं स्पष्टाञ्चितमहापथम् ।
शैलकल्पमहावप्रम् गिरिव्रजमिवापरम् ॥४२॥
पाण्डुराट्टालसुमुखं सुविभक्तान्तरापणम्[६] ।

---

१ P. M. यविनोद्दासा T.
२ P. M. बद्धगोष्ठाङ्गुलिवाणा T.
३ P. M. हस्तविष्ठित० T.
४ P. M. तां T.
५ P. M. व्याजा T.
६ P. M. ०रायनम् ।

हर्म्यमालापरिक्षिप्तम् कुक्षिं हिमगिरेरिव ॥४३॥
वेदवेदाङ्गविदुषः तस्थुषः षट्सु कर्म्मसु ।
शान्तये वृद्धये चैव यत्र विप्रानजीजपन् ॥४४॥
तद्भूमेरभियोक्तॄणाम् प्रयुक्तान् विनिवृत्तये ।
यत्र स्वेन प्रभावेन भृत्यैर्दण्डानजीजपन् ॥४५॥
चारित्रधनसम्पन्नान् सलज्जान् दीर्घदर्शिनः ।
अर्हतोऽतिष्ठपन् पैत्रे शूरान् दक्षान् कुटुम्बिनः ॥४६॥
व्यस्तैस्तैस्तैर्गुणैर्युक्तान् मतिवाग्विक्रमादिभिः ।
कर्म्मसु प्रतिरूपेषु सचिवांस्तान् न्ययूयुजन् ॥४७॥
वसुमद्भिरविभ्रान्तैरलंविद्यैरविस्मितैः ।
यद्बभासे नरैः कीर्णम् मन्दरः किन्नरैरिव ॥४८॥
यत्र ते हृष्टमनसः पौरप्रीतिचिकीर्षया ।
श्रीमन्त्युद्यानसंज्ञानि यशोधामान्यचीकरन् ॥४९॥
शिवाः पुष्करिणीश्चैव परमार्घ्यगुणाम्भसः ।
नाज्ञया चेतनोत्कर्षात् दिक्षु सर्व्वास्वचीखनन् ॥५०॥
मनोज्ञा[ः] श्रीमतीः प्रष्ठीः[१] पथिषूपवनेषु च ।
सभाः कूपवतीश्चैव समन्तात् प्रत्यतिष्ठिपन् ॥५१॥
हस्त्यश्वरथसङ्कीर्णं असङ्कीर्णमनाकुलम् ।
अनिगूढार्थ[२]विभवम् निगूढज्ञानपौरुषम् ॥५२॥

---

१ P. M. पष्ठीः ।
२ P. M. अनिगूढार्थि० ।

सन्निधानमिवार्थानाम् आधानमिव तेजसाम् ।
निकेतमिव विद्यानाम् सङ्केतमिव सम्पदाम् ॥५ ३॥
वासवृक्षं गुणवताम् आश्रयं शरणैषिणाम् ।
आनर्त्तं कृतशास्त्राणाम् आलानं बाहुशालिनाम्[१] ॥५ ४॥
समाजैरुत्सवैः दायैः[२] क्रियाविधिभिरेव च ।
अलंचक्रुरलंवीर्य्यास्ते जगद्धाम तत्पुरम् ॥५ ५॥
यस्मादन्यायतस्ते च कञ्चिन्नाचीकरत्करम् ।
तस्मादल्पेन कालेन तत्तदापूपुरन् पुरम् ॥५ ६॥
कपिलस्य च तस्यर्षेस्तस्मिन्नाश्रमवास्तुनि ।
यस्मात्ते तत् पुरञ्चक्रुः तस्मात् कपिलवास्तु तत् ॥५ ७॥
ककन्दस्य मकन्दस्य[३] कुशाम्बस्येव चाश्रमे ।
पुर्य्यो यथा हि श्रूयन्ते तथैव कपिलस्य तत् ॥५ ८॥

आपुः पुरं तत् पुरुहूतकल्पा-
स्ते तेजसार्य्येण न विस्मयेन ।
आपुर्यशो गन्धमतश्च शश्वत्
सुता ययातेरिव कीर्त्तिमन्तः ॥५ ९॥
तन्नाथवत्तैरपिराजपुत्रै-
रराजकं नैव रराज राष्ट्रम् ।

---

१. P. M. आह्लानां बाहुसालिनाम् । P. L. M. आलानां बाहु-शान्दिनाम् । २ P. M. दाश्रियैः । ३ P. M. मकन्दस्य ।

तारासहस्रैरपि दीप्यमानैः
अनुत्थिते[1] चन्द्र इवान्तरीक्षम् ॥६०॥

यो ज्यायानथ वयसा गुणैश्च तेषाम्
भ्रातृणाम् वृषभ इवौजसा वृषाणाम् ।
ते तत्र प्रियगुरवस्तमभ्यषिञ्च-
न्नादित्या दशशतलोचनं दिवीव ॥६१॥

आचारवान् विनयवान् नयवान् क्रियावान्
धर्माय ने[2]न्द्रियसुखाय धृतातपत्रः ।
तद्भ्रातृभिः परिवृतः स जुगोप राष्ट्रम्
संक्रन्दनो दिवमिवानुसृतो मरुद्भिः ॥६२॥

सौन्दरनन्द[3]-महाकाव्ये कपिलवस्तुवर्णनो नाम
प्रथमः सर्गः ।

---

१ P. M. अनुदिते । २ P. M. धर्मायतेन्द्रिय०
३ P. M. सौन्दरानन्द० ।

# द्वितीयः सर्गः

ततः कदाचित् कालेन तदवाप कुलं क्रमात् ।
राजा शुद्धोदनो नाम शुद्धकर्म्मा जितेन्द्रियः ॥१॥
यः स सज्जिनकामेषु श्रीप्राप्तौ न विसिस्मिये ।
नावमेने परान् ऋद्ध्या परेभ्यो [1]नापि विव्यथे ॥२॥
बलीयान् सत्त्वसम्पन्नः श्रुतवान् बुद्धिमानपि ।
विक्रान्तो नयवांश्चैव धीरः सुमुख एव च ॥३॥
वपुष्मांश्च न च स्तब्धो दक्षिणो न च नार्ज्जवः ।
तेजस्वी न च न क्षान्तः कर्त्ता च न च विस्मितः ॥४॥
आक्षिप्त[ः] शत्रुभिः सं[स]ख्ये सुहृद्भि[श्च] व्यपाश्रितः ।
अभवद्यो न विमुखः तेजसा दित्सयैव च ॥५॥
यः पूर्वैं राजभिर्यातां यियासुर्धर्म्मपद्धतिम् ।
राज्यं दीक्षामिव वहन् वृत्तेनान्वगमत्पितॄन् ॥६॥
यस्य सुव्यवहाराच्च रक्षणाच्च सुखं प्रजाः ।
शिश्यिरे विगतोद्वेगाः पितुरङ्कगता इव ॥७॥
कृतशास्त्रः कृतास्त्रो वा जातो वा विपुले कुले ।
अकृतार्थो न ददृशे योऽस्य दर्शनमीयिवान् ॥८॥

---

१ P. M. नामि ।

हितं विप्रियमप्युक्तो यः शुश्राव न चुक्षुभे ।
दुष्कृतं बह्वपि त्यक्त्वा सस्मार कृतमण्वपि ॥९॥
प्रणताननुजग्राह विजग्राह कुलद्विषः ।
आपन्नान् परिजग्राह निजग्राह स्थिता[न्] पथि ॥१०॥
प्रायेण विषये तस्य तच्छीलमनुवर्त्तिनः ।
अर्ज्जयन्तो ददृशिरे धनानीव गुणानपि ॥११॥
अध्यै(ध्य)ष्ट यः परं ब्रह्म नाध्यै(ध्या)ष्ट सततं धृतेः ।
दानान्यदित पात्रेभ्यः पापं नाकृत किञ्चन ॥१२॥
धृत्या [1]रक्षीत्प्रतिज्ञां स सद्वाजीवोद्यतां धुरम् ।
नह्यकाङ्क्षीत् च्युतः[2] सत्यान्मुहूर्त्तमपि जीवितम् ॥१२॥
विदुषः पर्य्युपासिष्ट व्यकाशिष्टात्मवत्तया ।
व्यरोचिष्ट च शिष्टेभ्यः मासीषे चन्द्रमा इव ॥१४॥
अवेदीत् बुद्धिशास्त्राभ्याम् इह चामुत्र च क्षमम् ।
अरक्षीत् धैर्य्यवीर्य्याभ्यां इन्द्रियाण्यपि च प्रजाः ॥१५॥
अहार्षी[त्] दुःखमार्त्तानाम् द्विषतां चोर्जितं यशः ।
अचैषीत् च नयैर्भूमिं भूयसा यशसैव च ॥१६॥
अप्यासीत् दुःखितान् पश्यन् प्रकृत्या करुणात्मकः ।
नाधौषीत् च यशोलोभात् अन्यायाधिगतैर्धनैः ॥१७॥
सौहार्द्ददृढभक्तित्वात् मैत्रेषु विगुणेष्वपि ।
नादिदासीत् अदित्सीत्तु सौमुख्यात् सस्वं(स्व)मर्थवत् ॥१८॥

---

१ P. M. ०राक्षीत् ।
२ P. M. न ह्यवाक्षराच्युतः P. L. M. indistinct भावत ।

अनिर्वेद्याग्र्यमर्हज्ञो नालिचत् किञ्चिदद्भुतः ।
गामधर्म्मेण नाधुचत् खरतर्षेण गामिव ॥१९॥
नास्तृचत् कलिमप्राप्तम् नारुचत्मानमैश्वरम् ।
आगमैर्बुद्धिमाधिचत् धर्म्माय न तु कीर्त्तये ॥२०॥
क्लेशार्हानपि कांश्चित्तु नाक्लिष्ट क्लिष्टकर्म्मणः ।
आर्य्यभावाच्च नाद्विचत्[1] द्विषतोऽपि सतो गुणान् ॥२१॥
आक्तचत् वपुषा दृष्टीः प्रजानाम् चन्द्रमा इव ।
परस्वं भुवि नाम्टचत् महाविषमिवौ(वो)रगम् ॥२२॥
नाक्रचत् विषये तस्य कश्चित् कैश्चित् क्वचित् चतः[2] ।
अदिचत् तस्य हस्तस्थमार्त्तेभ्यो ह्यभयं धनुः ॥२३॥
कृतागसोऽपि प्रणतान् प्रागेव प्रियकारिणः ।
आदर्शस्निग्धया दृष्ट्या श्लक्ष्णेन वचसासिचत् ॥२४॥
बह्वीरध्यगमत् विद्या विषयेष्वकुतूहलः ।
स्थितः कार्त्तयुगे धर्म्मे धर्म्मात् कृच्छ्रेऽपि नास्त्रसत् ॥२५॥
अवर्द्धिष्ट गुणैः शश्वदवृधत् मित्रसम्पदा ।
अवर्त्तिष्ट च वृद्धेषु नावृतत् गर्हिते पथि ॥२६॥
शरैरशीशमच्छत्रून् गुणै[3]र्बन्धूनरीरमत् ।
रन्ध्रैर्नाचूचुदत् भृत्यान् करैः नापीपिडत् प्रजाः ॥२७॥
रक्षणात् चैव शौर्य्याच्च निखिलां गामवीवपत् ।

---

१ P. M. नाद्युच्चत् T. २ P. M. कुतः ।
३ P. M. शार्गैः ।

स्पृष्ट्या दण्डनीत्या च रात्रिसत्त्वानवीवपत् ॥२८॥
कुलं राजर्षिवृत्तेन यशोगन्धमवीवपत् ।
दीप्त्या तम इवादित्यः तेजसारीनवीवपत् ॥२९॥
अपप्रथत् पितृंश्चैव सत्पुत्रसदृशैः गुणैः ।
सलिलेनेव चाम्भोदो[१] वृत्तेनाजिह्लदत्[२] प्रजाः ॥३०॥
दानैरजस्रविपुलैः सोमं विप्रान् असूषवत् ।
राजधर्म्मस्थितत्वाच्च कालं सस्यमसूषवत् ॥३१॥
अधर्म्मिष्ठामचकथन्नकथामकथंकथः ।
चक्रवर्त्तीव च परान् धर्म्मायाभ्युदसी[३]षहत् ॥३२॥
राष्ट्रमन्यत्र च बलेर्न स किञ्चिददीदपत् ।
भृत्यैरेव च सोद्योगं द्विषद्दर्पमदीदपत् ॥३३॥
स्वैरेवादीदपत् चापि भूयो भूयो गुणैः कुलम् ।
प्रजा नादीदपच्चैव सर्व्वधर्म्मव्यवस्थया ॥३४॥
अश्रान्तः समये यज्वा यज्ञभूमिममीमपत् ।
पालनाच्च द्विजान् ब्रह्म निरुद्विग्नानमीमपत् ॥३५॥
गुरुभिर्विधिवत् काले सौम्यः[४] सोमममीमपत् ।
तपसा तेजसा चैव द्विषत्सैन्यममीमपत् ॥३६॥
प्रजाः परमधर्म्मज्ञः सूक्ष्मं धर्म्ममवीवपत् ।

---

१ P. M. चाम्तो दो ।  २ P. M. अजिक्रदत् ।
३ P. M. परां धर्म्मायाभ्यदसीवत. ।
४ P. L. M. सोम्यः ।

दर्शनाच्चैव धर्मस्य काले स्वर्गमवी[व]पत् ॥२७॥
व्यक्तमप्यर्थकृच्छ्रेषु नाधर्म्मिष्ठमतिष्ठिपत्[१]।
प्रिय इत्येव चाशक्तं न संरागात् अवीवृधत् ॥२८॥
तेजसा च त्विषा चैव रिपून् दृप्तान् अवीभसत्[२]।
यशोदीपेन दीप्तेन पृथिवीञ्च व्यवीभसत् ॥२९॥
आनृशंस्यान्न यशसे तेनादायि सदार्थिने।
द्रव्यं महदपि त्यक्त्वा न चैवाकीर्त्ति किञ्चन ॥४०॥
तेनारिरपि दुःखार्त्तो नात्याजि शरणागतः।
जित्वा दृप्तानपि रिपून् न तेनाकारि विस्मयः ॥४१॥
न तेनाभेदि मर्य्यादा कामाद् द्वेषाद् भयादपि।
तेन सत्स्वपि भोगेषु नासेवीन्द्रियवृत्तिता ॥४२॥
न तेनादर्शि विषमं कार्य्यं[३] क्वचन किञ्चन।
विप्रियप्रिययोः कृत्ये न तेनागामि निक्रिया ॥४३॥
तेनापायि यथाकल्पं सोमश्च यश एवच।
वेदश्चाम्नायि सततं वेदोक्तो धर्म्म एवच ॥४४॥
एवमादिभिरत्यक्तो बभूव सुलभैः गणैः।
अशक्यशक्यसामन्तः शाक्यराजः स शक्रवत् ॥४५॥

अथ तस्मिन् तथा काले धर्म्मकामा दिवौकसः।
विचेरुर्दिशि लोकस्य धर्म्मचर्य्यां दिदृक्षवः ॥४६॥

---

१ P. M. नावर्म्मिष्ठ मतिष्ठपत्। २ P. M. अवीदृसत्।
३ P. M. न तेनादाधि विषमं कार्म्यं।

धर्म्मात्मानः चरन्तस्ते धर्म्मजिज्ञासया जगत् ।
ददृशुस्तं विशेषेण धर्म्मात्मानं नराधिपम् ॥४७॥
देवेभ्यस्तुषितेभ्योऽथ बोधिसत्त्वः क्षितिं व्रजन् ।
उपपत्तिं प्रणिदधे कुले तस्य महीपते[:] ॥४८॥
तस्य देवी नृदेवस्य माया नाम तदाभवत् ।
वीत[१]क्रोधतमा माया मायेव दिवि देवता ॥४९॥
स्वप्नेऽथ समये गर्भमाविशन्तं ददर्श सा ।
षड्दन्तं वारणं श्वेतम् ऐरावतमिवौजसा ॥५०॥
तं विनिर्दिदिशुः श्रुत्वा स्वप्नं स्वप्नविदो द्विजाः ।
तस्य जन्म कुमारस्य लक्ष्मीधर्म्मयशोभृतः ॥५१॥
तस्य सत्त्वविशेषस्य जातौ जातिक्षयैषिणः ।
साचला प्रचचालोर्व्वी तरङ्गाभिहतेव नौः ॥५२॥
सूर्य्यरश्मिभिरक्लिष्टं पुष्पवर्ष[ं] पपात खात् ।
दिग्वारणकराधूतात् वनाच्चैत्ररथादिव ॥५३॥
दिवि दुन्दुभयो नेदुः दीव्यताम् मरुतामिव ।
दिदीपेत्यधिकं सूर्य्यः शिवश्च पवनो ववौ ॥५४॥
तुतुषुस्तुषिताश्चैव शुद्धावासाश्च देवताः ।
सधर्म्मबहुमानेन सत्त्वानां चानुकम्पया ॥५५॥
समाययौ यशःकेतुं श्रेयस्केतुकरः परः ।

---

१ P. M. वीत० T.

बभ्राजे शान्तया लक्ष्म्या धर्मो विग्रहवानिव ॥५६॥

देव्यामपि यवीयस्यामरण्यामिव पावकः ।
नन्दो नाम सुतो जज्ञे नित्यानन्दकरः कुले ॥५७॥

दीर्घबाहुर्महावक्षाः सिंहांसो वृषभेक्षणः ।
वपुषाग्र्येण यो नाम सुन्दरोपपदं दधे ॥५८॥

मधुमास इव प्राप्तश्चन्द्रो नव इवोदितः ।
अङ्गवानिव चानङ्गः स बभौ कान्तया श्रिया ॥५९॥

स तौ संवर्द्धयामास नरेन्द्रः परया मुदा ।
अर्थः सज्जनहस्तस्थो धर्मकामौ महानिव ॥६०॥

तस्य कालेन सत्पुत्रौ वव्रधाते भयापहौ (सतौ) ।
आर्य्यस्यारम्भमहतो धर्मार्थाविव भूतये ॥६१॥

तयोः सत्पुत्रयोर्मध्ये शाक्यराजो रराज सः ।
मध्यदेश इव व्यक्तो हिमवत्पारिपात्रयोः ॥६२॥

ततस्तयोः संस्कृतयोः क्रमेण
नरेन्द्रसून्वोः कृतविद्ययोश्च ।
कामेष्वजस्रं प्रममाद नन्दः
सर्व्वार्थसिद्धस्तु[१] न संररञ्ज ॥६३॥

स प्रेक्ष्यैव हि जीर्णमातुरञ्च मृतञ्च
विमृशन् जगदनभिज्ञमार्त्तहृदयः ।

---

१ P. M. ०सिद्धिस्तु ।

गतपरमशङ्कं [न] विषयरतिमगमत्
जननमरणभयमभितो विजिघांसुः ॥६४॥

उद्वेगात् अपुनर्भवे मनः प्रणिधाय
स ययौ शयितवराङ्गनादनास्थः ।
निशि नृपतिनिलयनात् वनगमनकृतमनाः
सरस इव मथितनलिनात् कलहंसः ॥६५॥

सौन्दरनन्दे महाकाव्ये राजवर्णनो नाम द्वितीयः सर्गः ।

# तृतीयः सर्गः

तपसे ततः कपिलवास्तु हयगजरथौघसङ्कुलम् ।
श्रीमदभयमनुरक्तजनं स विहाय निश्चितमना वनं ययौ ॥१॥
विविधागमांस्तपसि तांश्च विविधनियमाश्रयान् मुनीन् प्रेक्ष्य ।
स विषयतृषाकृपणान् अनवस्थितं तम इति न्यवर्त्तत ॥२॥
अथ मोक्षवादिनमराडमुपशममतिं तथोद्रकम् ।
तत्त्वकृतमतिरुपास्य जहावयमप्यमार्ग इति मार्गकोविदः ॥३॥
स विचारयन् जगति किन्नु परममिति तन्तमागमम् ।
निश्चयमनधिगतः परतः परमं चचार तप एव दुष्करम् ॥४॥
अथ नैषमार्ग इति वीक्ष्य तदपि विपुलं जहौ तपः ।
व्याधि[1] विषयमवगम्य परम् बुभुजे नरान्नममृतलवुद्धये ॥५॥
स सुवर्णपीनयुगवाहुः ऋषभगतिरायतेक्षणः ।
प्लक्षमवनिरुहमभ्यगमत् परमस्य निश्चयविधेर्बुभुत्सया ॥६॥
उपविश्य तत्र कृतबुद्धिरचलधृतिरद्रिराजवत् ।
मारबलमजयदुग्रमथो बुबुधे पदं शिवमहार्य्यमव्ययम् ॥७॥
अवगम्य तं च[2] कृतकार्य्यममृतमनसो दिवौकसः ।
हर्षमतुलमगमन्मुदिता विमुखी तु मारपरिषत् प्रचुक्षुभे ॥८॥
सनगा च भूः प्रविचचाल हुतवहसखः शिवो[3] ववौ ।
नेदुरपि च सुरदुन्दुभयः प्रववर्ष चाम्बुधरवर्जितं नभः ॥९॥

---

१ P. L. M. ध्यान० । २ P. M. तम । ३ P. M. प्रियो ।

अवबुध्य चैव परमार्थमजरमनुकम्पया विभुः ।
नित्यममृतमुपदर्शयितुम् स वरणसापरिकरामयात् पुरीम् ॥१०॥
अथ धर्म्मचक्रमृतनाभि धृतिमतिसमाधिनेमिमत् ।
तत्र विनयनियमारमृषिर्जगतो हिताय परिषद्यवर्त्तयत् ॥११॥
इति दुःखमेतदियमस्य समुदयलता प्रवर्त्तिका ।
शान्तिरियमयमुपाय इति प्रविभागशः परमिदं चतुष्टयम् ॥१२॥
अभिधाय च त्रिपरिवर्त्तमतुलमनिवर्त्त्य[1]मुत्तमम् ।
द्वादशनियतविकल्पमपि विनिनाय कौण्डिनसगोत्रमादितः ॥१३॥
स हि दोषसागरमगाधमुपधिजलमाधिजन्तुकम् ।
क्रोधमदभयतरङ्गचपलं प्रततार लोकमपि चाप्यतारयत् ॥१४॥
स विनीय काशिषु गयेषु बहुजनमथो गिरिव्रजे ।
पित्र्यमपि परमकारुणिको नगरं ययावनुजिघृक्षया तदा ॥१५॥
विषयात्मकस्य हि जनस्य बहुविविधमार्गसेविनः ।
सूर्य्यसदृशवपुरभ्युदितो विजहार सूर्य्य इव गौतमस्तमः ॥१६॥
अभितस्ततः कपिलवास्तु परमशुभवास्तुसंस्तुतम् ।
व[ा]स्तुमतिशुचिशिवोपवनम् स ददर्श निस्पृहतया यथा वनम् ॥१७॥
अपरिग्रहः स हि बभूव नियतिमतिरात्मनीश्वरः ।
नैकविधभयकरेषु किमु स्वजनः स्वदेश [2]एव मित्रवस्तुषु ॥१८॥
प्रतिपूजया न स जहर्ष न च शुचमवज्ञयागमत् ।
निश्चितमतिरसिचन्दनयोः न जगाम सुखदुःखयोश्च विक्रियाम् ॥१९॥

---

१ P. M. अनित्यम् ।

२ P. M. एन P. L. M. lacuna. T.

अथ पार्थिवः समुपलभ्य [1]सुतमुपगतम् तथागतम् ।
तूर्णमबहुतुरगानुगतः सुतदर्शनोत्सुकतयाभिनिर्ययौ ॥२०॥
सुगतस्तथागतमपेक्ष्य नरपतिमधीरमानसतया ।
शेषमपि जनमश्रुमुखम् विनिनीषया गगनमुत्पपात ह ॥२१॥
स विचक्रमे दिवि भुवीव पुनरुपविवेश तस्थिवान् ।
निश्चलमतिः शिशयिषुः पुनर्बहुधाभवत् पुनरभूत् तथैकधा ॥२२॥
सलिले क्षिताविव चचार जलमिव विवेश मेदिनीम् ।
मेघ इव दिवि व[व]र्ष पुनः पुनरुज्ज्वलन्नव इवोदितो रविः ॥२३॥
युगपज्ज्वलन् ज्वलनवच्च जलमवसृजंश्च मेघवत् ।
तप्तकनकसदृशप्रभया स बभौ प्रदीप्त इव सन्ध्यया घनः ॥२४॥
तमुदीक्ष्य हेममणिजालवलयिनमिवोत्थितं ध्वजम् ।
प्रीतिमगमदतुलां नृपतिर्जनता नताश्च बहुमानमभ्ययुः ॥२५॥

अथ भाजनीकृतमवेक्ष्य मनुजपतिमृद्धिसम्पदा ।
पौरजनमपि च तत्प्रसवेन निजगाद धर्मविनयं विनायकः ॥२६॥
नृपतिस्ततः प्रथममाप फलममृतधर्मसिद्धयोः ।
धर्ममतुलमधिगम्य मुनेः मुनये ननाम स यतो गुराविव ॥२७॥
बहवः प्रसन्नमनसोऽथ जननमरणार्त्तिभीरवः ।
शाक्यतनयवृषभाः कृतिनो वृषभा इवानलभयात् प्रवव्रजुः ॥२८॥
विजहुस्तु येपि न गृहाणि तनयपितृमात्रपेक्षया ।
तेऽपि नियमविधिमामरणात् जगृहुश्च युक्तमनसश्च दधिरे ॥२९॥

---

[1] P. M. सुगत० ।

न जिहिंस सूक्ष्ममपि जन्तुमपि परवधोपजीवनः ।
किं बत विपुलगुणः कुलजः सदयः सदा किमु मुनेरुपासया ॥२०॥
अक्लिष्टोद्यमः कृषधनोऽपि परपरिभवासहोऽपि सन् ।
नान्यधनमपजहार तथा भुजगादिवान्यविभवात् विविव्यथे ॥२१॥
विभवान्वितोऽपि तरुणोऽपि विषयचपलेन्द्रियोऽपि सन् ।
नैव च परयुवतीरगमत् परमहिला[1] दहनतोप्यमन्यत ॥२२॥
अनृतं जगाद न च कश्चित् ऋतमपि जजल्प नाप्रियम् ।
श्लक्ष्णमपि न जगावहितम् हितमप्युवाच न च पैशुनाय यत् ॥२३॥
मनसा लुलोभ न च जातु परवसुषु बद्धमानसः[2] ।
कामसुखमसुखतो विमृशन् विजहार तृप्त इव तत्र सज्जनः ॥२४॥
न परस्य कश्चित् अपघातमपि च सघृणो व्यचिन्तयत् ।
मातृपितृसुतसुहृत्सदृशं स ददर्श तत्र हि परस्परं जनः ॥२५॥
नियतम् भविष्यति परत्र भवदपि च भूतमप्यथो ।
कर्म्मफलमपि च लोकगतिर्नियतेति दर्शनमवाप साधु च ॥२६॥
इति कर्म्मणा दशविधेन परमकुशलेन भूरिणा ।
भ्रंशिनि शिथिलगुणेऽपि युगे विजहार तत्र मुनिसंश्रयाज्जनः ॥२७॥
न च तत्र कश्चिदुपपत्तिसुखमभिललाष तैर्गुणैः ।
सर्व्वमशिवमवगम्य भवम् भवसंक्षयाय ववृते न जन्मने ॥२८॥

---

१ P. M. P. L. M. परमहिता T.

२ P. L. M. गृद्धमानसः ।

अकथंकथाग्रहिन एव परमपरिशुद्धदृष्टयः ।
स्रोतसि हि ववृतिरे बहवो रजसस्तनुत्वमपि चक्रिरे परे[1] ॥३९॥
ववृतेऽत्र योऽपि विषमेषु विभवसदृशेषु कश्चन ।
त्यागविनयनियमाभिरतो विजहार सोऽपि न चचाल सत्पथात् ॥४०॥
अपि च स्वतोऽपि परतोऽपि न भयमभवत् न दैवतः ।
तत्र च सुखसुभिक्षगुणैः जहृषुः प्रजाः कृतयुगे राज्ञो मनोरिव ॥४१॥
इति मुदितमनामयन्निरापत्कुरुरघुपुरुपुरोपमं पुरं तत् ।
अभवभयदैशिके महर्षौ विहरति तत्र शिवाय वीतराग इति ॥४२॥

सौन्दरनन्दे महाकाव्ये तथागतवर्णनो नाम
तृतीयः सर्गः ॥३॥

---

१ P. M. स्रोतसिक्षो स ततरे बहवोरजसत्वतमपि चक्रिरे परे ।

## चतुर्थः सर्गः

मुनौ ब्रुवाणेऽपि तु तत्र धर्म्मम् धर्म्मं प्रति ज्ञातिषु चादृतेषु ।
प्रासादसंस्थो मदनैककार्य्यः प्रियासहायो विजहार नन्दः ॥१॥
स चक्रवाक्येव हि चक्रवाकस्तया समेतः प्रियया प्रियार्हः ।
नाचिन्तयद्वैश्रमणं न शक्रम् तत्स्थानहेतोः कृत एव धर्म्मः ॥२॥
लक्ष्म्या च रूपेण च सुन्दरीति स्तम्भेन गर्व्वेण च मानिनीति ।
दीप्त्या च मानेन च भामिनीति यासौ बभाषे त्रिविधेन नाम्ना ॥३॥
सा हासहंसा नयनद्विरेफा पीनस्तनाभ्युन्नतपद्मकोषा ।
भूयो बभासे स्वकुलोदितेन स्त्रीपद्मिनी नन्ददिवाकरेण ॥४॥
रूपेण चात्यन्तमनोहरेण रूपानुरूपेण च चेष्टितेन ।
मनुष्यलोके हि तदा बभूव सा सुन्दरी स्त्री पुरुषेषु नन्दः ॥५॥
सा देवता नन्दनचारिणीव कुलस्य नान्दीजननश्च नन्दः ।
अतीत्य मर्त्त्याननुपेत्य देवान् सृष्टावभूतामिव भूतधात्रा ॥६॥
तां सुन्दरीं चेत् न लभेत नन्दः सा वा निषेवेत न तं नतभ्रूः ।
द्वन्द्वं ध्रुवं तत् विकलं न शोभेतान्योन्यहीनाविव रात्रिचन्द्रौ ॥७॥
कन्दर्परत्योरिव लक्ष्मभूतम् प्रमोदनान्द्योरिव नीडभूतम् ।
प्रहर्षतुष्ट्योरिव पात्रभूतम् द्वन्द्वं सहार[ ]स्त मदान्धभूतम् ॥८॥
परस्परोद्वीक्षणतत्पराक्षं परस्परं व्याहृतसक्तचित्तम् ।
परस्पराश्लेषहृताङ्गरागम् परस्परं तन्मिथुनं जहार ॥९॥
भावानुरक्तौ गिरिनिर्झरस्थौ तौ किन्नरीकिंपुरुषाविवोभौ ।
चिक्रीडतुश्चापि विरेजतुश्च रूपश्रियान्योन्यमिवाक्षिपन्तौ ॥१०॥

अन्योन्यसंरागविवर्द्धनेन तद्द्वन्द्वमन्योन्यमरीरमच्च ।
क्लमान्तरे तर्षबलेन तेन[1] सलीलमन्योन्यममीमदच्च ॥११॥

विभूषयामास ततः प्रि(प)यां स सिषेविषुस्तां न मृजावहार्थम् ।
स्वेनैव रूपेण विभूषिता हि विभूषणानामपि भूषणं सा ॥१२॥

दत्वाथ सा दर्पणमस्य हस्ते ममाग्रतो धारय तावदेनम् ।
विशेषकं यावदहं करोमीत्युवाच कान्तं स च तं बभार ॥१३॥

भर्त्तुस्ततः श्मश्रु निरूप्यमाणा विशेषकं भासि[2] चकार तादृक् ।
निश्वासवातेन च दर्पणस्य चिकित्सयित्वा निजघान नन्दः ॥१४॥

सा तेन चेष्टाललितेन भर्त्तुः शाठ्येन चान्तर्मनसा[3] जहास ।
भवेच्च रुष्टा किल नाम तस्मै ललाटजिह्मां भ्रुकुटिं चकार ॥१५॥

चिक्षेप कर्णोत्पलमस्य चांसे करेण सव्येन मदालसेन ।
पत्राङ्गुलिं चार्द्धनिमीलिताक्षे वक्त्रेऽस्य तामेव विनिर्दुधाव ॥१६॥

ततश्चलन्नूपुरयन्त्रिताभ्याम् नखप्रभोद्भासितराङ्गुलिभ्याम् ।
पद्भ्यां प्रियाया नलिनोपमाभ्याम् मूर्द्ध्ना भयान्नाम ननाम नन्दः ॥१७॥

स मुक्तपुष्पोन्मिषितेन मूर्द्ध्ना ततः प्रियायाः प्रियकृत् बभासे ।
सुवर्णवेद्यां अनिलावभग्नः पुष्पातिभारादिव नागवृक्षः ॥१८॥

सा तं स्तनोद्वर्त्तितहारयष्टिरुत्थापयामास निपीड्य दोर्भ्याम् ।
कथं कृतोसीति जहास चोच्चैः मुखेन साचीकृतकुण्डलेन ॥१९॥

---

१ P. M. तर्थबलेह्रतेन ।

२ P. M. भासापिषि, not in P. L. M. T.

३ P. M. साध्येन चातुर्मनसा ।

पत्युस्ततो दर्पणसक्तपाणेः मुहुर्मुहुर्वक्त्रमवेक्षमाणा ।
तमालपत्रार्द्रतले कपोले समाधयामास विशेषकं तत् ॥२०॥
तस्या मुखं तत् सतमालपत्रं ताम्राधरोष्ठं चिकुरायताक्षम् ।
रक्ताधिकाग्रं पतितद्विरेफं सशैवलं पद्ममिवावभासे ॥२१॥
नन्दस्ततो दर्पणमादरेण बिभ्रत् तदा मण्डनसाक्षिभूतम् ।
विशेषकावेक्षणकेकराक्षो लडत् प्रियाया वदनं ददर्श ॥२२॥
तत्कुण्डलादष्टविशेषकान्तं कारण्डवक्लिष्टमिवारविन्दम् ।
नन्दः प्रियाया मुखमीक्षमाणो भूयः प्रियानन्दकरो बभूव ॥२३॥

विमानकल्पे स विमानगर्भे ततस्तथा चैव ननन्द नन्दः ।
तथागतश्चागतभैक्षकालो भैक्षाय तस्य प्रविवेश वेश्म ॥२४॥
अवाङ्मुखो निष्प्रणयश्च तस्थौ भ्रातुर्गृहेऽन्यस्य गृहे यथैव ।
तस्मादथो प्रेष्यजनप्रमादात् भिक्षामलब्ध्वैव पुनर्जगाम ॥२५॥
काचित् पिपेषाङ्गविलेपनं हि वासोऽङ्गना काचिदवासयच्च ।
अयोजयत् स्नानविधिं तथान्या जग्रन्थुरन्याः सुरभीः स्रजश्च ॥२६॥
तस्मिन् गृहे भर्तुरतश्चरन्त्यः क्रीडानुरूपं लडितं नियोगम् ।
काश्चिन्न बुद्धं ददृशुर्युवत्यः बुद्धस्य वैषा नियतं मनीषा ॥२७॥
काचित् स्थिता तत्र तु हर्म्यपृष्ठे गवाक्षपक्षे प्रणिधाय चक्षुः ।
विनिष्पतन्तं सुगतं ददर्श पयोदगर्भादिव दीप्तमर्कम् ॥२८॥
सा गौरवं तत्र विचार्य भर्तुः स्वया च भक्त्यार्हतयार्हतश्च ।
नन्दस्य तस्थौ पुरतो विवक्षुः तदाज्ञया चेति तदाचचक्षे ॥२९॥
अनुग्रहायास्य जनस्य शङ्के गुरुर्गृहं नो भगवान् प्रविष्टः ।
भिक्षामलब्ध्वा गिरमासनं वा शून्यादरण्यादिव याति भूयः ॥३०॥

श्रुत्वा महर्षेः स गृहप्रवेशं सत्कारहीनञ्च पुनः प्रयाणम् ।
चचाल चित्राभरणाम्बरस्रग् कल्पद्रुमो धूत इवानिलेन ॥२१॥
कृत्वाञ्जलिं मूर्द्धनि पद्मकल्पं ततः स कान्तां गमनं ययाचे ।
कर्त्तुं गमिष्यामि गुरौ प्रणामम् मामभ्यनुज्ञातुमिहार्हसीति ॥२२॥
सा वेपमाना परिसस्वजे तं शालं लता वातसमीरितेव ।
ददर्श चाश्रुप्लुतलोलनेत्रा दीर्घञ्च निश्वस्य वचोऽभ्युवाच ॥२३॥
नाहं यियासोर्गुरुदर्शनार्थम् अर्हामि कर्त्तुं तव धर्म्मपीडाम्[1] ।
गच्छार्य्यपुत्रैहि च शीघ्रमेव विशेषको यावदयं न शुष्कः ॥२४॥
स चेत् भवेस्त्वम् खलु दीर्घसूत्रो दण्डं महान्तम् त्वयि पातयेयम् ।
मुहुर्मुहुस्त्वां शयितम् कुचाभ्याम् विबोधयेयञ्च न चालयेयम् ॥२५॥
अथाप्यनाश्यानविशेषकायां अप्येष्यसि त्वं त्वरितम् ततः त्वाम् ।
निपीडयिष्यामि भुजद्वयेन विभूषणेनार्द्रविलेपनेन ॥२६॥
इत्येवमुक्तश्च निपीडितश्च तया स वेणुस्वनया जगाम ।
एवं करिष्यामि विमुञ्च चण्डि यावद्गुरुर्दूरगतो न मे सः ॥२७॥
ततस्तनोद्वर्त्तितचन्दनाभ्याम् मुक्तो भुजाभ्याम् न तु मानसेन ।
विहाय वेषम् मदनानुरूपम् तत्कालयोग्यम् स वपुर्बभार ॥२८॥
सा तं प्रयान्तम् रमणं प्रदध्यौ प्रध्यानशून्यस्थितनिश्चलाक्षी ।
स्थितोच्चकर्णा व्यपविद्धशष्पा भ्रान्तं मृगं भ्रान्तमुखी मृगीव ॥२९॥
दिदृक्षयाक्षिप्तमना मुनेस्तु नन्दः प्रयाणं प्रति तत्वरे च ।
विवृत्तदृष्टिश्च शनैर्ययौ ताम् करीव पश्यन् स लडत्करेणुम् ॥४०॥

---

१ P. L. M. धर्म्मयाच्ञां ।

शातोदरीं पीनपयोधरोरूम् स सुन्दरीं रुक्मदरीमिवाद्रेः ।
काक्षेण पश्यन् न ततर्प नन्दः पिबन्निवैकेन जलं करेण ॥४१॥

तं गौरवं बुद्धगतम् चकर्ष भार्य्यानुरागः पुनराचकर्ष ।
सोऽनिश्चयात् नापि ययौ न तस्थौ तरंस्तरङ्गेष्विव राजहंसः ॥४२॥

अदर्शनं भूयगतस्य तस्या हर्म्यात्ततश्चावततार तूर्णम् ।
श्रुत्वा ततो नूपुरनिस्वनं स पुनर्ललम्बे हृदये गृहीतः ॥४३॥

स कामरागेण निगृह्यमाणो धर्म्मानुरागेण च कृष्यमाणः ।
जगाम दुःखेन विवर्त्त्यमानः प्लवः प्रतिस्रोत इवापगायाः ॥४४॥

ततः क्रमैर्दीर्घतमैः प्रचक्रमे कथं नु यातो न गुरुर्भवेदिति ।
स्वजेय तां चैव विशेषकप्रियां कथं प्रियामार्द्रविशेषकामिति ॥४५॥

अथ स पथि ददर्श मुक्तमानं पितृनगरेपि तथा गताभिमानम् ।
दशबलमभितो विलम्बमानम् ध्वजमनुयान इवैन्द्रमर्च्यमानम् ॥४६॥

सौन्दरनन्दे महाकाव्ये भार्य्यायाचितको नाम
चतुर्थः सर्गः ॥४॥

---

# पञ्चमः सर्गः

अथावतीर्य्याश्वरथद्विपेभ्यः शाक्या यथास्वर्द्धि[१] गृहीतवेषाः ।
महापणेभ्यो व्यवहारिणश्च महामुनौ भक्तिवशात् प्रणेमुः ॥१॥
केचित् प्रणम्यानुययुर्मुहूर्त्तम् केचित् प्रणम्यार्थवशेन जग्मुः ।
केचित् स्वकेष्वावसथेषु तस्थुः कृत्वाञ्जलीन् वीक्षणतत्पराक्षाः ॥२॥
बुद्धस्ततस्तत्र नरेन्द्रमार्गे स्रोतो महत् भक्तिमतो जनस्य ।
जगाम दुःखेन विगाह्यमानो जलागमे स्रोत इवापग[ा]याः ॥३॥
अथो महद्भिः पथि सम्पतद्भिः सम्पूज्यमानाय तथागताय ।
कर्त्तुं प्रणामं न शशाक नन्दस्तेनाभिरेमे तु गुरोर्महिम्ना ॥४॥
स्वञ्चावसङ्गम् पथि निर्मुमुक्षुः भक्तिं जनस्यान्यमतेश्च रक्षन् ।
नन्दञ्च गेहाभिमुखं जिघृक्षन् मार्गं ततोऽन्यं सुगतः प्रपेदे ॥५॥
ततो विविक्तञ्च विविक्तचेताः सन्मार्गवित् मार्गमभिप्रतस्थे ।
गत्वाग्रतश्चाग्र्यतमाय तस्मै नान्दीविमुक्ताय ननाम नन्दः ॥६॥
शनैर्व्रजन्नेव स गौरवेण पटावृतांशो विनतार्द्धकायः ।
अधोनिबद्धाञ्जलिरूर्द्ध्वनेत्रः सगद्गदम् वाक्यमिदं बभाषे ॥७॥
प्रासादसंस्थो भगवन्तमन्तःप्रविष्टमश्रौषमनुग्रहाय ।
अतस्त्वरावानहमभ्युपेतो गृहस्य कक्षा[न्][२] महतोभ्यसूयन् ॥८॥
तत् साधु साधुप्रिय मत्प्रियार्थम् तत्रास्तु भिक्षूत्तम भैक्षकालः ।
असौ हि मध्यं नभसो यियासुः कालं प्रतिस्मारयतीव सूर्य्यः ॥९॥

---

१ P. M. मृद्धि ।

२ P. M. कक्षामहतो, P. L. M. कक्ष्यामहतः ।

इत्येवमुक्तः प्रणयेन तेन स्नेहाभिमानोन्मुखलोचनेन ।
तादृङ्निमित्तं सुगतश्चकार नाहार[१]कृत्यं स यथा विवेद ॥१०॥
ततः स कृत्वा मुनये प्रणामं गृहप्रयाणाय मतिं चकार ।
अनुग्रहार्थं सुगतस्तु तस्मै पात्रं ददौ पुष्करपत्रनेत्रः ॥११॥
ततः स लोके ददतः फलार्थं पात्रस्य तस्याप्रतिमस्य पात्रम् ।
जग्राह चापग्रहणक्षमाभ्यां पद्मोपमाभ्याम् प्रयतः कराभ्याम् ॥१२॥
पराङ्मुखन्त्वन्यमनस्कमारात् विज्ञाय नन्दः सुगतं गतास्थम् ।
हस्तस्थपात्रोऽपि गृहं यियासुः ससार मार्गात् मुनिमीक्षमाणः ॥१३॥
भार्य्यानुरागेण यदा गृहं स पात्रं गृहीत्वापि यियासुरेव ।
विमोहयामास मुनिस्ततस्तं रथ्यामुखस्यावरणेन तस्य ॥१४॥
निर्मो(र्यो)क्षबीजं[२] हि ददर्श तस्य ज्ञानं मृदु(ं) क्लेशरजश्च तीव्र(ः)म् ।
क्लेशाकुलान् [तान्] विषयान् स तस्य नन्दं यतस्तं मुनिराचकर्ष ॥१५॥
संक्लेशपक्षो द्विविधश्च दृष्टस्तथा द्विकल्पो व्यवदानपक्षः ।
आत्माश्रयो हेतुबलाधिकस्य बाह्याश्रयः प्रत्ययगौरवस्य ॥१६॥
अयत्नतो हेतुबलाधिकस्तु निर्मुच्यते घट्टितमात्र एव ।
यत्नेन तु प्रत्ययनेयबुद्धिः विमोक्षमाप्नोति पराश्रयेण ॥१७॥
नन्दः स च प्रत्ययनेयचेता[३] यं शिश्रिये तन्मयतामवाप ।
यस्मादिमं तत्र चकार यत्नं तत्स्नेहपङ्कान् मुनिरुज्जिहीर्षन् ॥१८॥

---

१ P. M. ०कारं वाह्वार ।
२ P. M. निर्य्योक्ष० ।
३ P. M. प्रत्ययने प्रचेता T.

नन्दस्तु दुःखेन विचेष्टमानः शनैरगत्या गुरुमन्वगच्छत् ।
भार्य्यामुखं वीक्षणलोलनेत्रं विचिन्तयन्नार्द्रविशेषकं तत् ॥१९॥

ततो मुनिस्तम् प्रियमाल्यहारम् वसन्तमासेन कृताभिहारम् ।
निनाय भग्नप्रमदाविहारं विद्याविहाराभिमतं विहारम् ॥२०॥
दीनं महा[का]रुणिकस्ततस्तम् दृष्ट्वा मुहूर्त्तं करुणायमानः ।
करेण चक्राङ्कतलेन मूर्द्धि पस्पर्श चैवेदमुवाच चैनम् ॥२१॥
यावन्न हिंस्रस् समुपैति कालः शमाय तावद् कुरु सौम्य बुद्धिम् ।
सर्व्वास्ववस्थास्विह वर्त्तमानं सर्व्वाभिसारेण निहन्ति मृत्युः ॥२२॥
साधारणात् स्वप्ननिभादसारात् लोलं मनः कामसुखान्नियच्छ ।
हव्यैरिवाग्नेः पवनेरितस्य लोकस्य कामैर्न हि तृप्तिरस्ति ॥२३॥
श्रद्धाधनं श्रेष्ठतमं धनेभ्यः प्रज्ञारसस्तृप्तिकरो रसेभ्यः ।
प्रधानमध्यात्मसुखं सुखेभ्योऽविद्यारतिः दुःखतमा रतिभ्यः ॥२४॥
हितस्य वक्ता प्रवरः सुहृद्भ्यो धर्म्माय खेदो गुणवान् श्रमेभ्यः ।
ज्ञानाय कृत्यम् परमं प्रियाभ्यः किमिन्द्रियाणामुपगम्य दास्यम् ॥२५॥
तन्निश्चितं भीक्षमशुग्वियुक्तम् परेष्वनायत्तमहार्य्यमन्यैः ।
नित्यं शिवं शान्तिसुखं वृणीष्व किमिन्द्रियार्थार्थमनर्थमूढ्वा ॥२६॥
जरा समा नास्त्यमृजा प्रजानाम् व्याधेः समो नास्ति जगत्यनर्थः ।
मृत्योः समं नास्ति भयं पृथिव्यां एतत्त्रयं खल्ववशेन सेव्यम् ॥२७॥
स्नेहेन कश्चिन्न समोऽस्ति पाशः स्रोतो न तृष्णासममस्ति हारि ।
रागाग्निना नास्ति समस्तथाग्निस्तच्चेत् त्रयं नास्ति सुखं च तेऽस्ति ॥२८॥
अवश्यभावी प्रियविप्रयोगः तस्माच्च शोको नियतं निषेव्यः ।
शोकेन चोन्मादमुपेयिवांसो राजर्षयोन्येऽप्यवशा विचेलुः ॥२९॥

प्रज्ञामयं वर्म्म बधान तस्मात् नेष्यन्ति[1] निघ्नस्य हि शोकबाणाः ।
महच्च दग्धुं भवकक्षजालं संधुक्षयाल्पाग्निमिवात्मतेजः ॥२०॥
यथौषधैर्हस्तगतैः स वैद्यो न दश्यते कश्चन पन्नगेन ।
तथानपेक्ष्योजितलोकमोहो न दश्यते शोकभुजङ्गमेन ॥२१॥
आस्थाय योगं परिगम्य तत्त्वं न त्रासमागच्छति मृत्युकाले ।
आबद्धवर्म्मा सुधनुः कृतास्त्रो जिगीषया शूर इवाहवस्थः ॥२२॥

इत्येवमुक्तः स तथागतेन सर्व्वेषु भूतेष्वनुकम्पकेन ।
धृष्टं गिरान्तर्हृदयेन सीदंस्तथेति नन्द[:] सुगतं बभाषे ॥२३॥
अथ प्रमादाच्च तमुज्जिहीर्षन् मत्वागमस्यैव च पात्रभूतम् ।
प्रव्राजयानन्द शमाय नन्दं इत्यब्रवीत् मैत्रमना महर्षिः ॥२४॥
नन्दं ततोऽन्तर्मनसा रुदन्तम् एहीति वैदेहमुनिर्जगाद ।
शनैस्ततस्तं समुपेत्य नन्दो न प्रव्रजिष्याम्यहमित्युवाच ॥२५॥

श्रुत्वाथ नन्दस्य मनीषितं तत् बुद्धाय वैदेहमुनि[:] शशंस ।
संश्रुत्य तस्मादपि तस्य भावम् महामुनिर्नन्दमुवाच भूयः ॥२६॥
मय्यग्रजे प्रव्रजिते जितात्मन् भ्रातृष्वनु प्रव्रजितेषु चास्मान् ।
ज्ञातींश्च दृष्ट्वा व्रतिनो गृहस्थान् संविन्न चित्तेऽस्ति न वास्ति चेतः ॥२७॥
राजर्षयस्ते विदिता न नूनम् वनानि ये शिश्रियिरे हसन्तः ।
निष्ठीव्य कामान् उपशान्तिकामाः कामेषु नैवं कृपणेषु सक्ताः ॥२८॥
भूयः समालोक्य गृहेषु दोषान् निशाम्य तत् त्यागकृतं च शर्म्म ।
नैवास्ति मोक्तुं मतिरालयं ते देशं मुमूर्षोरिव सोपसर्गम् ॥२९॥

---

१ Both MSS. नेष्यान्ति ।

संसारकान्तारपरायणस्य शिवे कथं ते पथि नारुरुक्षा ।
आरोप्यमाणस्य तमेव मार्गं भ्रष्टस्य सार्थादिव सार्थिकस्य ॥४०॥
यः सर्वतो वेश्मनि दह्यमाने शयीत मोहात् न ततो व्यपेयात् ।
कालाग्निना व्याधिजराशिखेन लोके प्रदीप्ते[1] स भवेत् प्रमत्तः ॥४१॥
प्रणीयमानश्च यथा वधाय मत्तो हसेच्च प्रलपेच्च वध्यः ।
मृत्यौ तथा तिष्ठति पाशहस्ते शोच्यः प्रमाद्यन् विपरीतचेताः ॥४२॥
यदा नरेन्द्राश्च कुटुम्बिनश्च विहाय बन्धूंश्च परिग्रहांश्च ।
ययुश्च यास्यन्ति च यान्ति चैव प्रियेष्वनित्येषु कुतोऽनुरोधः ॥४३॥'
किञ्चिन्न पश्यामि रतस्य यत्र तदन्यभावेन भवेन्न दुःखम् ।
तस्मात् क्वचिन्न क्षमते प्रसक्तिर्यदि क्षमस्तद्विगमान्न शोकः ॥४४॥
तत् सौम्य लोलं परिगम्य लोकं मायोपमं चित्तमिवेन्द्रजालम् ।
प्रियाभिधानं त्यज (तो) मोहजालं छेत्तुं मतिस्ते यदि दुःखजालम् ॥
४५॥
वर[ं] हितोदर्कमनिष्टमन्नम् न स्वादु यत्स्यादहितानुबद्धम् ।
यस्मादहं (न) त्वां विनियोजयामि शिवे शुचौ वर्त्मनि विप्रियेऽपि ॥
४६॥
बालस्य धात्री विनिगृह्य लोष्टं यथोद्धरत्यास्यपुटप्रविष्टम् ।
तथोज्जिहीर्षुः खलु रागशल्यं तत्त्वामवोचं परुषं हिताय ॥४७॥
अनिष्टमप्यौषधमातुराय ददाति वैद्यश्च यथा निगृह्य ।
तद्वन्मयोक्तम् प्रतिकूलमेतत् तुभ्यं हितोदर्कमनुग्रहाय ॥४८॥

---

१ Both P. L. M. and P. M. प्रदीपे स T.

तद्यावदेव क्षणसन्निपातो न मृत्युरागच्छति यावदेव ।
यावद्वयो योगविधौ समर्थं बुद्धिं कुरु श्रेयसि तावदेव ॥४९॥

इत्येवमुक्तः स विनायकेन हितैषिणा कारुणिकेन नन्दः ।
कर्त्तास्मि सर्व्वं भगवन् वचस्ते तथा यथाज्ञापयसीत्युवाच ॥५०॥

आदाय वैदेहमुनिस्ततस्तम् निनाय संश्लिष्य विचेष्टमानम् ।
व्ययोजयच्चाश्रुपरिप्लुताक्षं केशश्रियं छत्रनिभस्य मूर्द्ध्नः ॥५१॥

अथो रुतं तस्य मुखं सबाष्पम् प्रवास्यमानेषु शिरोरुहेषु ।
वक्राग्रनालं नलिनं तडागे वर्षोदकक्लिन्नमिवावभासे ॥५२॥

नन्दस्ततः तरुकषायविविक्तवासा-
श्चिन्तावशो नवगृहीत इव द्विपेन्द्रः ।
पूर्णः शशी बहुलपक्षगतः क्षपान्ते
बालातपेन परिषिक्त इवावभासे ॥५३॥

सौन्दरनन्दमहाकाव्ये नन्दप्रव्राजनं नाम पञ्चमः सर्गः ।

# षष्ठः सर्गः

ततो हृते भर्त्तरि गौरवेण प्रीतौ हृतायामरतौ कृतायां ।
तत्रैव हर्म्म्योपरि वर्त्तमाना न सुन्दरी सैव तदा बभासे ॥१॥
सा भर्त्तुरभ्यागमनप्रतीक्षा गवाक्षमाक्रम्य पयोधराभ्याम् ।
द्वारोन्मुखी हर्म्म्यतलाल्ललम्बे मुखेन [१]तिर्य्यङ्नतकुण्डलेन ॥२॥
विलम्बहारा चलयोक्त्रका सा तस्माद् विमानाद्विनता चकाशे ।
तपःक्षयादप्सरसां वरेव च्युतं[२] विमानात् प्रियमीक्षमाणा ॥३॥
सा खेदसंस्विन्नललाटकेन निश्वासनिष्पीतविशेषकेण ।
चिन्ताचलाक्षेण मुखेन तस्थौ भर्त्तारमन्यत्र विशङ्कमाना ॥४॥
ततश्चिरस्थानपरिश्रमेण स्थितेव पर्य्यङ्कतले पपात ।
तिर्य्यक्च शिश्ये प्रविकीर्णहारा सपादुकैवार्द्धविलम्बपादा ॥५॥
अथात्र काचित् प्रमदा सबाष्पां तां दुःखितां द्रष्टुमनीप्समाना ।
प्रासादसोपानतलप्रणादं चकार पद्भ्यां सहसा रुदन्ती ॥६॥
तस्याश्च सोपानतलप्रणादं श्रुत्वैव तूर्णं पुनरुत्पपात ।
प्रीत्या प्रसक्तेव च संजहर्ष प्रियोपयानं परिशङ्कमाना ॥७॥
सा त्रासयन्ती वलभीपुटस्थान् पारावतान् नूपुरनिःस्वनेन ।
सोपानकुक्षिं प्रससार हर्षात् भ्रष्टं दुकूलान्तमचिन्तयन्ती ॥८॥
तामङ्गनां प्रेक्ष्य च विप्रलब्धा निश्वस्य भूयः शयनं प्रपेदे ।
विवर्णवक्त्रा न रराज चाशु विवर्णचन्द्रेव हिमागमे द्यौः ॥९॥
सा दुःखिता भर्त्तुरदर्शनेन कामेन कोपेन च दह्यमाना ।
कृत्वा करे वक्त्रमथोपविष्टा चिन्तानदीं शोकजलां ततार ॥१०॥

---

१ P. M. निर्य्यन्नत० । २ P. M. च्युता ।

तस्या मुखं पद्मसपत्नभूतम् पाणौ स्थितं पल्लवरागताम्रे ।
छायामयस्याम्भसि पङ्कजस्य बभौ नतं पद्ममिवोपरिष्टात् ॥११॥
सा स्त्रीस्वभावेन विचिन्त्य तत्तत् दृष्टानुरागेऽभिमुखेऽपि पत्यौ ।
धर्माश्रिते तत्त्वमविन्दमाना संकल्प्य तत्तत् विललाप तत्तत् ॥१२॥
एष्याम्यनाश्यानविशेषकायां त्वयीति कृत्वा मयि तां प्रतिज्ञां ।
कस्मान्नु हेतोर्दयितप्रतिज्ञः सोद्य प्रियो मे वितथप्रतिज्ञः ॥१३॥
आर्य्यस्य साधोः करुणात्मकस्य मन्नित्यभीरोरतिदक्षिणस्य ।
कुतो विकारोयमभूतपूर्व्वः स्वेनापरागेण ममापचारात् ॥१४॥
रतिप्रियस्य प्रियवर्त्तिनो मे प्रियस्य नूनं हृदयं विरक्तम् ।
तथा हि रागो यदि तस्य हि स्यात् मच्चित्तरक्षी न स नागतः[1] स्यात् ॥१५॥
रूपेण भावेन न च यत् विशिष्टा प्रियेण दृष्टा नियतं ततोऽन्या ।
तथा हि कृत्वा मयि मोघसान्त्वं लग्नां सतीं मामगमत् विहाय ॥१६॥
भक्तिं स बुद्धं प्रति यामवोचत् तस्य प्रयातुं मयि सोऽपदेशः ।
मुनौ प्रसादो यदि तस्य हि स्यात् मृत्योरिवोग्रादनुतत् बिभीयात् ॥१७॥
लेखार्थ[2]मादर्शमनन्यचित्तो विभूषयन्त्या मम धारयित्वा ।
बिभर्त्ति सोऽन्यस्य जनस्य तच्चेत् नमोस्तु तस्मै चलसौहृदाय ॥१८॥
नेच्छन्ति याः शोकमवाप्तुमेवं[3] श्रद्धातुमर्हन्ति न ता नराणाम् ।
क्व चानुवृत्तिर्मयि सास्य पूर्व्वं त्यागः क्व चायं जनवत् क्षणेन ॥१९॥
इत्येवमादि प्रियविप्रयुक्ता प्रियेऽन्यदाशङ्क्य च सा जगाद ।
सम्भ्रान्तमारुह्य च तत् विमानं सा स्त्री सबाष्पा गिरमित्युवाच ॥२०॥

---

१ P. M. न समागतः स्यात् ।

२ P. M. लेवार्थं P. L. M. lacuna T. ३ P. L. M. रतम् ।

युवापि तावत् प्रियदर्शनोऽपि सौभाग्यभाग्याभिजनान्वितोऽपि ।
यस्त्वां प्रियो नाभ्यचरत्[1] कदाचित् तमन्यथा यास्यसि कातरासि ॥२१॥
मा स्वामिनं स्वामिनि दोषमागाः प्रियं प्रियार्हं प्रियकारिणं तम् ।
न स त्वदन्यां प्रमदामवैति स्वचक्रवाक्या इव चक्रवाकः ॥२२॥
स तु त्वदर्थं गृहवासमीप्सन् जिजीविषुस्त्वत्परितोषहेतोः ।
भ्रात्रा किलार्य्येण तथागतेन प्रव्राजितो नेत्रजलार्द्रवक्त्रः ॥२३॥

श्रुत्वा ततो भर्त्तरि तां प्रवृत्तिं सवेपथुः सा सहसोत्पपात ।
प्रगृह्य बाहू विरुराव चोच्चैः हृदीव[ि]दग्धाभिहता करेणुः ॥२४॥
सा रोदनारोषितरक्तदृष्टिः सन्तापसंक्षोभितगात्रयष्टिः ।
पपात शीर्णाकुलहारयष्टिः फलातिभारादिव चूतयष्टिः ॥२५॥
सा पद्मरागं वसनं वसाना पद्मानना पद्मदलायताक्षी ।
पद्मा विपद्मा पतिताक्षलाक्षी शुशोष [प]द्मस्रगिवातपेन ॥२६॥
संचिन्त्य संचिन्त्य गुणांश्च भर्त्तुर्दीर्घं निशश्वास तताम चैव ।
विभूषणश्रीर्निहिता प्रको[तो]ष्ठे ताम्रे कराग्रे च विनिर्दुधाव ॥२७॥
न भूषणे[णा]ऽर्थो मम संप्रतीति सा दिक्षु चिक्षेप विभूषणानि ।
निर्भूषणा सा पतिता चकाशे विशीर्णपुष्पस्तवका लतेव ॥२८॥
धृतः प्रियेणायमभूत् ममेति रुक्मत्सरुं दर्पणमालिलिङ्ग ।
यत्नाच्च विन्यस्ततमालपत्रौ रुष्टेव धृष्टं प्रममार्ज गण्डौ ॥२९॥
सा चक्रवाकीव भृशं चुकूज श्येनाग्रपक्षक्षतचक्रवाका ।
विस्पर्द्धमानेव विमानसंस्थैः पारावतैः कूजनलोलकण्ठैः ॥३०॥
विचित्रमृद्वास्तरणेऽपि सुप्ता वैदूर्य्यवज्रप्रतिमण्डितेऽपि ।

---

१ P. M. नाभ्यच[र]त् ।

रुक्माङ्गपादे शयने महार्हे न शर्म्म लेभे परिचेष्टमाना ॥२१॥
संदृश्य भर्त्तुश्च विभूषणानि वासांसि वीणाप्रभृतीश्च लीडाः ।
तमो विवेशाभिननाद चोच्चैः पङ्कावतीर्णेव च संससाद ॥२२॥
सा सुन्दरी श्वासचलोदरी हि वज्राग्निसंभिन्नदरीगुहेव ।
शोकाग्निनान्तर्हृदि दह्यमाना विभ्रान्तचित्तेव तदा बभूव ॥२३॥
ररोद मम्लौ विरुराव जग्लौ बभ्राम तस्थौ विललाप दध्यौ ।
चकार रोषं विचकार माल्यं चकर्त्त वक्त्रं विचकर्ष वस्त्रम् ॥२४॥

तां चारुदन्तीं प्रसभं रुदन्तीं संश्रुत्य नार्य्यः परमाभितप्ताः ।
अन्तर्गृहादारुरुहुर्विमानं त्रासेन किन्नर्य्य इवाद्रिपृष्ठम् ॥२५॥
बाष्पेण ताः क्लिन्नविषण्णवक्त्रा वर्षेण पद्मिन्य इवार्द्रपद्माः ।
स्थानानुरूपेण यथाभिमानं निलिल्यिरे तामनुदह्यमानाः ॥२६॥
ताभिर्वृता हर्म्यतलेऽङ्गनाभिश्चिन्तातनुः सा सुतनुर्बभासे ।
शतह्रदाभिः परिवेष्टितेव शशाङ्कलेखा शरदभ्रमध्ये ॥२७॥

या तत्र तासां वचसोपपन्ना मान्या च तस्या वयसाधिका च ।
सा पृष्ठतस्तां तु[१] समालिलिङ्ग प्रमृज्य चाश्रूणि वचांस्युवाच ॥२८॥
राजर्षिवध्वास्तव नानुरूपो धर्म्माश्रिते भर्त्तरि जातु शोकः ।
इक्ष्वाकुवंशे ह्यभिकाङ्क्षितानि दायाद्यभूतानि तपोवनानि ॥२९॥
प्रायेण मोक्षाय विनिःसृतानाम् शाक्यर्षभाणां विदिताः स्त्रियस्ते[२] ।
तपोवनानीव गृहाणि यासां साध्वीव्रतं[३] कामवदाश्रितानाम् ॥४०॥
यद्यन्यया रूपगुणाधिकत्वात् भर्त्ता हृतस्ते कुरु बाष्पमोक्षम् ।

---

१ P. M. च । २ P. M. स्त्रियस्ता ।
३ P. M. साध्विपथं, P. L. M. साध्विव्रतम् T.

मनस्विनी रूपवती गुणाढ्या हृदि क्षते काच हि नास्रु मुञ्चेत् ॥४१॥
अथापि किञ्चित् व्यसनं प्रपन्नो मा चैव तद्भूत् सदृशोऽत्र बाष्पः ।
अतो विशिष्टं न हि दुःखमस्ति कुलोद्गतायाः पतिदेवतायाः ॥४२॥
अथ त्विदानीं [1]लडितः सुखेन स्वस्थः फलस्थो व्यसनान्यदृष्ट्वा ।
वीतस्पृहो धर्म्ममनुप्रपन्नः किं विक्लवे[2] रोदिषि हर्षकाले ॥४३॥

इत्येवमुक्तापि बहुप्रकारम् स्नेहात्[3] तया नैव धृतिं चकार ।
अथापरा तां मनसोनुकूलं कालोपपन्नम् प्रणयादुवाच ॥४४॥
ब्रवीमि सत्यं सुविनिश्चितं मे प्राप्तं प्रियं द्रक्ष्यसि शीघ्रमेव ।
त्वया विना स्थास्यति तत्र नासौ सत्त्वाश्रयश्चेतनयेव हीनः ॥४५॥
अङ्केपि लक्ष्म्याः न स निर्वृतः स्यात् त्वं तस्य पार्श्वे यदि तत्र न स्याः ।
आपत्सु कृच्छ्रास्वपि चागतासु त्वां पश्यतस्तस्य भवेन्न दुःखम् ॥४६॥
त्वं निर्वृतिं गच्छ नियच्छ बाष्पम् तप्ताश्रुमोचात् परिरक्ष चक्षुः ।
यस्तस्य भावस्त्वयि यश्च रागो न रंस्यते त्वद्विरहात् स धर्म्मे ॥४७॥
स्यादत्र नासौ कुलसत्त्वयोगात् काषायमादाय विहास्यतीति ।
अनात्मनादाय गृहोन्मुखस्य पुनर्विमोक्तुं क इवास्ति दोषः ॥४८॥

इति युवतिजनेन सान्त्व्यमाना
हृतहृदया रमणेन सुन्दरी सा ।
द्रमिडमभिमुखे पुरेव रम्भा
क्षितिमगमत् परिवारिताप्सरोभिः ॥४९॥

सौन्दरनन्दे महाकाव्ये भार्य्याविलापो नाम षष्ठः सर्गः ।

---

१ P. M. चलितः । २ P. M. विक्लवा । ३ P. M. स्तदा ।

## सप्तमः सर्गः

लिङ्गं ततस्तास्तु विधिप्रदिष्टम् गात्रेण बिभ्रन्न तु चेतसा तत् ।
भार्य्यागतैरेव मनोवितर्कैः यो ह्रीयमानो न ननन्द नन्दः ॥१॥
स पुष्पमासस्य च पुष्पलक्ष्म्या सर्व्वाभिसारेण च पुष्पकेतोः ।
यानीयभावेन च यौवनस्य विहारसंस्थो न शमं जगाम ॥२॥
स्थितः स दीनः सहकारवीथ्यामालीनसंमूर्च्छितषट्पदायाम् ।
भृशं जजृम्भे युगदीर्घबाहुः ध्यात्वा प्रियां चापमिवाचकर्ष ॥३॥
स पातकक्षोदमिव प्रतीच्छ[न्] चूतद्रुमेभ्यस्तनुपुष्पवर्षम् ।
दीर्घं निशश्वास विचिन्त्य भार्य्यां नवग्रहो नाग इवावबुद्धः[१] ॥४॥
शोकस्य हर्त्ता शरणागतानाम् शोकस्य कर्त्ता प्रतिगर्व्वितानाम् ।
अशोकमालम्ब्य स जातशोकः प्रियां प्रियाशोकवनां शुशोच ॥५॥
प्रियां प्रियायाः प्रतनुं प्रियङ्गुं[२] निशाम्य भीतामिव निष्पतन्तीम् ।
सस्मार तामश्रुमुखीं सबाष्पः प्रियां प्रियङ्गुप्रसवावदाताम्[३] ॥६॥
पुष्पावनद्धे तिलकद्रुमस्य दृष्ट्वान्यपुष्टां शिखरे निविष्टाम् ।
सङ्कल्पयामास शिखां प्रियायाः शुक्लांशुकाट्टालमपाश्रितायाः ॥७॥
लतां प्रफुल्लामतिमुक्तकस्य चूतस्य पार्श्वे परिरभ्य जाताम् ।
निशाम्य चिन्तामगमत् तदेवं श्लिष्टा भवेत् मामपि सुन्दरीति ॥८॥
पुष्पै[र]राला[४] अपि नागवृक्षा दान्तैः समुद्गैरिव[५] हेमगर्भैः ।
कान्तारवृक्षा इव दुःखितस्य न चक्षुराचिक्षिपुरस्य तत्र ॥९॥

---

१ P. M. इव नागावबुद्धः T. २ P. M. प्रियं भूः T.
३ P. M. प्रियां प्रियं सप्रसवावदाता T. ४ P. M. पुष्पोकृभरगा ।
५ P. M. दान्तैः समुद्गैः P. L. M. lacuna.

गन्धं वमन्तोपि च गन्धपूर्णा गन्धर्व्वदेश्या इव गन्धपूर्णाः ।
तस्यान्यचित्तस्य शुगात्मकस्य[१] घ्राणं न जह्रु[२]र्हृदयं प्रतेपुः ॥१०॥
संरक्तकण्ठैरपि [३]नीलकण्ठैः तुष्टैः प्रहृष्टैरपि चान्यपुष्टैः ।
लेलिह्यमानैश्च मधु द्विरेफैः स्वनद्वनं तस्य मनो नुनोद[४] ॥११॥
स तत्र भार्य्यारणिसम्भवेन वितर्कधूमेन तमःशिखेन ।
कामाग्निनान्तर्हृदि दह्यमानो[५] विहाय धैर्य्यं विललाप तत्तत् ॥१२॥

अद्यावगच्छामि सुदुष्करं ते चक्रुः करिष्यन्ति च कुर्व्वते च ।
त्यक्ता प्रियामश्रुमुखीं तपो[६] ये चेरुश्चरिष्यन्ति चरन्ति चैव ॥१३॥
तावद्दृढं बन्धनमस्ति लोके न दारवं तान्तव[७]मायसं वा ।
यावद्दृढं बन्धनमेतदेव मुखं चलाक्षम् ललितञ्च वाक्यम् ॥१४॥
छित्त्वा च भित्त्वा च हि यान्ति तानि स्वपौरुषाच्चैव सुहृद्बलाच्च ।
ज्ञानाच्च रौद्र्याच्च विना विमोक्तुं न शक्यते स्नेहमयस्तु पाशः ॥१५॥
ज्ञानं न मे तच्च शमाय यत् स्यात् न चास्ति रौद्रं करुणात्मकोस्मि ।
कामात्मकश्चास्मि गुरुश्च बुद्धः स्थितोऽन्तरे चक्रगतेरिवास्मि ॥१६॥
अहं गृहीत्वापि हि भिक्षुलिङ्गं भ्रातृर्षिणा द्विगुरुणानुशिष्टः ।
सर्व्वास्ववस्थासु लभे न शान्तिं प्रियावियोगादिव चक्रवाकः ॥१७॥
अद्यापि तन्मे हृदि वर्त्तते च यद्दर्पणे व्याकुलिते मया सा ।
कृतानृतक्रोधकमब्रवीन्मां कथं कृतोसी[८]ति शठं हसन्ती ॥१८॥

---

१ P. M. सुखात्मकस्य । २ P. M. जघ्रुः । ३ P. L. M. संरक्तकण्ठैश्च विनील० । ४ P. M. ननानुमोद P. L. M. has only the lower halves of the five letters remaining.
५ P. M. तद्वविदह्यमानो । ६ P. M. तथा ये ।
७ P. M. वास्करं । ८ P. M. हतोसीति ।

यथैष्यनाख्यानविशेषकायां मयीति यन्मामवदच्च साश्रु ।
पारिप्लवाक्षेण मुखेन बाला तन्मे वचोऽद्यापि मनो रुणद्धि ॥१९॥
बद्धासनं पादपनिर्झरस्थः स्वस्थो यथा ध्यायति भिक्षुरेषः ।
शक्तः क्वचिन्नाहमिवैष नूनम् शान्तस्तथा तृप्त इवोपविष्टः ॥२०॥
पुंस्कोकिलानामविचिन्त्य घोषं वसन्तलक्ष्म्यामविचार्य्य चक्षुः ।
शास्त्रं यथाभ्यस्यति चैष युक्तः शङ्के प्रियाकर्षति नास्य चेतः ॥२१॥
अस्मै नमोस्तु स्थिरनिश्चयाय निवृत्तकौतूहलविस्मयाय ।
शान्तात्मनेऽन्तर्गतमानसाय चङ्क्रम्यमानाय[१] निरुत्सुकाय ॥२२॥
निरीक्षमाणस्य जलं सपद्मम् वनञ्च पुण्यम् परपुष्टजुष्टम् ।
कस्यास्ति वीर्य्यं नवयौवनस्य मासे मधौ धर्म्मसपत्नभूते ॥२३॥
भावेन गर्व्वेण गतेन लक्ष्म्या स्मितेन कोपेन मदेन वाग्भिः ।
जह्रुः स्त्रियो देवनृपर्षिसंघान् कस्माद्धि नास्मद्विधमाक्षिपेयुः ॥२४॥
कामाभिभूतो हि हिरण्यरेताः स्वाहां सिषेवे मघवानहल्यां ।
सत्वेन सर्गेण च तेन हीनः स्त्रीनिर्जितः किं बत मानुषोऽहम् ॥२५॥
सूर्य्यः स रम्भां प्रति जातरागस्तत्प्रीतये नष्ट इति श्रुतं नः ।
यामश्वभूतोऽश्ववधूं समेत्य र(य)तोऽश्विनौ तौ जनयाम्बभूव ॥२६॥
स्त्रीकारणं वैरविषक्तबुद्ध्योर्वैवस्वताग्न्योश्चलितात्मधृत्योः ।
बहूनि वर्षाणि बभूव युद्धं कः स्त्रीनिमित्तं न चलेदिहान्यः ॥२७॥
भेजे श्वपाकीं मुनिरक्षमालां कामाद् वशिष्ठश्च स सद्वरिष्ठः ।
यस्यां विवस्वानिव भूजलादः सुतः प्रसूतोऽस्य कपिञ्जलादः ॥२८॥
पराशरः शापशरस्तथर्षिः काली[ ] सिषेवे झषगर्भयोनिं ।

---

१ Both P. M. and P. L. M. यं क्रम्यमानाय T.

अतोऽस्य यस्यां सुषुवे[1] महात्मा द्वैपायनो वेदविभागकर्त्ता ॥२९॥
द्वैपायनो धर्म्मपरायणश्च रेमे समं काशिषु वेश्यवध्वा[2] ।
यया हतोऽभूत् चलनूपुरेण पादेन विद्युल्लतयेव मेघः ॥३०॥
तथाङ्गिरा रागपरीतचेताः सरस्वतो[ं] ब्रह्मसुतः सिषेवे ।
सारस्वतो यत्र सुतोऽस्य जज्ञे नष्टस्य वेदस्य पुनःप्रवक्ता ॥३१॥
तथा नृपर्षेर्दिलिपस्य य(जं)ज्ञे स्वर्गस्त्रियां काश्यप आगतास्थः ।
स्रुचं गृहीत्वा स्रवदात्मतेजः चिक्षेप वह्ना[3]वसितो यतोऽभूत् ॥३२॥
तथाङ्गदोऽन्त[ं]तपसोऽपि गत्वा कामाभिभूतो यमुनामगच्छत् ।
धीमत्तरं यत्र रथीतरं स सारङ्गजुष्टं जनयाम्बभूव ॥३३॥
निशाम्य शान्तां नरदेवकन्यां वनेऽपि शान्तेऽपि च वर्त्तमानः ।
चचाल धैर्य्यात् मुनिर्ऋष्यशृङ्गः[4] शैलो महीकम्प इवोच्चशृङ्गः ॥३४॥
ब्रह्मर्षिभावार्थमपास्य राज्यं भेजे वनं यो विषयेष्वनास्थः ।
स गाधिजश्चापहृतो घृताच्या समा दशैकं[5] दिवसं विवेद ॥३५॥
तथैव कन्दर्पशराभिमृष्टो रम्भां प्रति स्थूलशिरा मुमूर्च्छ ।
यः कामरोषात्मतयानपेक्ष[ः] शशाप तामप्रतिगृह्यमाणः ॥३६॥
प्रमत्वरायां च रुरुः प्रियायां भुजङ्गमेनापहृतेन्द्रियायां ।
संदृश्य संदृश्य जघान सर्व्वेन्द्रियं[6] न रोषेण तपो ररक्ष[7] ॥३७॥

---

१ P. M. यस्यामसुषुवे ।    २ P. L. M. lacuna P. M. वेश्यवर्या ।    ३ P. M. वह्निं T.    ४ P. M. धैर्य्यन्मुनि ऋष्यिशृङ्गः P. L. M. धैर्य्यान्मुनि ऋष्यशृङ्गः ।    ५ P. M. दशौकं T.
६ सर्व्वान्द्रियं (both P. L. M. and P. M.) T
७ P. M. तथोररक्षं ।

नप्ता शशाङ्कस्य यशोगुणाङ्को बुधस्य सूनुर्विबुधप्रभावः ।
तथोर्व्वशीमप्सरसं विचिन्त्य राजर्षिरुन्मादमगच्छदैडः ॥२८॥

रक्तो गिरेर्मूर्द्धनि मेनकायां कामात्मकत्वाच्च स तालजङ्घः ।
पादेन विश्वावसुना सरोषम् वज्रेण हिंताल इवाभिजघ्ने ॥२९॥

नाशङ्गतायां परमाङ्गनायां गङ्गाजलेऽनङ्गपरीतचेताः ।
जह्नुश्च गङ्गां नृपतिर्भुजाभ्याम् रुरोध मैनाक[1] इवाचलेन्द्रः ॥४०॥

भूपश्च गङ्गाविरहात् जुघूर्ण गङ्गाम्भसा शाल इवात्तमूलः ।
कुलप्रदीपः प्रतिपस्य सूनु[:] श्रीमत्तनु[:] शान्तनुरस्वतन्त्रः ॥४१॥

हृताच्च सौनन्दकिनानुशोचन् प्राप्तामिवोर्व्वीं स्त्रियमुर्व्वशीं तां ।
सद्वृत्तवर्म्मा किल सोमवर्म्मा बभ्राम चित्तोद्भवभिन्नधर्म्मा ॥४२॥

भार्य्यां मृतां चानुममार राजा भीमप्रभावो भुवि भौमकः सः ।
बलेन सेनाक इति प्रकाशः सेनापतिर्द्देव इवार्त्तसेनः ॥४३॥

स्वर्गं गते भर्त्तरि शान्तनौ च कालीं जिहीर्षन् जनमेजयः सः ।
अवाप भीष्मात् समवेत्य मृत्युं न तद्गतं मन्मथमुत्ससर्ज ॥४४॥

शप्तश्च पाण्डुर्मदनेन नूनम् स्त्रीसङ्गमे मृत्युमवाप्स्यसीति ।
जगाम माद्रीं न महर्षिशापात् असेव्यमेतत् विममर्ष मृत्युम् ॥४५॥

एवंविधा देवनृपर्षिसङ्घा स्त्रीणां वशं कामवशेन जग्मुः ।
धिया च सारेण च दुर्व्वलः स प्रियामपश्यन् किमु विक्लवोऽहम् ॥४६॥

यास्यामि तस्मात् गृहमेव भूयः कामं करिष्ये विधिवत्सकामम् ।
नह्यन्यचित्तस्य चलेन्द्रियस्य लिङ्गं क्षमं धर्म्मपथाच्च्युतस्य ॥४७॥

---

१ P. M. मनामक ।

पाणौ कपालमवधाय विधाय मौण्ड्यम्
मानं निधाय विकृतं परिधाय वासः ।
यस्योद्भवो न धृतिरस्ति न शान्तिरस्ति
चित्रप्रदीप इव सोऽस्ति च नास्ति चैव ॥४८॥

यो निःसृतश्च न च निःसृतकामरागः
काषायमुद्वहति यो न च निष्कषायः ।
पात्रं बिभर्त्ति च गुणैर्न च पात्रभूतो
लिङ्गं वहन्नपि स नैव गृही न भिक्षुः ॥४९॥

न न्याय्यमन्वयवतः परिगृह्य लिङ्गम्
भूयो विमोक्तुमिति योऽपि हि मे विचारः ।
सोऽपि प्रणश्यति विचिन्त्य नृपप्रवीरां
स्तान् ये तपोवनमपास्य गृहाण्यतीयुः ॥५०॥

शाल्वाधिपो हि ससुतोपि तथाम्बरीषो
रामोन्ध एव स च साङ्कृतिरन्तिदेवः ।
चीराण्यपास्य दधिरे पुनरंशुकानि
छित्त्वा जटाश्च कुटिला मुकुटानि बभ्रुः ॥५१॥

तस्माद् भिक्षार्थं मम गुरुरितो यावदेव प्रयातः
त्यक्त्वा काषायं गृहमहमितस्तावदेव प्रयास्ये ।
पूज्यं लिङ्गं हि स्खलितमनसो बिभ्रतः क्लिष्टबुद्धेः
नामुत्रार्थः स्यात् उपहतमतेर्नाप्ययं जीवलोकः ॥५२॥

इति सौन्दरनन्दे महाकाव्ये नन्दविलापो नाम सप्तमः सर्गः ॥

## अष्टमः सर्गः

अथ नन्दमधीरलोचनम् गृहयानोत्सुकमुत्सुकोत्सुकम् ।
अभिगम्य शिवेन चक्षुषा श्रमणः कश्चिदुवाच मैत्रया[१] ॥१॥
किमिदं मुखमश्रुदुर्द्दिनम् हृदयस्थं विवृणोति ते भ्रमः ।
धृतिमेहि नियच्छ विक्रियां न हि बाष्पश्च शमश्च शोभते ॥२॥
द्विविधा समुदेति वेदना नियतं चेतसि देह एव च ।
श्रुतविध्युपचा[र]कोविदा द्विविधा एव तयोश्चिकित्सकाः ॥३॥
तदियं यदि कायिकी रुजा भिषजे तूर्णमसौ समुच्यताम्[२] ।
विनिगुह्य हि रोगमातुरो नचिरात्तीव्रमनर्थमृच्छति ॥४॥
अथ दुःखमिदं मनोमयं वद वक्ष्यामि यदत्र भेषजम् ।
मनसो हि रजस्तमःसतां[३] भिषजोऽध्यात्मविदः परीक्षकाः ॥५॥
निखिलेन च सत्यमुच्यताम् यदि वाच्यं मयि सौम्य मन्यसे ।
गतयो विविधा हि चेतसाम् बहु[गु]ह्यानि महाकुलानि च ॥६॥
इति तेन स बोधितस्तदा व्यवसायं प्रविवक्षुरात्मनः ।
अवलम्ब्य करेण करेण तं प्रविवेशान्यतरत्[४] वनान्तरम् ॥७॥
अथ तत्र शुचौ लतागृहे कुसुमोद्गारिणि तौ निषेदतुः ।
मृदुभिर्मृदुमारुतेरितैः उपगूढावि[व] बालपल्लवैः ॥८॥
स जगाद ततश्चिकीर्षितम् घननिश्वासगृहीतमन्तरा ।
श्रुतवाग्विभवाय[५] भिक्षवे विदुषा प्रव्रजितेन दुर्वचम् ॥९॥

---

१ P. M. मैत्रयः ।　　२ P. M. मभूनमुच्यतां T.
३ P. M. ०सत्त्व T.　　४ P. M. प्रविश्यस्थान्यतराद् T.
५ P. M. वाग्भिसदाय T.

सदृशं यदि धर्म्मचारिणः सततं प्राणिषु मैत्रचेतसः ।
अधृतौ यदियं हितैषिता मयि ते स्यात् करुणात्मनः सतः ॥१०॥
अत एव च मे विशेषतः प्रविवक्षा क्षयवादिनि त्वयि ।
न हि भावमिमं चलात्मने कथयेयं ब्रुवतेऽप्यसाधवे ॥११॥
तदिदं शृणु मे समासतो न रमे धर्म्मविधावृते प्रियां ।
गिरिसानुषु कामिनीमृते कृतरेता इव किन्नरश्चरन् ॥१२॥
वनवाससुखात् पराङ्मुखः प्रयियासा गृहमेव येन मे ।
न हि शर्म्म लभे तया विना नृपतिर्हीन इवोत्तमश्रिया ॥१३॥
अथ तस्य निशम्य तद्वचः प्रियभार्य्याभिमुखस्य शोचतः ।
श्रमणः स शिरः प्रकम्पयन् निजगादात्मगतं शनैरिदम् ॥१४॥
कृपणं बत यूथलालसो महतो व्याधभयाद्विनिःसृतः ।
प्रविविक्षति वागुरां मृगश्चपलो गीतरवेण वञ्चितः ॥१५॥
विहगः खलु जालसंवृतो हितकामेन जनेन मोचितः ।
विचरन् फलपुष्पवद् वनम् प्रविविक्षुः स्वयमेव पञ्जरम् ॥१६॥
कलभः करिणा खलूद्धृतो बहुपङ्कात् विषमात् नदीतलात् ।
जलतर्षवशेन तां पुनः सरितं ग्राहवतीं तितीर्षति ॥१७॥
शरणे सभुजङ्गमे स्वपन् प्रतिबुद्धेन परेण बोधितः ।
तरुणः खलु जातविभ्रम[ः] स्वयमुग्रं भुजगं जिघृक्षति ॥१८॥
महता खलु जातवेदसा ज्वलितादुत्पतितो वनद्रुमात् ।
पुनरिच्छति नीडतृष्णया पतितुं तत्र गतव्यथो द्विजः ॥१९॥
अवशः खलु काममूर्च्छया प्रियया श्येनभयाद् विनाकृतः ।
न धृतिं समुपैति न ह्रियं करुणं जीवति जीवजीवकः ॥२०॥

अकृतात्मतया तृषान्वितो घृणया चैव धिया च वर्ज्जितः ।
अशनं खलु वान्तमात्मना कृपण[ः] श्वा पुनरत्तुमिच्छति ॥२१॥

इति मन्मथशोककर्षितम् तमनुध्याय मुहुर्निरीक्ष्य च ।
श्रमणः स हिताभिकाङ्क्षया गुणवद् वाक्यमुवाच विप्रियम् ॥२२॥
अविचारयतः शुभाशुभम् विषयेष्वेव निविष्टचेतसः ।
उपपन्नमलब्धचक्षुषो न रतिः श्रेयसि चेत् भवेत्तव ॥२३॥
श्रवणे ग्रहणेऽथ धारणे परमार्थावगमे मनःशमे ।
अविषक्तमतेश्चलात्मनो न हि धर्म्मेऽभिरतिर्विधीयते ॥२४॥
विषयेषु तु दोषदर्शिनः परितुष्टस्य शुचेरमानिनः ।
शमकर्म्मसु युक्तचेतसः कृतबुद्धेर्न रतं न विद्यते[1] ॥२५॥
रमते तृषितो धनश्रिया रमते कामसुखेन बालिशः ।
रमते प्रशमेन सज्जनः परिभोगान् परिभूय विद्यया ॥२६॥
अपि च प्रथितस्य धीमतः कुलजस्यार्च्चितलिङ्गधारिणः ।
सदृशी न गृहाय चेतना प्रणतिर्वायुवशात् गिरेरिव ॥२७॥
स्पृहयेत् परसंश्रिताय यः परिभूयात्मवशां स्वतन्त्रतां ।
उपशान्तिपथे शिवे स्थितः स्पृहयेद्दोषवते गृहाय सः ॥२८॥
व्यसनाभिहतो यथा विशेत् परिमुक्तः पुनरेव बन्धनम् ।
समुपेत्य वनं तथा पुनः गृहसंज्ञं मृगयेत बन्धनम् ॥२९॥
पुरुषश्च विहाय यः कलिम् पुनरिच्छेत् कलिमेव सेवितुम् ।
स विहाय भजेत बालिशः कलिभूतामजितेन्द्रियः स्त्रियम् ॥३०॥
सविषा इव संश्रिता लताः परिमृष्टा इव सोरगा गुहाः ।

---

१ P. M. न रतिर्न्नविन्ते ।

विवृता इव चाशयो धृता व्यसनान्ता हि भवन्ति योषितः ॥२१॥
प्रमदाः समदा मदप्रदाः प्रमदा वीतमदा भयप्रदाः ।
इति दोषभयावहाश्च ताः कथमर्हन्ति निषेवणं नु ताः ॥ २२ ॥
स्वजनः स्वजनेन भिद्यते सुहृदश्चापि सुहृज्जनेन यत् ।
परदोषविचक्षणाश्रयास्तदनार्य्याः प्रचरन्ति योषितः ॥२३॥
सुजनाः (कुराजा) कृपणीभवन्ति यत् यदयुक्तम् प्रचरन्ति साहसम् ।
प्रविशन्ति च यत्त्वमूमुखं रभसा तत्र[1] निमित्तमङ्गना ॥२४॥
वचनेन हरन्ति वर्णना[2] निशितेन प्रह[र]न्ति चेतसा ।
मधु तिष्ठति वाचि योषितां हृदये हालहलम्[3] महद् विषम् ॥२५॥
प्रदहन् दहनोऽपि गृह्यते विशरीरः पवनोऽपि गृह्यते ।
कुपितो भुजगोऽपि गृह्यते प्रमदानां तु मनो न गृह्यते ॥२६॥
न वपुर्विमृशन्ति न श्रि(पि)यम् न मतिं नापि कुलं न विक्रमम् ।
प्रहरन्त्यविशेषतः स्त्रियः सरितो ग्रा[ह]कुलाकुला इव ॥२७॥
न वचो मधुरं न लालनम्[4] स्मरति स्त्री न [च] सौहृदम् [कदा] ।
कलिता वनितेव चञ्चला तदितरा भुवने न विद्यते[5] ॥२८॥
प्रददत्सु भवन्ति नर्म्मदाः प्रददत्सु प्रविशन्ति विभ्रमम् ।
प्रणतेषु भवन्ति गर्व्विता प्रमदास्तृप्ततराश्च मानिषु ॥२९॥
गुणवत्सु चरन्ति भर्त्तृवत् गुणहीनेषु चरन्ति शत्रुवत्[6] ।

---

१ Both P. L. M. and P. M. स्तत्र ।
२ P. M. वचनेन न हन्ति वर्णना ।
३ P. M. हलाहलं T. ४ P. M. राडनं T.
५ P. M. तदिदरेष्ठि वनावद्यते P. L. M. lacuna T.
६ P. M. सूतवत् ।

धनवत्सु चरन्ति तृष्णया धनहीनेषु चरन्त्यवज्ञया ॥४०॥
विषयाद् विषयान्तरं गता प्रचरत्येव यथा हृतापि गौः ।
अनवेक्षितपूर्व्वसौहृदा रमतेऽन्यत्र गता तथाङ्गना ॥४१॥
प्रविशन्त्यपि हि स्त्रियः चितामनुबध्नन्त्यपि मुक्तजीविताः ।
अपि बिभ्रति नैव यन्त्रणा न तु भावेन वहन्ति सौहृदम् ॥४२॥
रमयन्ति पतीन् कथञ्चन प्रमदा याः पतिदेवताः क्वचित् ।
चलचित्ततया सहस्रशो रमयन्ते हृदयं स्वमेव ताः ॥४३॥
श्वपचं किल शक्रजित्सुता बकमीनरिपुं कुमुद्वती ।
मृगराजमथो बृहद्रथा प्रमदानामगतिर्न विद्यते ॥४४॥
कुरुहैहयवृष्णिवंशजा बहुमायाकवचोऽथ शंबरः ।
मुनिरुद्भ्रान्तमनाश्च गौतमः समवापुर्वनितोद्धुतं रजः ॥४५॥
अकृतज्ञमनार्य्यमस्थिरम् वनितानामिदमीदृशं मनः ।
कथमर्हति तासु पण्डितो हृदयं सञ्जयितुं चलात्मसु ॥४६॥
अथ सूक्ष्ममतिः प्रियाशया लघुता सा हृदयं न पश्यसि ।
किमु कायमसद्गृहं स्रवत् वनितानाश्चरितं न पश्यसि ॥४७॥
यदहन्यहनि प्रधावनैर्वसनैश्चाभरणैश्च संस्कृतम् ।
अशुभं तमसावृतेक्षण शुभतो गच्छसि नावगच्छसि ॥४८॥
अथवा समवैषि तत्तनुम् अशुभं त्वम् न तु संविदस्ति ते ।
सुरभिं विदधासि हि क्रियां अशुचेस्तत्प्रभवस्य शान्तये ॥४९॥
अनुलेपनमञ्जनं स्रजो मणिमुक्तातपनीयमंशुकम् ।
यदि साधु किमत्र योषितां सहजं तासु विचीयतां[1] शुचि ॥५०॥

---

१ P. M. विनीयताम् ।

मलपङ्कधरा दिगम्बरा प्रकृतिस्थैर्नखदन्तरोमभिः ।
यदि सा तव सुन्दरी भवेत् नियतं तेऽद्य न सुन्दरी भवेत् ॥५१॥
स्रवतीमशुचिं स्पृशेच्च कः सघृणो जर्ज्जरभाण्डवत् स्त्रियम् ।
यदि केवलया त्वचावृता न भवेन्मक्षिकपत्रमात्रया ॥५२॥
त्वचवेष्टितमस्थिपञ्जरम् यदि कायं समवैषि योषिताम् ।
मदनेन च कृष्यसे बलादघृणः खल्वधृतिश्च मन्मथ[ः] ॥५३॥
शुभतामशुभेषु कल्पयन् नखदन्तत्वचकेशरोमसु ।
अविचक्षण किं न पश्यसि प्रकृतिञ्च प्रभवञ्च योषिताम् ॥५४॥
तदवेत्य मनःशरीरयोर्वनिता दोषवतीर्विशेषतः ।
चपलं भवतोत्सुकं मनः प्रतिसङ्ख्यानबलेन वार्य्यताम् ॥५५॥

श्रुतवान् मतिमान् कुलोद्गतः परमस्य प्रशमस्य भाजनम् ।
उपगम्य यथा तथा पुन र्न हि भेत्तुं नियमं त्वमर्हसि ॥५६॥
अभिजनमहतो मनस्विनः प्रिययशसो बहुमानमिच्छतः ।
निधनमपि वरं स्थिरात्मनः च्युतविनयस्य नचैव[1] जीवितम् ॥५७॥

बद्ध्वा यथा हि कवचम् प्रगृहीतचापो
निन्द्यो भवत्यपसृतः समराद्रथस्थः ।
भैक्षाकमभ्युपगतः परिगृह्य लिङ्गम्
निन्द्यस्तथा भवति कामहृतेन्द्रियाश्वः ॥५८॥

हास्यो यथा च परमाभरणाम्बरस्रग्
भैक्ष्यं चरन् धृतधनुश्चलचित्रमौलिः ।

---

१ P. M. तवैव ।

वैरूप्यमभ्युपगतः परपिण्डभोजी
हास्यस्तथा गृहसुखाभिमुखः सतृष्णः ॥५९॥

यथा स्वन्नं भुक्त्वा परमशयनीयेऽपि शयितो
वराहो निर्मुक्तः पुनरशुचि धावेत् परिचितम् ।
तथा श्रेयः शृण्वन् प्रशमसुखमास्वाद्य गुणवद्
वनं शान्तं हित्वा गृहमभिलषेत् कामतृषितः ॥६०॥

यथोल्का हस्तस्था दहति पवनप्रेरितशिखा
यथा पादाक्रान्तो दशति भुजगः क्रोधरभसः ।
यथा हन्ति व्याघ्रः शिशुरपि गृहीतो गृहगतः
तथा स्त्रीसंसर्गो बहुविधमनर्थाय भवति ॥६१॥

तद्विज्ञाय मनःशरीरनियतान् नारीषु दोषानिमान्
मत्वा कामसुखं नदीजलचलं क्लेशाय शोकाय च ।
दृष्ट्वा दुर्ब्बलमाम[1]पात्रसदृशम् मृत्यूपसृष्टं जगत्
निर्मोक्षाय कुरुष्व बुद्धिमतुलामुत्कण्ठितुं नार्हसि ॥६२॥

इति सौन्दरनन्दे महाकाव्ये स्त्रीविघातो नाम
अष्टमः सर्गः ।

---

१ P. M. ०मान० ।

## नवमः सर्गः

अथैवमुक्तोऽपि स तेन भिक्षुणा
जगाम नैवोपशमं प्रियां प्रति ।
तथाहि तामेव तदा स चिन्तयन्
न तस्य शुश्राव विसंज्ञवान्धवः[१] ॥१॥

यथा हि वैद्यस्य चिकीर्षतः शिवम्
वचो न गृह्णाति मुमूर्षुरातुरः ।
तथैव मत्तो बलरूपयौवनैः
हितं न जग्राह स तस्य तद्वचः ॥२॥

न चात्र चित्रं यदि रागपाप्मना
मनोऽभिभूयेत तमोवृतात्मनः ।
नरस्य पाप्मा हि तदा निवर्त्तते
यदा भवत्यन्तगतं तमस्तनु ॥३॥

ततस्तथाक्षिप्तमवेक्ष्य तं तदा
बलेन रूपेण च यौवनेन च ।
गृहप्रयाणं प्रति च व्यवस्थितं
शशास नन्दं श्रमणः स शान्तये ॥४॥

बलञ्च रूपञ्च नवञ्च यौवनम्
तथावगच्छामि यथावगच्छसि ।

---

१ P. L. M. lacuna. P. M. विसंज्ञा० ।

अहन्त्विदं ते वयमव्यवस्थितम्
यथावबुद्धो न तथा च बुध्यसे ॥५॥

इदं हि रोगायतनं जरावशम्
नदीतटानोकहवच्चलाचलम् ।
न वेत्सि देहं जलफेनदुर्ब्बलम्
बलस्थतामात्मनि येन मन्यसे ॥६॥

यदान्नपानाशनयानकर्म्मणा-
मसेवनादप्यतिसेवनादपि ।
शरीरमासन्नविपत्ति दृश्यते
बलेऽभिमानस्तव केन हेतुना ॥७॥

हिमातपव्याधिजराक्षुदादिभिः
यदाप्यनर्थैरुपनीयते जगत् ।
जलं शुचौ मास इवार्करश्मिभिः
क्षयं व्रजेत् किं बलदृप्त मन्यसे ॥८॥

त्वगस्थिमांसक्षतजात्मकं यदा
शरीरमाहारवशेन तिष्ठति ।
अजस्रमार्त्तं सततप्रतिक्रियम्
बलान्वितोऽस्मीति कथं विहन्यसे ॥९॥

यथा घटं मृण्मयमाममाश्रितो
नरस्तितीर्षेत् क्षुभितं महार्णवम् ।
समुच्छ्रयं तद्वदसारमुद्वहन्-
बलं व्यवस्येत् विषयार्थमुद्यतः ॥१०॥

शरीरमामादपि मृण्मयाद् घटात्
इदन्तु निःसारतमं मतं मम ।
चिरं हि तिष्ठेत् विधिवद्धृतो घ[टः]
समुच्छ्रयोऽयं सुधृतोऽपि भिद्यते ॥११॥

यदाम्बुभूवाय्वनलाश्च धातवः
सदा [नि]रुद्धा विषमा इवोरगाः ।
भवन्त्यनर्थाय शरीरमाश्रिताः
कथं बलं रोगविधौ व्यवस्यसि ॥१२॥

प्रयान्ति मन्त्रैः प्रशमं भुजङ्गमा
न मन्त्रसाध्यास्तु भवन्ति धातवः ।
केचिच्च कञ्चिच्च दशन्ति पन्नगाः
सदा च सर्व्वञ्च तुदन्ति धातवः ॥१३॥

इदं हि शय्याशनपानभोजनैः
गुणैः शरीरं चिरमप्यवेक्षितम् ।
न मर्षयत्येकमपि व्यतिक्रमम्
यतो [1]महाशीविषवत् प्रकुप्यति ॥१४॥

यदा हिमार्त्तो ज्वलनं निषेवते
हिमं निदाघाभिहतोऽभिकाङ्क्षति ।
क्षुधान्वितोऽन्नं सलिलं तृषान्वितो
बलं कुतः किञ्च कथञ्च कस्य च ॥१५॥

---

१ P. M. महाहौ० ।

तदेवमाज्ञाय शरीरमातुरम्
बलान्वितोऽस्मीति न मन्तुमर्हसि ।
असारमस्वन्तमनिश्चितं जगत्
जगत्यनित्ये बलमव्यवस्थितम् ॥१६॥

क्व कार्त्तवीर्य्यस्य बलाभिमानिनः
सहस्रबाहोर्बलमर्ज्जुनस्य तत् ।
चकर्त्त बाहून् युधि यस्य भार्गवो
महान्ति शृङ्गाण्यशनिर्गिरेरिव ॥१७॥

क्व तद्बलं कंसविकर्षिणो हरे-
स्तुरङ्गराजस्य पुटावभेदिनः[१] ।
यमेकबाणेन निजघ्निवान् जरा
क्रमागता रूपमिवोत्तमं जरा ॥१८॥

दिते[ः] सुतस्यामररोषकारिणः
चमूरुचेर्वा नमुचेः क्व तद्बलम् ।
यमाहवे क्रुद्धमिवान्तकं स्थितम्
जघान फेनावयवेन वासवः ॥१९॥

बलं कुरूणां क्व च तत्तदाभवत्
युधि ज्वलित्वा तरसौजसा च ये ।
समित्समिद्धा ज्वलना इवाध्वरे
हतासवो भस्मनि पर्य्यवस्थिताः ॥२०॥

---

१ P. M. पुच्येर ।

अतो विदित्वा बलवीर्य्य[१]मानिनाम्
बलान्वितानामवमर्द्दितं बलम् ।
जगज्जरामृत्युवशं विचारयन्
[२]बलेऽभिमानं न विधातुमर्हसि ॥२१॥

बलं महद्वा यदि येन मन्यसे
कुरुष्व युद्धं सह तावदिन्द्रियैः ।
जयश्च [३]तेऽत्रास्ति महच्च ते बलं
पराजयश्चेद् वितथं च ते बलम् ॥२२॥

तथा हि वीराः पुरुषा न ते मता
जयन्ति ये साश्वरथद्विपानरीन् ।
यथा मता वीरतरा मनीषिणो
जयन्ति लोलानि ष[डि]न्द्रियाणि ये ॥२३॥

अहं वपुष्मानिति यच्च मन्यसे
विचक्षणं नैतदिदं च गृह्यताम् ।
क्व तद्वपुः सा च वपुष्मती तनुः
गदस्य साम्यस्य च सारणस्य च ॥२४॥

यथा मयूरश्चलचित्रचन्द्रको
बिभर्त्ति रूपं गुणवत् स्वभावतः ।
शरीरसंस्कारगुणादृते तथा
बिभर्षि रूपं यदि रूपवानसि ॥२५॥

---

१ P. M. P. L. M. ०विर्य्य ।
२ P. M. परे, P. L. M. पले ।  ३ P. M. तेन ।

यदि प्रतीपं वृणुयान्न वाससा
न शौचकाले यदि संस्पृशेदपः ।
मृजाविशेषं यदि नाददीत वा
वपु र्वपुष्मन् वद कीदृशं भवेत् ॥२६॥

नवं वयश्चात्मगतं निशाम्य यद्
गृहोन्मुखं ते विषयाप्तये मनः ।
नियच्छ तच्छैलनदी[१]रयोपमम्
द्रुतं हि गच्छत्यनिवर्त्ति यौवनम् ॥२७॥

ऋतुर्व्यतीतः परिवर्त्तते पुनः
क्षयं प्रयातः पुनरेति चन्द्रमाः ।
गतं गतं नैव तु संनिवर्त्तते
जलं नदीनाञ्च नृणाञ्च यौवनम् ॥२८॥

विवर्णितश्मश्रु बलीविकुञ्चितम्
विशीर्णदन्तं शिथिलभ्रु निष्प्रभम् ।
यदा मुखं द्रक्ष्यसि जर्ज्जरं तदा
जराभिभूतो विमदो भविष्यसि ॥२९॥

निषेव्य पानं मदनीयमुत्तमम्
निशाविवासेषु चिराद्विमाद्यति ।
नरस्तु मत्तो बलरूपयौवनैः
न कश्चिदप्राप्य जरां विमाद्यति ॥३०॥

यथेक्षुरभ्यन्तरसंप्रपिण्डितो

---

१ P. M. तलेनदी० ।

भुवि प्रविद्धो दहनाय शुष्यते ।
तथा जरायन्त्रनिपिण्डिता तनु-
र्निपीतसारा मरणाय तिष्ठति ॥२१॥
यथा हि नृभ्यां करपत्रपीडितम्
समुच्छ्रितं दारु भिनत्त्यनेकधा ।
तथोच्छ्रितां पातयति प्रजामिमाम्
अहर्निशाभ्यामुपसंहिता जरा ॥२२॥
स्मृतेः प्रमोषो वपुषः पराभवो
रतेः क्षयो वा श्रुतिचक्षुषां ग्रहः ।
श्रमस्य योनि र्बलवीर्य्ययो र्वधो
जरासमो नास्ति शरीरिणां रिपुः ॥२३॥
इदं विदित्वा [वि]निधत्स्व दैशिकम्
जराभिधानं जगतो महद्भयम् ।
अहं वपुष्मान् करवान् युवेति वा
न मा[न]मारोढुमनार्य्यमर्हसि ॥२४॥
अहं ममेत्येव च रक्तचेतसाम्
शरीरसंज्ञो भवज(य): कलौ ग्रहः ।
तमुत्सृजैवं यदि शाम्यते भवात्
भयं ह्यहं चेति ममेति वर्द्धति ॥२५॥
यदा शरीरं न वशोऽस्ति[१] कस्यचित्
निरस्यमानं विविधैरुपप्लवैः ।

---

१ P. M. शरीरे न वशोऽस्ति ।

कथं क्षमं वेत्तुमहं ममेति वा
शरीरसंज्ञं गृहमापदामिदम् ॥३६॥

सपन्नगे यः कुगृहे सदाऽशुचौ
रमेत नित्यं प्रतिसंस्कृतेऽबले ।
स दुष्टधातावशुचौ चलाचले
रमेत काये विपरीतदर्शनः ॥३७॥

यथा प्रजाभ्यः कुनृपो बलाद् बली
हरत्यशेषं च न चाभिरक्षति ।
तथैव कायो व्यसनादिसाधनम्
हरत्यशेषञ्च न चानुवर्त्तते ॥३८॥

यथा प्ररोहन्ति गृहाण्ययत्नतः
क्षितौ प्रयत्नात्तु भवन्ति शालयः ।
तथैव दुःखानि भवन्त्ययत्नतः
सुखानि यत्नेन भवन्ति वा न वा ॥३९॥

शरीरमार्त्तं परिकर्षतश्चलम्
न चास्ति किञ्चित् परमार्थतः सुखम् ।
सुखं हि दुःखप्रतिकारसेवया
स्थिते च दुःखे तनुनि व्यवस्यति ॥४०॥

यथानपेक्ष्याग्र्यमपीप्सितं सुखम्
प्रबाधते दुःखमुपेतमण्वपि ।
तथानवेक्ष्यात्मनि दुःखमागतम्
न विद्यते किञ्चन कस्यचित् सुखम् ॥४१॥

शरीरमीदृक् बहुदुःखमध्रुवम्
फलानुरोधादथवावगच्छसि ।
इवत् फलेभ्यो धृतिरश्मिभिर्मनो-
ऽभिगृह्यतां गौरिव शस्यलालसा ॥४२॥
न कामभोगा हि भवन्ति तृप्तये
हवींषि दीप्तस्य विभावसोरिव ।
यथा यथा कामसुखेषु वर्त्तते
तथा तथेच्छा विषयेषु वर्द्धते ॥४३॥
यथा च कुष्ठव्यसनेन दुःखितः
प्रतापयन्नैव शमं निगच्छति ।
तथेन्द्रियार्थेष्वजितेन्द्रियश्चरन्
न कामभोगैरुपशान्तिमृच्छति ॥४४॥
यथा हि भैषज्यसुखाभिकाङ्क्षया
भजेत रोगान्न भजेत तत्क्षमम् ।
तथा शरीरे बहुदुःखभाजने
रमेत मोहाद् विषयाभिकाङ्क्षया ॥४५॥
अनर्थकामः पुरुषस्य यो जनः
स तस्य शत्रुः किल तेन कर्म्मणा ।
अनर्थमूला विषयाश्च केवला
ननु प्रहेया विषया यथारयः ॥४६॥
इहैव भूत्वा रिपवो वधात्मकाः
प्रयान्ति काले पुरुषस्य मित्रताम् ।

परत्र चैवेह च दुःखहेतवो
भवन्ति कामा न तु कस्यचित् शिवाः ॥४७॥
यथोपयुक्तम् रसवर्णगन्धवत्
वधाय किम्पाकफलम् न पुष्टये ।
निषेव्यमाणा विषयाश्चलात्मनो
भवन्त्यनर्थाय तथा न भूतये ॥४८॥
तदेतदाज्ञाय विपाप्मनात्मना
विमोक्षधर्म्या ह्युपसंहितं हितम् ।
जुषस्व मे सज्जनसम्मतं मतम्
प्रचक्ष्व वा निश्चयमुद्गिरन् गिरम् ॥४९॥
इति हितमपि बह्वपीदमुक्तः
श्रुतमहता श्रमणेन तेन नन्दः ।
न धृतिमुपययौ च न शर्म्म लेभे
द्विरद इवातिमदो मदान्धचेताः ॥५०॥
नन्दस्य भावमवगम्य ततः स भिक्षुः
पारिप्लवं गृहसुखाभिमुखं न धर्म्मे ।
सत्त्वाशयानुशयभावपरीक्षकाय ।
बुद्धाय तत्त्वविदुषे कथयाञ्चकार ॥५१॥

सौन्दरनन्दे महाकाव्ये मदापवादो नाम
नवमः सर्गः ॥

# दशमः सर्गः

श्रुत्वा ततः सद्व्रतमुत्सिसृक्षुं भार्य्यांदिदृक्षुं भवनं विविक्षुम् ।
नन्दं निरानन्दमपेतधैर्य्यं अभ्युज्जिहीर्षुर्मुनिराजुहाव ॥१॥
तं प्राप्तमप्राप्तविमोक्षमार्गं पप्रच्छ चित्तस्खलितं सुचित्तः ।
स ह्रीमते ह्रीविततो जगाद स्वं निश्चयं निश्चयकोविदाय ॥२॥
नन्दं विदित्वा सुगतस्ततस्तं भार्य्याभिधाने तमसि भ्रमन्तम् ।
पाणौ गृहीत्वा वियदुत्पपात मलं जले साधुरिवोज्जिहीर्षुः ॥३॥

काषायवस्त्रौ कनकावदातौ विरेजतुस्तौ नभसि प्रसन्ने ।
अन्योन्यसंश्लिष्टविकीर्णपक्षौ सरःप्रकीर्णाविव चक्रवाकौ ॥४॥
तौ देवदारूत्तमगन्धवन्तम् नदीसरःप्रस्रवणौघवन्तम् ।
आजग्मतुः काञ्चन धातुमन्तम् देवर्षिमन्तं हिमवन्तमाशु ॥५॥
तस्मिन् गिरौ चारणसिद्धजुष्टे शिवे हविर्धूमकृतोत्तरीये ।
अगम्यपारस्य निराश्रयस्य तौ तस्थतुर्द्वीप इवाम्बरस्य ॥६॥
शान्तेन्द्रिये तत्र मुनौ स्थिते तु सविस्मयं दिक्षु ददर्श नन्दः ।
दरीश्च कुञ्जांश्च वनौकसश्च विभूषणं रक्षणमेव चाद्रेः ॥७॥
बह्वायते तत्र सिते हि शृङ्गे संक्षिप्तबर्हः शयितो मयूरः ।
भुजे बलस्यायतपीनबाहोः वैदूर्य्यकेयूर इवाबभासे ॥८॥
मनःशिलाधातुशिलाश्रयेण पीतीकृताङ्गो[1] विरराज सिंहः ।
[2]सन्तप्तचामीकरभक्तिचित्रम् रूप्याङ्गदं शीर्णमिवाम्बरस्य ॥९॥
व्याघ्रः क्लमव्यायतखेलगामी लाङ्गूलचक्रेण कृतापसव्यः ।
बभौ गिरेः प्रस्रवणं पिपासुर्दित्सन् पितृभ्योऽम्बु इवावतीर्णः ॥१०॥

---

१ P. M. तापीकृताङ्गो T.  २ P. M. तं तप्त T.

चलत्कदम्बे हिमवन्नितम्बे तरौ प्रलम्बे चमरो ललम्बे ।
छेत्तुं विलग्नं न शशाक बालं कुलोद्गतः प्रीतिमिवार्य्यवृत्तः ॥ ११ ॥

सुवर्णगौराश्च किरातसंघा मयूरपिच्छो[१]ज्ज्वलगात्ररेखाः ।
शार्दूलपातप्रतिमा गुहाभ्यो निष्पेतुरुद्गार इवाचलस्य ॥ १२ ॥

दरीचरीणामतिसुन्दरीणां मनोहरश्रोणिकुचोदरीणाम् ।
वृन्दानि रेजुर्दिशि किन्नरीणां पुष्पोत्किराणामिव वल्लरीणाम् ॥ १३ ॥

नगान्नगस्योपरि देवदारूनायासयन्तः कपयो विचेरुः ।
तेभ्यः फलं नापुरतोऽपजग्मुः मोघप्रसादेभ्य इवेश्वरेभ्यः ॥ १४ ॥

तस्मात्तु यूथादपसार्य्यमाणां निष्पीडितालक्तकरक्तवक्त्राम् ।
शाखामृगीमेकविपन्नदृष्टिं दृष्ट्वा मुनिर्नन्दमिदं बभाषे ॥ १५ ॥

का नन्द रूपेण च चेष्टया च संपश्यतश्चारुतरा मता ते ।
एषा मृगी वैकविपन्नदृष्टिः स वा जनो यत्र गता तवेष्टिः ॥ १६ ॥

इत्येवमुक्तः सुगतेन नन्दः कृत्वा स्मितं किञ्चिदिदं जगाद ।
क चोत्तमस्त्री भगवन् वधूस्ते मृगी नगक्लेशकरी क चैषा ॥ १७ ॥

ततो मुनिस्तस्य निशम्य वाक्यं हेत्वन्तरं किञ्चिदवेक्षमाणः ।
आलम्ब्य नन्दं प्रययौ तथैव क्रीडावनं वज्रधरस्य राज्ञः ॥ १८ ॥

ऋतावृतावाकृतिमेक एके क्षणे क्षणे बिभ्रति यत्र वृक्षाः ।
चित्रां समस्तामपि केचिदन्ये षण्णामृतूनां श्रियमुद्वहन्ति ॥ १९ ॥

पुष्यन्ति केचित् सुरभीरुदारा मालाः स्रजश्च ग्रथिता विचित्राः ।
कर्णानुकूलानवतंसकांश्च प्रत्यर्थिभूतानिव कुण्डलानाम् ॥ २० ॥

---

१ P. M. ०पिच्छो० ।

रक्तानि फुल्लाः कमलानि यत्र प्रदीपवृक्षा इव भान्ति वृक्षाः ।
प्रफुल्लनीलोत्पलरोहिणोऽन्ये सोन्मीलिताक्षा इव भान्ति वृक्षाः ॥२१॥
नानाविरागाण्यथ पाण्डराणि सुवर्णभक्तिव्यवभासितानि ।
अतान्तवान्येकघनानि यत्र सूक्ष्माणि वासांसि फलन्ति वृक्षाः ॥२२॥
हारान् मणीनुत्तमकुण्डलानि केयूरवर्य्याण्यथ नूपुराणि ।
एवंविधान्याभरणानि यत्र स्वर्गानुरूपाणि फलन्ति वृक्षाः ॥२३॥
वैदूर्य्यनालानि च काञ्चनानि पद्मानि वज्राङ्कुरकेशराणि ।
स्पर्शक्षमाण्युत्तमगन्धवन्ति रोहन्ति निष्कम्पतला नलिन्यः ॥२४॥
पक्षायतांस्त्रैव ततांश्च तांस्तान् वाद्यस्य हेतून् सुखरान् घनांश्च ।
फलन्ति वृक्षा मणिहेमचित्रा क्रीडासहायांस्त्रिदशालयानाम् ॥२५॥
मन्दारवृक्षांश्च कुशेशयांश्च पुष्पानतान् कोकनदांश्च वृक्षान् ।
आक्रम्य माहात्म्यगुणैर्व्विराजन् राजायते यत्र स पारिजातः ॥२६॥
कृष्टे तपःशीलफलैरखिन्नैस्त्रिपिष्टपक्षेत्रतले प्रसूताः ।
एवंविधा यत्र सदानुवृत्ता दिवौकसां भोगविधानवृक्षाः ॥२७॥
मनःशिलाभैर्वदनैर्विहङ्गा यत्राक्षिभिः स्फाटिकसन्निभैश्च ।
शादैश्च पक्षैरतिलोहितान्तैः माञ्जिष्ठकैरर्द्धसितैश्च पादैः ॥२८॥
चित्रैः सुवर्णच्छदनैस्तथान्यैः वैदूर्य्यनीलैर्नयनैः प्रसन्नैः ।
विहङ्गमा शिञ्जिरिकाभिधाना रुतैर्मनः श्रोत्रहरैर्भ्रमन्ति ॥२९॥
रक्ताभिरग्रेषु च वल्लरीभिर्मध्येषु चामीकरपिञ्जराभिः ।
वैदूर्य्यवर्णाभिरुपान्तमध्येष्वलङ्कृता यत्र खगाश्चरन्ति ॥३०॥
रोचिष्णवो नाम पतत्रिणोऽन्ये दीप्ताग्निवर्णोज्ज्वलितैरिवास्यैः ।
भ्रमन्ति दृष्टीर्वपुषाक्षिपन्तः स्वनैः शुभैरप्सरसो हरन्तः ॥३१॥

यथेष्टचेष्टाः सततप्रहृष्टा निरर्त्तयो निर्ज्जरसो विशोकाः ।
स्वैः कर्म्मभिर्हीनविशिष्टमध्याः स्वयंप्रभाः पुण्यकृतो रमन्ते ॥२२॥
नित्योत्सवं तञ्च निशाम्य लोकं निस्तन्द्रिनिद्रारतिशोकरोगम् ।
नन्दो जरामृत्युवशं सदार्त्तं मेने श्मशानप्रतिमं नृलोकम् ॥२३॥
ऐन्द्रं वनं तञ्च ददर्श नन्दः समन्ततो विस्मयफुल्लदृष्टिः ।
हर्षान्विताश्चाप्सरसः परीयुः सगर्व्वमन्योन्यमवेक्षमाणाः ॥२४॥
सदा युवत्यो मदनैककार्य्याः साधारणाः पुण्यकृतां विहाराः ।
दिव्याश्च निर्द्दोषपरिग्रहाश्च तपःफलस्याश्रयणं सुराणाम् ॥२५॥
तासां जगुर्धीरमुदात्तमन्याः पद्मानि काश्चित् ललितं बभञ्जुः ।
अन्योन्यहर्षात् ननृतुस्तथान्याश्चित्राङ्गहाराः स्तनभिन्नहाराः ॥२६॥
पूर्व्वं तपोमूल्यपरिग्रहेण स्वर्गक्रयार्थं कृतनिश्चयानाम् ।
मनांसि खिन्नानि तपोधनानां हरन्ति यत्राप्सरसो लडन्त्यः ॥२७॥
कासाञ्चिदासां वदनानि रेजुर्वनान्तरेभ्यश्चलकुण्डलानि ।
व्याविद्धपर्णेभ्य इवाकरेभ्यः पद्मानि कादम्बविघट्टितानि ॥२८॥
ता निःसृताः प्रेक्ष्य वनान्तरेभ्यस्तडित्पताका इव तोयदेभ्यः ।
नन्दस्य रागेण तनुर्विवेपे जले चले चन्द्रमसः प्रभेव ॥२९॥
वपुश्च दिव्यं ललिताश्च चेष्टास्ततः स तासां मनसा जहार ।
कौतूहलावर्ज्जितया तु दृष्ट्या संश्लेषतर्षादिव जातरागः ॥४०॥
स जाततर्षोऽप्सरसः पिपासुः तत्प्राप्तयेऽधिष्ठितविक्लवार्त्तः ।
लोलेन्द्रियाश्वेन मनोरथेन जेह्रीयमाणो न धृतिं जगाम ॥४१॥
यथा मनुष्या मलिनं हि वासः क्षारेण भूयो मलिनीकरोति ।
मलक्षयार्थं न मलोद्भवार्थं रजस्तथास्मै मुनिराचकर्ष ॥४२॥

दोषा[ं]श्च (स्व)काया[द्] भिषगुज्जिहीर्षु र्भूयो यथा क्लेशयितुं यतेत ।
रागं तथा तस्य मुनिर्जिघांसुर्भूयस्तरं रागमुपानिनाय ॥४२॥

दीपप्रभां हन्ति यथा च काले सहस्ररश्मेरुदितस्य दीप्तिः ।
मनुष्यलोके द्युतिमङ्गनानामन्तर्दधात्यप्सरसां तथा श्रीः ॥४४॥

महच्च रूपं स्वणु हन्ति रूपं शब्दो महान् हन्ति च शब्दमल्पम् ।
गुर्वी रुजा हन्ति रुजां मृद्वीं सर्व्वो महान् हेतुरणोर्वधाय ॥४५॥

मुनेः प्रभावाच्च शशाक नन्दस्तद्दर्शनं सोढुमसह्यमन्यैः ।
अवीतरागस्य हि दुर्ब्बलस्य मनो दहेदप्सरसां वपुःश्रीः ॥४६॥

मत्वा ततो नन्दमुदीर्णरागं भार्य्यानुरोधादपवृत्तरागम् ।
रागेण रागं प्रतिहन्तुकामो मुनिर्विरागो गिरमित्युवाच ॥४७॥

एताः स्त्रियः पश्य दिवौकसस्त्वं निरीक्ष्य च ब्रूहि यथाथ तत्त्वम् ।
एताः कथं रूपगुणैर्मतास्ते स वा जनो यत्र गतं मनस्ते ॥४८॥

अथाप्सरस्स्वेव निविष्टदृष्टी रागाग्निनान्तर्हृदये प्रदीप्तः ।
सगद्गदं कामविषक्तचेताः कृताञ्जलिर्वाक्यमुवाच नन्दः ॥४९॥

हर्य्यङ्गनासौ मुषितैकदृष्टिर्यदन्तरे स्यात् तव नाथ वध्वाः ।
तदन्तरेऽसौ कृपणा वधूस्ते वपुष्मतीरप्सरसः प्रतीत्य ॥५०॥

आस्था यथा पूर्वमभून्न काचित् अन्यासु मे स्त्रीषु निशाम्य भार्य्याम् ।
तस्यां तथा संप्रति काचिदास्था न मे निशाम्यैव हि रूपमासाम् ॥५१॥

यथा प्रतप्तो मृदुनातपेन दह्येत कश्चिन्महतानलेन ।
रागेण पूर्व्वं मृदुनाभितप्तो रागाग्निनानेन तथाभिदह्ये ॥५२॥

वाग्वारिणा मां परिषिञ्च तस्माद् यावन्न दह्ये स इवाब्जचक्षुः ।
रागाग्निरद्यैव हि मां दिधक्षुः कक्षं स वृक्षाग्रमिवोत्थितोऽग्निः ॥५३॥

प्रसीद सीदामि विमुञ्च मां मुने वसुन्धराधैर्य्य न धैर्य्यमस्ति मे ।
असून् विमोच्यामि विमुक्तमानसः प्रयच्छ वा वागमृतं मुमूर्षवे ॥५४॥
अनर्थभोगेन विघातदृष्टिना प्रमाददंष्ट्रेण तमोविषाग्निना ।
अहं हि दष्टो हृदि मन्मथाहिना विधत्स्व तस्मादगदं महाभिषक् ॥५५॥
अनेन दष्टो मदनाहिनाऽहिना न कश्चिदात्मन्यनवस्थितः स्थितः ।
मुमोह बोध्यो[र्हि] चलात्मनो मनो बभूव धीमांश्च स शन्तनुस्तनुः॥५६॥
स्थिते विशिष्टे त्वयि संश्रये श्रये यथा न यायी(मी) बङ्कसंदिशं

दिशम् ।

यथा च लब्ध्वा व्यसनक्षयं क्षयं व्रजामि तन्मे कुरु शंसतः सतः ॥५७॥

ततो जिघांसुर्हृदि तस्य तत्तमस्तमोनुदो नक्तमिवोत्थितं तमः ।
महर्षिचन्द्रो जगतस्तमोनुदस्तमःप्रहीणो निजगाद गौतमः ॥५८॥
धृतिं परिष्वज्य विधूय विक्रियां निगृह्य तावत् श्रुतिचेतसी शृणु ।
इमा यदि प्रार्थयसे त्वमङ्गना विधत्स्व शुल्कार्थमिहोत्तमं तपः ॥५९॥
[1]इमा हि शक्यन्न बलान्न सेवया न संप्रदानेन न रूपवत्तया ।
इमा ह्रियन्ते खलु धर्म्मचर्य्यया स चेत् प्रहर्षश्चर धर्म्ममादृतः ॥६०॥
इहाधिवासो दिवि दैवतैः समं वनानि रम्याण्यजराश्च योषितः ।
इदं फलं स्वस्य शुभस्य कर्म्मणः न दत्तमन्येन न वाप्यहेतुतः ॥६१॥
क्षितौ मनुष्यो धनुरादिभिः श्रमैः स्त्रियः कदाचिद् विलभेत वा न वा ।
असंशयं यत्त्विह धर्म्मचर्य्यया भवेयुरेता दिवि पुण्यकर्म्मणः ॥६२॥
तदप्रमत्तो नियमे समुद्यतो रमस्व यद्यप्सरसोऽभिलिप्ससे ।
अहं च तेऽत्र प्रतिभूः स्थिरे व्रते यथा त्वमाभिर्नियतं समेष्यसि ॥६३॥

---

१ P. L. M. इमा हि शक्य एव गात्र सेवया ।

अतःपरं परममिति व्यवस्थितः परां धृतिं परमसुनौ चकार सः ।
ततो मुनिः पवन इवाम्बरात् पतन् प्रगृह्य तं पुनरगमन् महीतलम् ॥
६४॥

इति सौन्दरनन्दे महाकाव्ये स्वर्गनिदर्शनो
नाम दशमः सर्गः ।

## एकादशः सर्गः

ततस्ता योषितो दृष्ट्वा नन्दो नन्दनचारिणीः ।
बबन्ध नियमस्तम्भे दुर्दमं चपलं मनः ॥१॥

सोऽनिष्टनैष्कर्म्यरसो म्लानतामरसोपमः ।
चचार विरसो धर्म्मं निवेश्याप्सरसो हृदि ॥२॥

तथा लोलेन्द्रियो भूत्वा दयितेन्द्रियगोचरः ।
इन्द्रियार्थवशादेव बभूव नियतेन्द्रियः ॥३॥

कामचर्य्यासु कुशलो भिक्षुचर्य्यासु विक्लवः ।
परमाचार्य्यविष्टब्धो ब्रह्मचर्य्यं चचार सः ॥४॥

संवृतेन च शान्तेन तीव्रेण मदनेन च ।
जलाग्न्यो[1]रिव संसर्गात् शशाम[2] च शुशोष च ॥५॥

स तावद् दर्शनीयोऽपि वैरूप्यमगमत् परम् ।
चिन्तयाप्सरसाञ्चैव नियमेनायतेन च ॥६॥

प्रस्तावेष्वपि भार्य्यायाः प्रियभार्य्यस्तथापि सः ।
वीतराग इवातस्थौ न जहर्ष न चुक्षुभे ॥७॥

तं व्यवस्थितमाज्ञाय भार्य्यारागात् पराङ्मुखम् ।
अभिगम्याब्रवीत् नन्दमानन्दः प्रणयादिदम् ॥८॥

अहो सदृशमारब्धं श्रुतस्याभिजनस्य च ।
निगृहीतेन्द्रियः स्वस्थो नियमे यदि संस्थितः ॥९॥

---

१ P. M. जलाग्नेः T. २ P. M. प्रशशास T.

अभिव्यक्तस्य कामेषु रागिणो विषयात्मनः ।
यदियं संविदुत्पन्ना नेयमल्पेन हेतुना ॥१०॥
व्याधिरल्पेन यत्नेन मृदुः प्रतिनिवार्य्यते ।
प्रबलः प्रबलैरेव यत्नैर्नश्यति वा न वा ॥११॥
दुर्हरो मानसो व्याधिर्बलवांश्च तवाभवत् ।
विनिवृत्तो यदि स ते सर्व्वथा धृतिमानसि ॥१२॥
दुष्करं साधनार्य्येण मानिना चैव मार्दवम् ।
अतिसर्गश्च लुब्धेन ब्रह्मचर्य्यञ्च रागिणा ॥१३॥
एकस्तु मम सन्देहस्तवास्यां नियमे धृतौ ।
अत्रानुनयमिच्छामि वक्तव्यं यदि मन्यसे ॥१४॥
आर्ज्जवाभिहितं वाक्यं न च गन्तव्यमन्यथा ।
रूक्षमप्याशये शुद्धे [1]रूक्षतां नेति सज्जनः ॥१५॥
अप्रियं हि हितं स्निग्धमस्निग्धमहितं प्रियम् ।
दुर्लभं तु प्रियहितं स्वादु पथ्यमिवौषधम् ॥१६॥
विश्वासश्चार्थचर्य्या च सामान्यं सुखदुःखयोः ।
मर्षणं प्रणयश्चैव मित्रवृत्तिरियं सताम् ॥१७॥
तदिदं त्वां विवक्षामि प्रणयान्न जिघांसया ।
त्वच्छ्रेयो हि विवक्षा मे यते नार्हाम्युपेक्षितुम् ॥१८॥
अप्सरोभृतको धर्मं चरसीत्यभिधीयसे ।
किमिदं भूतमाहोस्वित् परिहासोऽयमीदृशः ॥१९॥

---

१ P. L. M. रूक्षतो ।

यदि तावदिदं सत्यं वच्याम्यत्र यदौषधम् ।
औद्धत्यमथ वक्तृणामभिधास्यामि तद्रुजः ॥२०॥

स्नेहपूर्व्वमथो तेन हृदि सोऽभिहतस्तदा ।
ध्यात्वा दीर्घं निशश्वास किञ्चिच्चावाङ्मुखोऽभवत् ॥२१॥

ततस्तस्येङ्गितं ज्ञात्वा मनःसंकल्पसूचकम् ।
बभाषे वाक्यमानन्दो मधुरोदर्कमप्रियम् ॥२२॥

आकारेणावगच्छामि तव धर्म्मप्रयोजनम् ।
यज्ज्ञात्वा त्वयि जातं मे हास्यं कारुण्यमेव च ॥२३॥

यथासनार्थं स्कन्धेन कश्चिद् गुर्व्वीं शिलां वहेत् ।
तद्वत् त्वमपि कामार्थं नियमं वोढुमुद्यतः ॥२४॥

तिताडयिषया दृप्तो यथा मेषोऽपसर्पति ।
तद्वदब्रह्मचर्य्याय ब्रह्मचर्य्यमिदं तव ॥२५॥

चिक्रीषन्ति यथा पण्यं वणिजो लाभलिप्सया ।
धर्म्मचर्य्या तव तथा पण्यभूता न शान्तये ॥२६॥

यथा फलविशेषार्थं बीजं वपति कर्षकः ।
तद्वद्विषयकार्पण्यात् विषयांस्त्यक्तवानसि ॥२७॥

आकाङ्क्षेच्च यथा रोगं प्रतीकारसुखेप्सया ।
दुःखमन्विच्छति भवान् तथा विषयतृष्णया ॥२८॥

यथा पश्यति मध्वेव[१] न प्रपातमवेक्षते ।
पश्यस्यप्सरसस्तद्वद् भ्रंशमन्ते न पश्यसि ॥२९॥

---

१ P. L. M. मध्येव M. P. मध्येव ।

हृदि कामाग्निना दीप्ते कायेन वहतो व्रतम् ।
किमिदं ब्रह्मचर्य्यं ते मनसाऽब्रह्मचारिणः ॥२०॥
संसारे वर्त्तमानेन यदा चाप्सरसस्त्वया ।
प्राप्तास्त्यक्ताश्च शतशस्ताभ्यः किमिति ते स्पृहा ॥२१॥
तृप्तिर्नास्तीन्धनैरग्नेर्नाम्भसा लवणाम्भसः ।
नापि कामैरतृप्तस्य तस्मात् कामा न तृप्तये ॥२२॥
अतृप्तौ च कुतः शान्तिरशान्तौ च कुतः सुखम् ।
असुखे च कुतः प्रीतिरप्रीतौ च कुतो रतिः ॥२३॥
रिरंसा यदि ते तस्मादध्यात्मे धीयतां मनः ।
प्रशान्ता चानवद्या च नास्त्यध्यात्मसमा रतिः ॥२४॥
न तत्र कार्य्यं तूर्य्यैस्ते न स्त्रीभिर्न विभूषणैः ।
एकस्त्वं यत्र तत्रस्थस्तया रत्याभिरंस्यसे ॥२५॥
मानसं बलवद्दुःखं तर्षे तिष्ठति तिष्ठति ।
तं तर्षं छिन्धि दुःखं हि तृष्णा नास्ति च नास्ति च ॥२६॥
सम्पत्तौ वा विपत्तौ वा दिवा वा नक्तमेव वा ।
कामेषु हि सतृष्णस्य न शान्तिरुपपद्यते ॥२७॥
कामानां प्रार्थना दुःखा प्राप्तौ तृप्तिर्न विद्यते ।
वियोगान्नियतः शोको वियोगश्च ध्रुवो दिवि ॥२८॥
कृत्वापि दुष्करं कर्म्म स्वर्गं लब्ध्वापि दुर्लभम् ।
नृलोकं पुनरेवैति प्रवासात् स्वगृहं यथा ॥२९॥
यथा भ्रष्टस्य कुशलं शिष्टं किञ्चिन्न विद्यते ।
तिर्य्यक्षु पितृलोके वा नरके वोपपद्यते ॥४०॥

तस्य भुक्तवतः स्वर्गे विषयानुत्तमानपि ।
भ्रष्टस्यार्त्तस्य दुःखेन किमास्वादः करोति सः ॥४१॥

श्येनाय प्राणिवात्सल्यात् स्वमांसान्यपि दत्तवान् ।
शिबिः स्वर्गात् परिभ्रष्टस्तादृक् कृत्वापि दुष्करम् ॥४२॥

शक्रस्यार्द्धासनं गत्वा पूर्व्वपार्थिव एव यः ।
स देवत्वं गतः काले मान्धाताधः पुनर्ययौ ॥४३॥

राज्यं कृत्वापि देवानां पपात नहुषो भुवि ।
प्राप्तः किल भुजङ्गत्वं नाद्यापि परिमुच्यते ॥४४॥

तथैव द्विविडो राजा राजवृत्तेन संस्कृतः ।
स्वर्गं गत्वा पुनर्भ्रष्टः कूर्म्मीभूतः किलार्णवे ॥४५॥

भूरिद्युम्नो ययातिश्च एते चान्ये नृपर्षभाः ।
कर्म्मभिर्द्यामभिक्रीय तत्क्षयात्पुनरत्यजत् ॥४६॥

असुराः पूर्व्वदेवास्तु सुरैरपहृतश्रियः ।
श्रियं समनुशोचन्तः पातालं शरणं ययुः ॥४७॥

किञ्च राजर्षिभिस्तावदसुरैर्वा सुरादिभिः ।
महेन्द्राः शतशः पेतुर्माहात्म्यमपि न स्थिरम् ॥४८॥

संसदं शोभयित्वैन्द्रीमुपेन्द्रश्चण्डविक्रमः ।
क्षीणकर्म्मा पपातोर्व्वीं मध्यादप्सरसां रसन् ॥४९॥

हा चैत्ररथ हा वापि हा मन्दाकिनि हा प्रिये ।
इत्यार्त्ता विलपन्तोपि गां पतन्ति दिवौकसः ॥५०॥

तीव्रं ह्युत्पद्यते दुःखं धीमतां[१] यन्मुमूर्षताम् ।

---

१ P. M. ह्मिमतावत् T.

किं पुनः पततां स्वर्गाद्देवान्तसुखसेविनाम् ॥५१॥

रजो गृह्णाति वासांसि म्लायन्ति परमा[:]स्रजः ।
गात्रेभ्यो जायते स्वेदो रतिर्भवति नासने ॥५२॥
एतान्यादौ निमित्तानि च्युतौ स्वर्गाद्दिवौकसाम् ।
अनिष्टानीव मर्त्यानामरिष्टानि मुमूर्षताम् ॥५३॥
सुखमुत्पद्यते यच्च दिवि कामानुपाश्नताम् ।
त(य)च्च दुःखं निपततां दुःखमेवावशिष्यते ॥५४॥

तस्मादस्वन्तमत्राण(णा)मविश्वास्यमतर्पकम् ।
विज्ञाय चयिणं स्वर्गमपवर्गे मतिं कुरु ॥५५॥
अशरीरं भवाग्र्यं हि गत्वापि मुनिरुद्रकः ।
कर्मणोऽन्ते च्युतस्तस्मात् तिर्य्यग्योनिं प्रपत्स्यते ॥५६॥
मैत्रया सप्तवार्षिक्या ब्रह्मलोकमितो गतः ।
सुनेत्रः पुनरावृत्तो गर्भवासमुपेयिवान् ॥५७॥
यदा चैश्वर्य्यवन्तोपि चयिणः स्वर्गवासिनः ।
को नाम स्वर्गवासाय च्चिष्णवे स्पृहयेद्बुधः ॥५८॥

सूत्रेण बद्धोहि यथा विहङ्गो व्यावर्त्तते दूरगतोपि भूयः ।
अज्ञानसूत्रेण तथावबद्धो गतोपि दूरं पुनरेति लोकः ॥५९॥
कृत्वा[1] कालविलचणं प्रतिभुवा मुक्तो यथा बन्धनाद्
भुक्त्वा वेश्मसुखान्यतीत्य समयं भूयो विशेद् बन्धनम् ।
तद्वद् द्यां प्रतिभूवदात्मनियमै ध्यानादिभिः प्राप्तवान्
काले कर्मसु तेषु भुक्तविषयेष्वाकृष्यते गां पुनः ॥६०॥

---

१ P. M. कृत्वार्थे T.

अन्तर्जालगताः प्रमत्तमनसो मीनास्तडागे यथा
जानन्ति व्यसनं निरोधजनितं स्वस्थाश्चरन्त्यम्भसि ।
अन्तर्लोकगताः कृतार्थमतयस्तद्वद्दिवि ध्यायिनो
मन्यन्ते शिवमच्युतं ध्रुवमिति स्वं स्थानमावर्त्तकम् ॥६१॥

तज्जन्मव्याधिमृत्युव्यसनपरिगतं मत्वा जगदिदं
संसारे भ्राम्यमाणं दिवि नृषु नरके तिर्य्यक्पितृषु च ।
यत्त्राणं निर्भयं यत् शिवममरमजरं निःशोकममृतम्
तद्धेतोर्ब्रह्मचर्य्यं चर जहिहि चलं स्वर्गं प्रति रुचिम् ॥६२॥

इति सौन्दरनन्दे महाकाव्ये स्वर्गापवादो नाम
एकादशः सर्गः ॥

# द्वादशः सर्गः

अप्सरोभृतको धर्मं चरसीत्यथ चोदितः ।
आनन्देन तदा नन्दः परं व्रीडमुपागमत् ॥१॥
तस्य व्रीडेन महता प्रमोदो हृदि नाभवत् ।
अप्रामोद्येन विमुखं नावतस्थे व्रते मनः ॥२॥
कामरागप्रधानोऽपि परिहाससमोऽपि सन् ।
परिपाकगते हेतौ न स तन्ममृषे वचः ॥३॥
अपरीक्षकभावाच्च पूर्व्वं मत्वा दिवं ध्रुवम् ।
तस्मात् क्षिष्णुं परिश्रुत्य भृशं संवेगमीयिवान् ॥४॥
तस्य स्वर्गात् निववृते सङ्कल्पाश्वो मनोरथः ।
महारथ इवोन्मार्गादप्रमत्तस्य सारथेः ॥५॥
स्वर्गतर्षान्निवृत्तस्य सद्यः स्वस्थ इवाभवत् ।
मृष्टादपथ्याद्विरतो जिजीविषुरिवातुरः ॥६॥
विसस्मार प्रियां भार्य्यामप्सरोदर्शनाद् यथा ।
तथा नित्यतयोद्विग्नस्तत्याजाप्सरसोऽपि सः ॥७॥
महतामपि भूतानामावृत्तिरिति चिन्तयन् ।
संवेगाच्च सरागोऽपि वीतराग इवाभवत् ॥८॥
बभूव सहि संवेगः श्रेयसस्तस्य वृद्धये ।
[1]धातोरधिरिवाख्याते पठितोऽक्षरचिन्तकैः ॥९॥

---

१ P. L. M. धातु ।

न तु कामात्मनस्तस्य केनचित् जगृहे धृतिः ।
त्रिषु कालेषु सर्व्वेषु निपातोऽस्तिरिव स्मृतः ॥१०॥
खेलगामी महाबाहु र्गजेन्द्र इव निर्म्मदः ।
सोऽभ्यगच्छद् गुरुं काले विवक्षुर्भावमात्मनः ॥११॥
प्रणम्य च गुरौ मूर्ध्ना बाष्पव्याकुललोचनः ।
कृत्वाञ्जलिमुवाचेदं ह्रिया किञ्चिदवाङ्मुखः ॥१२॥
अप्सरःप्राप्तये यन्मे भगवन् प्रतिभूरसि ।
नाप्सरोभि र्ममार्थोऽस्ति प्रतिभूत्वं त्यजाम्यहम् ॥१३॥
श्रुत्वा ह्यावर्त्तकं स्वर्गं संसारस्य च चित्रताम् ।
न मर्त्त्येषु न देवेषु प्रवृत्तिर्म्मम रोचते ॥१४॥
यदि प्राप्य दिवं यत्नान्नियमेन दमेन च ।
अवितृप्ताः पतन्त्यन्ते स्वर्गाय त्यागिने नमः ॥१५॥
अतश्च निखिलं लोकं विदित्वा सचराचरम् ।
सर्व्वदुःखक्षयकरे त्वद्धर्म्मे परमे रमे ॥१६॥
तस्माद् व्याससमासाभ्यां तन्मे व्याख्यातुमर्हसि ।
यच्छ्रुत्वा शृण्वताम् श्रेष्ठ परमं प्राप्नुयां पदम् ॥१७॥
ततस्तस्याशयं ज्ञात्वा विपक्षाणीन्द्रियाणि च ।
श्रेयश्चैवामुखीभूतं निजगाद तथागतः ॥१८॥
अहो प्रत्यवमर्शोऽयं श्रेयसस्ते पुरोजवः ।
अरण्यां मथ्यमानायामग्नेर्धूम इवोत्थितः ॥१९॥
चिरमुन्मार्गविहृतो लोलैरिन्द्रियवाजिभिः ।
अवतीर्णोऽसि पन्थानं दिष्ट्या दृष्ट्याऽविमूढया ॥२०॥

अद्य ते सफलं जन्म लाभोऽद्य सुमहांस्तव ।
यस्य कामरसज्ञस्य नैष्कर्म्यायोत्सुकं मनः ॥२१॥
लोकेऽस्मिन्नालयारामे निवृत्तौ दुर्लभा रतिः ।
व्यथन्ते ह्यपुनर्भावात् प्रपातादिव बालिशाः ॥२२॥
दुःखं न स्यात् सुखं मे स्यादिति प्रयतते जनः ।
अत्यन्तदुःखोपरमं सुखं तच्च न बुध्यते ॥२३॥
अरिभूतेष्वनित्येषु सततं दुःखहेतुषु ।
कामादिषु जगत् सक्तं न वेत्ति सुखमव्ययम् ॥२४॥
सर्व्वदुःखापहं तत्तु हस्तस्थममृतं तव ।
विषं पीत्वा यदगदं समये पातुमिच्छसि ॥२५॥
अनर्हसंसारभयं मानार्हं ते चिकीर्षितम् ।
रागाग्निस्तादृशो यस्य धर्म्मोन्मुखपराङ्मुखः ॥२६॥
रागोद्दामेन मनसा सर्व्वथा दुष्करा धृतिः ।
सदोषं सलिलं दृष्ट्वा पथिकेन पिपासुना ॥२७॥
ईदृशी नाम बुद्धिस्ते निरुद्धा रजसाऽभवत् ।
रजसा चण्डवातेन विवस्वत इव प्रभा ॥२८॥
सा जिघांसुस्तमो हार्दं या संप्रति विजृम्भते ।
तमो नैशं प्रभा सौरी विनिर्गीर्णेव मेरुणा ॥२९॥
युक्तरूपमिदञ्चैव शुद्धसत्वस्य चेतसः ।
यत्ते स्यान्नैष्ठिके सूक्ष्मे श्रेयसि श्रद्दधानता ॥३०॥
धर्म्मच्छन्दमिमं तस्माद् विवर्द्धयितुमर्हसि ।
सर्व्वधर्म्मा हि धर्म्मज्ञ नियमाच्छन्दहेतवः ॥३१॥

सत्यां गमनबुद्धौ हि गमनाय प्रवर्त्तते ।
शय्याबुद्धौ च शयनं स्थानबुद्धौ तथा स्थितिः ॥२२॥
अन्तर्भूमिगतं ह्यम्भः श्रद्दधाति नरो यदा ।
अर्थित्वे सति यत्नेन तदा खनति गामिमाम् ॥२३॥
नार्थी यद्यग्निना वा स्यात् श्रद्दध्यात्तु न वारणौ ।
मथ्नीयान्नारणिं कश्चित् तद्भावे सति मथ्यते ॥२४॥
सस्योत्पत्तिं यदि न वा श्रद्दध्यात् कर्षकः क्षितौ ।
अर्थी सस्येन वा न स्याद् बीजानि न वपेद्भुवि ॥२५॥
अतश्च हस्त इत्युक्ता मया श्रद्धा विशेषतः ।
यस्माद् गृह्णाति सद्धर्मं दायं हस्त इवाक्षतः ॥२६॥
प्राधान्यादिन्द्रियमिति स्थिरत्वाद् बलमित्यतः ।
गुणदारिद्र्यशमनाद् धनमित्यभिवर्णिता ॥२७॥
रक्षणार्थेन धर्मस्य तथेषीके[1]त्युदाहृता ।
लोकेऽस्मिन् दुर्लभत्वाच्च रत्नमित्यभिभाषिता ॥२८॥
पुनश्च बीजमित्युक्ता निमित्तं श्रेयसो यदा ।
पावनार्थेन पापस्य नदीत्यभिहिता पुनः ॥२९॥
यस्माद्धर्मस्य चोत्पत्तौ श्रद्धा कारणमुत्तमम् ।
मयोक्ता कार्य्यतस्तस्मात् तत्र तत्र तथा तथा ॥४०॥
श्रद्धाङ्कुरमिमं तस्मात् संवर्द्धयितुमर्हसि ।
तद्वृद्धौ वर्द्धते धर्मो मूलवृद्धौ यथा द्रुमः ॥४१॥

---

१ P. M. ०चीके० ।

व्याकुलं दर्शनं यस्य दुर्ब्बलो यस्य निश्चयः ।
तस्य पारिप्लवा श्रद्धा न हि कृत्याय वर्त्तते ॥४२॥

यावत्तत्त्वं न भवति हि दृष्टं श्रुतं वा
तावच्छ्रद्धा न भवति बलस्था स्थिरा वा ।
दृष्टे तत्त्वे नियमपरिभूतेन्द्रियस्य
श्रद्धावृक्षो भवति सफलश्चाश्रयस्य ॥

इति सौन्दरनन्दे महाकाव्ये प्रत्यवमर्शो नाम
द्वादशः सर्गः ॥

## त्रयोदशः सर्गः

अथ संराधितो नन्दः श्रद्धां प्रति महर्षिणा ।
परिषिक्तोऽमृतेनेव युयुजे परया मुदा ॥१॥

कृतार्थमिव तम् मेने संबुद्धः श्रद्धया तया ।
मेने प्राप्तमिव श्रेयः स च बुद्धेन संस्कृतः ॥२॥

श्लक्ष्णेन वचसा कांश्चित् कांश्चित् परुषया गिरा ।
कांश्चिदाभ्यामुपायाभ्यां स विनिन्ये विनायकः ॥३॥

पांशुभ्यः काञ्चनं जातं विशुद्धं निर्म्मलं शुचि ।
स्थितं पांशुष्वपि यथा पांशुदोषै र्न लिप्यते ॥४॥

पद्मपर्णं यथा चैव जले जातं जले स्थितम् ।
उपरिष्टादधस्ताद् वा न जलेनोपलिप्यते ॥५॥

तद्वल्लोके मुनिर्जातो लोकस्यानुग्रहं चरन् ।
कृतित्वान्निर्म्मलत्वाच्च लोकधर्म्मै र्न लिप्यते ॥६॥

श्लेषं त्यागं प्रियं रूक्षं कथाञ्च ध्यानमेव च ।
मन्त्रकाले चिकित्सार्थं चक्रे नात्मानुवृत्तये ॥७॥

अतश्च सन्दधे कायं महाकरुणया तया ।
मोचयेयं कथं दुःखात् सत्वानीत्यनुकम्पकः ॥८॥

अथ संहर्षणान्नन्दं विदित्वा भाजनीकृतम् ।
अब्रवीद् ब्रुवतां श्रेष्ठः क्रमज्ञः श्रेयसां क्रमम् ॥९॥

अतः प्रभृति भूयस्त्वं श्रद्धेन्द्रियपुरःसरः ।
अमृतस्याप्तये सौम्य वृत्तं रक्षितुमर्हसि ॥१०॥

प्रयोगः कायवचसोः शुद्धो भवति ते यथा ।
उत्तानो विवृतो गुप्तोऽनवच्छिद्रस्तथा कुरु ॥११॥
उत्तानो भावकरणात् विवृतश्चाप्यगूहनात् ।
गुप्तो रक्षणतात्पर्य्यादच्छिद्रश्चानवद्यतः ॥१२॥
श[री]रवचसोः शुद्धौ सप्ताङ्गे चापि कर्म्मणि ।
आजीवसमुदाचारं शौचात् संस्कर्त्तुमर्हसि ॥१३॥
दोषाणां कुहनादीनां पञ्चानामनिषेवणात् ।
त्यागाच्च ज्योतिषादीनां चतुर्णां वृत्तिघातिनाम् ॥१४॥
प्राणिधान्यधनादीनां वर्ज्ज्यानामप्रतिग्रहात् ।
भैक्ष्याङ्गानां निसृष्टानां नियतानां प्रतिग्रहात् ॥१५॥
परितुष्टः शुचिर्मञ्जुश्चौक्षया जीवसम्पदा ।
कुर्य्याद्दुःखप्रतीकारं यावदेव विमुक्तये ॥१६॥
कर्म्मणो हि यथा दृष्टात् कायवाक्प्रभवादपि ।
आजीवः पृथगेवोक्तो दुःशोधत्वादयं मया ॥१७॥
गृहस्थेन हि दुःशोधा दृष्टि र्विविधदृष्टिना ।
आजीवो भिक्षुणा चैव परेष्वायत्तवृत्तिना ॥१८॥
एतावच्छीलमित्युक्तमाचारोयं समासतः ।
अस्य नाशेन नैव स्यात् प्रव्रज्या न गृह स्थिता ॥१९॥
तस्माच्चारित्रसम्पन्नो ब्रह्मचर्य्यमिदं चर ।
अणुमात्रेष्ववद्येषु भयदर्शी दृढव्रतः ॥२०॥
शीलमास्थाय वर्त्तन्ते सर्व्वा हि श्रेयसि क्रियाः ।
स्थानाद्यानीव कार्य्याणि प्रतिष्ठाय वसुन्धराम् ॥२१॥

मोक्षस्योपनिष सौम्यत् वैराग्यमिति गृह्यताम् ।
वैराग्यस्यापि संवेगः संविदो ज्ञानदर्शनम् ॥२२॥
ज्ञानस्योपनिषच्चैव समाधिरुपधार्य्यताम् ।
समाधेरप्युपनिषत् सुखं शारीरमानसम् ॥२३॥
प्रस्रब्धिः कायमनसः सुखस्योपनिषत्परा ।
प्रस्रब्धेरप्युपनिषत् प्रीतिरप्यवगम्यताम् ॥२४॥
तथा प्रीतेरुपनिषत् प्रामोद्यं परमं मतम् ।
प्रामोद्यस्याप्यहृल्लेखः कुकृतेष्वकृतेषु वा ॥२५॥
अविलेखस्य मनसः शीलन्तूपनिषच्छुचि ।
अतः शीलं नयत्यग्यमिति शीलं विशोधय ॥२६॥
शीलनात् शीलमित्युक्तं शीलनात् सेवनादपि ।
सेवनात्तन्निदेशाच्च निर्द्देशश्च तदाश्रयात् ॥२७॥
शीलं हि शरणं सौम्य कान्तार इव दैशिकः ।
मित्रं बन्धुश्च रक्षा च धनञ्च बलमेव च ॥२८॥
यतः शीलमतः सौम्य शीलं संस्कर्त्तुमर्हसि ।
एतत् स्थानमथान्ये च मोक्षारम्भेषु योगिनाम् ॥२९॥
ततः स्मृतिमधिष्ठाय चपलानि स्वभावतः ।
इन्द्रियाणीन्द्रियार्थेभ्यो निवारयितुमर्हसि ॥३०॥
भेतव्यं न तथा शत्रो र्नाग्ने र्नाहेर्नचाशनेः ।
इन्द्रियेभ्यो यथा स्वेभ्यस्तैरजस्रं हि हन्यते ॥३१॥
द्विषद्भिः शत्रुभिः कश्चित् कदाचित् पीड्यते न वा ।
इन्द्रियैर्बाध्यते सर्व्वः सर्व्वत्र च सदैव च ॥३२॥

न च प्रयाति नरकं शत्रुप्रभृतिभिर्हतः ।
कृष्यते तत्र निघ्नस्तु चपलैरिन्द्रियैर्हतः ॥२३॥
हन्यमानस्य तैर्दुःखं हार्दं भवति वा न वा ।
इन्द्रियैर्बाध्यमानस्य हार्दं शारीरमेव च ॥२४॥
सङ्कल्पविषदिग्धा हि पञ्चेन्द्रियमया[:] शराः ।
चिन्तापुङ्खा रतिफला विषयाकाशगोचराः ॥२५॥
मनुष्यहरिणान् घ्नन्ति कामव्याधेरिता हृदि ।
विहन्यन्ते यदि न ते ततः पतन्ति तैः क्षत[ाः] ॥२६॥
नियमाजिरसंस्थेन धैर्य्यकार्म्मुकधारिणा ।
निपतन्तो निवार्य्यास्ते महता स्मृतिवर्म्मणा ॥२७॥
इन्द्रियाणामुपशमादरीणां निग्रहादिव ।
सुखं स्वपिति वास्ते वा यत्र तत्र गतोद्धवः ॥२८॥
तेषां हि सततं लोके विषयानभिकाङ्क्षताम् ।
संविन्नैवास्ति कार्पण्याच्छुनामाशावतामिव ॥२९॥
विषयैरिन्द्रियग्रामो न तृप्तिमधिगच्छति ।
अजस्रं पूर्य्यमाणोऽपि समुद्रः सलिलैरिव ॥४०॥
अवश्यं गोचरे[:] स्वे[:] स्वैर्वर्त्तितव्यमिहेन्द्रियैः ।
निमित्तं तत्र न ग्राह्यमनुव्यञ्जनमेव च ॥४१॥
आलोक्य चक्षुषा रूपं धातुमात्रे व्यवस्थितः ।
स्त्री वेति पुरुषो वेति न कल्पयितुमर्हसि ॥४२॥
स चेत् स्त्रीपुरुषग्राहः क्वचिद् विद्येत कश्चन ।
शुभतः केशदन्तादीन् नानुप्रस्थातुमर्हसि ॥४३॥

नापनेयं ततः किञ्चित् प्रक्षेप्यं नापि किञ्चन ।
द्रष्टव्यं भूततो भूतं यादृशञ्च यथा च यत् ॥४४॥

एवं ते पश्यतस्तत्त्वं शश्वदिन्द्रियगोचरे ।
भविष्यति पदस्थानं नाभिध्यादौर्म्मनस्ययोः ॥४५॥

अभिध्या प्रियरूपेण हन्ति कामात्मकं जगत् ।
अरिर्मित्रमुखेनेव प्रियवाक् कलुषाशयः ॥४६॥

दौर्मनस्याभिधानस्तु प्रतिघो विषयाश्रितः ।
मोहाद् येनानुवृत्तेन परत्रेह च हन्यते ॥४७॥

अनुरोधविरोधाभ्यां शीतोष्णाभ्यामिवार्द्दितः ।
शर्म्म नाप्नोति न श्रेयश्चलेन्द्रियमतो जगत् ॥४८॥

नेन्द्रियं विषये तावत् प्रवृत्तमपि सज्जते ।
यावन्न मनसस्तत्र परिकल्पः प्रवर्त्तते ॥४९॥

इन्धने सति वायौ च यथा ज्वलति पावकः ।
विषयात् परिकल्पाच्च क्लेशाग्निर्जायते तथा ॥५०॥

अभूतपरिकल्पेन विषयस्य हि बध्यते ।
तमेव विषयं पश्यन् भूततः परिमुच्यते ॥५१॥

दृष्ट्वैकं रूपमन्यो हि रज्यतेऽन्यः प्रदुष्यति ।
कश्चिद् भवति मध्यस्थस्तत्रैवान्यो घृणायते ॥५२॥

अतो न वि[ष]यो हेतु र्बन्धाय न विमुक्तये ।
परिकल्पविशेषेण सङ्गो[१] भवति वा न वा ॥५३॥

---

१ P. M. संयोग T.

कार्य्यः परमयत्नेन तस्मादिन्द्रियसंवरः ।
इन्द्रियाणि ह्यगुप्तानि दुःखाय च भवाय च ॥५४॥

कामभोगभोगवद्भिरात्मदृष्टिदृष्टिभिः
प्रमादनैकमूर्द्धभिः प्रहर्षलोलजिह्वकैः ।
इन्द्रियोरगै र्मनोविलश्रयैः स्पृहाविषैः
शमागदादृते न[द]ष्टमस्ति यच्चिकित्सयेत्[1] ॥५५॥

तस्मादेषामकुशलकराणामरीणां
चक्षुर्घ्राणश्रवणरसनस्पर्शनानाम् ।
सर्व्वावस्थं भवति नियमादप्रमत्तो
मास्मिन्नर्थे क्षणमपि कृथास्त्वं प्रमादम् ॥५६॥

सौन्दरनन्दे महाकाव्ये शीलेन्द्रियजयो नाम
त्रयोदशः सर्गः ।

---

१ P. M. शमागतादृते नष्टमस्ति यश्चिकित्सेत् T.

## चतुर्दशः सर्गः

अथ स्मृतिकपाटेन पिधायेन्द्रियसंवरम् ।
भोजने भव म[ा]त्र[ा]ज्ञो ध्यानायानामयाय च ॥१॥
प्राणापानौ निगृह्णाति ग्लानिनिद्रे प्रयच्छति ।
कृतो ह्यत्यर्थमाहारो विहन्ति च पराक्रमम् ॥२॥
यथा चात्यर्थमाहा[र]ः कृतोऽनर्थाय कल्पते ।
उपयुक्तस्तथात्यल्पो न सामर्थ्याय कल्पते ॥३॥
आचयं द्युतिमुत्साहं प्रयोगं बलमेव च ।
भोजनं कृतमत्यल्पं शरीरस्यापकर्षति ॥४॥
यथा भारेण नमते लघुनोन्नमते तुला ।
समा तिष्ठति युक्तेन भोज्येनेयं तथा तनुः ॥५॥
तस्मादभ्यवहर्त्तव्यं स्वशक्तिमनुपश्यता ।
नातिमात्रं न चात्यल्पं मेयं मानवशादपि ॥६॥
अभ्याक्रान्तो हि कायाग्नि र्गुरुणान्नेन शाम्यति ।
अवच्छन्न इवाल्पोऽग्निः सहसा महतेन्धसा ॥७॥
अत्यन्तमपि संहारो नाहारस्य प्रशस्यते ।
अनाहारो हि निर्व्वाति निरिन्धन इवानलः ॥८॥
यस्मान्नास्ति विनाहारात् सर्व्वप्राणभृतां स्थितिः ।
तस्माद्दुष्यति नाहारो विकल्पोऽत्र तु वार्य्यते ॥९॥
न ह्येकविषयेऽन्यत्र सज्यन्ते प्राणिनस्तथा ।
अविज्ञाते यथाहारे बोद्धव्यं तत्र कारणम् ॥१०॥

चिकित्सार्थं यथा धत्ते व्रणस्यालेपनं व्रणी ।
क्षुद्विघातार्थमाहारस्तद्वत् सेव्यो मुमुक्षुणा ॥११॥
भारस्योद्वहनार्थञ्च रथाक्षोऽभ्युज्यते यथा ।
भोजनं प्राणयात्रार्थं तद्वद्विद्वान्निषेवते ॥१२॥
समभिक्रमणार्थञ्च कान्तारस्य यथाध्वगौ ।
पुत्रमांसानि खादेतां दम्पती भृशदुःखितौ ॥१३॥
एवमभ्यवहर्त्तव्यं भोजनं प्रतिसंख्यया ।
न भूषार्थं न वपुषे न मदाय न दृप्तये ॥१४॥
धारणार्थं शरीरस्य भोजनं हि विधीयते ।
उपस्तम्भः पिपतिषो दुर्ब्बलस्येव वेश्मनः ॥१५॥
प्लवं यत्नात् यथा कश्चिद् बध्नीयाद् धारयेदपि ।
न तत्स्नेहेन यावत्तु महौघस्योत्तितीर्षया ॥१६॥
तथोपकरणैः कायं धारयन्ति परीक्षकाः ।
न तत्स्नेहेन यावत्तु दुःखौघस्य तितीर्षया ॥१७॥
शोचता पीड्यमानेन दीयते शत्रवे यथा ।
न भक्त्या नापि तर्षेण केवलं प्राणगुप्तये ॥१८॥
योगाचारस्तथाहारं शरीराय प्रयच्छति ।
केवलं क्षुद्विघातार्थं न रागेण न भक्तये ॥१९॥
मनोधारणया चैव परिणाम्यात्मवानहः ।
विधूय निद्रां योगेन निशामप्यतिनामयेत् ॥२०॥
हृदि यत् संज्ञिनश्चैव निद्रा प्रादुर्भवेत्तव ।
गुणवत्संज्ञितां संज्ञां तदा मनसि मा कृथाः ॥२१॥

धातुरारम्भधृत्योश्च स्थामविक्रमयोरपि ।
नित्यं मनसि कार्य्यस्ते बाध्यमानेन निद्रया ॥२२॥
आम्नातव्याश्च विशदं ते धर्म्मा ये परिश्रुताः ।
परेभ्यश्चोपदेष्टव्याः सञ्चिन्त्याः स्वयमेव च ॥२३॥
प्रक्लेद्यमद्भिर्वदनं विलोक्याः सर्व्वतो दिशः ।
चार्य्या दृष्टिश्च तारासु जिजागरिषुणा सदा ॥२४॥
अन्तर्गतैरचपलै र्वशस्थायिभिरिन्द्रियैः ।
अविक्षिप्तेन मनसा चंक्रम्यस्वास्व वा निशि ॥२५॥
भये प्रीतौ च शोके च निद्रया नाभिभूयते ।
तस्मान्निद्राभियोगेषु सेवितव्यमिदं त्रयम् ॥२६॥
भयमागमनान्मृत्योः प्रीतिं धर्म्मपरिग्रहात् ।
जन्मदुःखादपर्य्यन्तात् शोकमागन्तुमर्हसि ॥२७॥
एवमादिः क्रमः सौम्य कार्य्यो जागरणं प्रति ।
बन्ध्यं हि शयनादायुः कः प्राज्ञः कर्त्तुमर्हति ॥२८॥
दोषव्यालानतिक्रम्य व्यालान् गृहगतानिव ।
क्षमं प्राज्ञस्य न स्वप्तुं निस्तितीर्षोर्महद्भयम् ॥२९॥
प्रदीप्ते जीवलोके हि मृत्युव्याधिजराग्निभिः ।
कः शयीत निरुद्वेगः प्रदीप्त इव वेश्मनि ॥३०॥
तस्मात् तम इति ज्ञात्वा निद्रां नावेष्टुमर्हसि ।
अप्रशान्तेषु दोषेषु सशस्त्रेष्विव शत्रुषु ॥३१॥

पूर्व्वयामं त्रियामायाः प्रयोगेनातिनाम्यतु ।
सेव्या शय्या शरीरस्य विश्रामार्थमतन्द्रिणा ॥३२॥

दक्षिणेन तु पार्श्वेन स्थितया लोकसंज्ञया ।
प्रबोधं हृदयं कृत्वा शयीथाः शान्तिमानसः ॥२३॥
यामे तृतीये चोत्थाय चरन्नासीन एव वा ।
भूयो योगं मनःशुद्धौ कुर्व्वीथा नियतेन्द्रियः ॥२४॥
अथासनगत[ा]स्था न प्रेक्षितव्या हृतादिषु ।
सम्प्रजानन् क्रियाः सर्व्वाः स्मृतिमाधातुमर्हसि ॥२५॥
द्वाराध्यक्ष इव द्वारि यस्य प्रणिहिता स्मृतिः ।
धर्षयन्ति न तं दोषाः पुरं गुप्तमिवारयः ॥२६॥
न तस्योत्पद्यते क्लेशो यस्य कायगता स्मृतिः ।
चित्तं सर्व्वास्ववस्थासु बालं धात्रीव रक्षति ॥२७॥
शरव्यः स तु दोषाणां यो हीनः स्मृतिवर्म्मणा ।
रणस्थः प्रतिशत्रूणां विहीन इव वर्म्मणा ॥२८॥
अनाथं तन्मनो ज्ञेयं यत् स्मृतिर्नाभिरक्षति ।
निर्णेता दृष्टिरहितो विषयेषु चरन्निव ॥२९॥
अनर्थेषु प्रसक्ताश्च स्वार्थेभ्यश्च पराङ्मुखाः ।
यद्भये सति नोद्विग्नाः स्मृतिनाशोऽत्र कारणम् ॥४०॥
स्वभूमिषु गुणाः सर्व्वे ये च शीलादयः स्थिताः ।
विकीर्णा इव गा गोपः स्मृतिस्ताननुगच्छति ॥४१॥
प्रनष्टममृतम् तस्य यस्य विप्रसृता स्मृतिः ।
हस्तस्थममृतं तस्य यस्य कायगता स्मृतिः ॥४२॥
आर्य्यो न्यायः कुतस्तस्य स्मृतिर्यस्य न विद्यते ।
यस्यार्य्यो नास्ति च न्यायः प्रनष्टस्तस्य सतपथः ॥४३॥

प्रनष्टो यस्य सन्मार्गो नष्टं तस्यामृतं पदम् ।
प्रनष्टममृतम् यस्य स दुःखान्न विमुच्यते ॥४४॥

तस्माच्चरन् चरोऽस्मीति स्थितोस्मीति च तिष्ठतः ।
एवमादिषु कालेषु स्मृतिमाधातुमर्हसि ॥४५॥

योगानुलोमं विजनं[१] विशब्दं
शय्यासनं सौम्य तथा भजस्व ।
कायस्य कृत्वा हि विवेकमादौ
सुखोऽधिगन्तुं मनसो विवेकः ॥४६॥

अलब्धचेतःप्रशमः सरागो
यो न प्रचारं भजते विविक्तम् ।
स क्षण्यते ह्यप्रतिलब्धमार्गः
चरन्निवोर्व्यां बहुकण्टकायाम् ॥४७॥

अदृष्टतत्त्वेन परीक्षकेण
स्थितेन चित्रे विषयप्रचारे ।
चित्तं निषेद्धुं न सुखेन शक्यं
कृष्टोदका गौरिव सस्यमध्यात् ॥४८॥

अनीर्य्यमाणस्तु यथानिलेन
प्रशान्तिमागच्छति चित्रभानुः ।
अल्पेन यत्नेन तथा विविक्ते-
ष्वघट्टितं शान्तिमुपैति चेतः ॥४९॥

---

१ P. M. विजलं ।

क्वचिद्भुक्त्वा यत्तद्वसनमपि यत्तत्परिहितो
वसन्नात्मारामः क्वचन विजने योऽभिरमते ।
कृतार्थः स ज्ञेयः शमसुखरसज्ञः कृतमतिः
परेभ्यः संसर्गं परिहरति यः कण्टकमिव ॥५०॥

यदि द्वन्द्वारामे जगति विषयव्यग्रहृदये
विविक्ते निर्द्वन्द्वो विहरति कृती शान्तहृदयः ।
ततः पीत्वा प्रज्ञारसममृतवत् तृप्तहृदयो
विविक्तः संसक्तं विषयकृपणं शोचति जगत् ॥५१॥

वसन् शून्यागारे यदि सततमेकोऽभिरमते
यदि क्लेशोत्पादैः सह न रमते शत्रुभिरिव ।
चरन्नात्मारामो यदि च पिबति प्रीतिसलिलं
ततो भुङ्क्ते श्रेष्ठं त्रिदशपतिराज्यादपि सुखम् ॥५२॥

सौन्दरनन्दे महाकाव्ये आदिप्रस्थानो नाम
चतुर्दशः सर्गः ।

## पञ्चदशः सर्गः

यत्र तत्र विविक्ते तु[१] बद्ध्वा पर्य्यङ्कमुत्तमम् ।
ऋजुं कायं समाधाय स्मृत्याभिमुखयान्वितः ॥१॥
नासाग्रे वा ललाटे वा भ्रुवोरन्तर एव वा ।
कुर्व्वीथाश्चपलं चित्तमालम्बनपरायणम् ॥२॥
स चेत् कामवितर्कस्त्वां धर्षयेन्मानसो ज्वरः ।
क्षेप्तव्यो नाधिवास्यः स वस्त्रे रेणुरिवागतः ॥३॥
यद्यपि प्रतिसंख्यानात् कामानुत्सृष्टवानसि ।
तमांसीव प्रकाशेन प्रतिपक्षेण तान् जहि ॥४॥
तिष्ठत्यनुशयस्तेषां छन्नोऽग्निरिव भस्मना ।
स ते भावनया सौम्य प्रशाम्योऽग्निरिवाम्बुना ॥५॥
ते हि तस्मात् प्रवर्त्तन्ते भूयो बीजादिवाङ्कुराः ।
तस्य नाशेन ते न स्युः बीजनाशादिवाङ्कुराः ॥६॥

अर्ज्जनादीनि कामेभ्यो दृष्ट्वा दुःखानि कामिनाम् ।
तस्मात् तान् मूलतश्छिन्धि मित्रसंज्ञानरीनिव ॥७॥
अनित्या मोषधर्म्माणो रिक्ता व्यसनहेतवः ।
बहुसाधारणाः कामाः वर्ज्या ह्याशीविषा इव ॥८॥
ये मृग्यमाणा दुःखाय रक्ष्यमाणा न शान्तये ।
भ्रष्टाः शोकाय महते प्राप्ताश्च न वितृप्तये ॥९॥
तृप्तिं वित्तप्रकर्षेण स्वर्गावाप्त्या कृतार्थताम् ।
कामेभ्यश्च सुखोत्पत्तिं यः पश्यति स नश्यति ॥१०॥

---

१ P. M. च ।

चलानपरिनिष्पन्नानसारानवस्थितान् ।
परिकल्पसुखान् कामान् न तान् स्मर्त्तुमिहार्हसि ॥११॥

व्यापादो वा विहिंसा वा क्षोभयेद् यदि ते मनः ।
प्रसाद्यं तद् विपक्षेण मणिनेवाकुलं जलम् ॥१२॥
प्रतिपक्षस्तयोर्ज्ञेयो मैत्री कारुण्यमेव च ।
विरोधो हि तयोर्नित्यं प्रकाशतमसोरिव ॥१३॥
निवृत्तं यस्य दौःशील्यं व्यापादश्च प्रवर्त्तते ।
हन्ति पांशुभिरात्मानं सुस्नात इव वारणः ॥१४॥
दुःखितेभ्यो हि मर्त्त्येभ्यो व्याधिमृत्युजरादिभिः ।
आर्य्यः को दुःखमपरं सघृणो धातुमर्हति ॥१५॥
दुष्टेन चेह मनसा बाध्यते वा परो न वा ।
सद्यस्तु दह्यते तावत् स्वंमनो दुष्टचेतसः ॥१६॥
तस्मात् सर्व्वेषु भूतेषु मैत्रीं कारुण्यमेव च ।
न व्यापादं विहिंसां वा विकल्पयितुमर्हसि ॥१७॥

यद्यदेव प्रसक्तं हि वितर्क्कयति[1] मानवः ।
अभ्यासात् तेन तेनास्य [2]रतिर्भवति चेतसः ॥१८॥
तस्मादकुशलं त्यक्त्वा कुशलं ध्यातुमर्हसि ।
यत्ते स्यादिह चार्थाय परमार्थस्य चाप्तये ॥१९॥
संवर्धन्ते ह्यकुशला वितर्काः सम्भृता हृदि ।
अनर्थजनकास्तुल्यमात्मनश्च परस्य च ॥२०॥

---

१ P. M. विवर्ज्जयति । २ P. M. नति० T.

श्रेयसो विघ्नकरणात् भवन्त्यात्मविपत्तये ।
पात्रीभावोपघातं तु परभक्तिविपत्तये ॥२१॥
मनः कर्म्मसु विक्षेप्यमपि वा वक्तुमर्हसि[1] ।
[2]नत्वेवाकुशलं सौम्य वितर्कयितुमर्हसि ॥२२॥
या त्रिकामोपभोगाय चिन्ता म[न]सि वर्त्तते ।
न च तं गुणमाप्नोति बन्धनाय च कल्पते ॥२३॥
सत्वानामुपघाताय परिक्लेशाय वा मनः ।
मोहं व्रजति कालुष्यं नरकाय च वर्त्तते ॥२४॥
तद्वितर्कैरकुशलैर्नात्मानं हन्तुमर्हसि ।
सुशस्त्रं रत्नविकृतं मृद्धतीर्गाः खनन्निव ॥२५॥
अनभिज्ञो यथा जात्यं दहेदगुरुकाष्ठवत् ।
अन्यायेन मनुष्यत्वमुपहन्यादिदं तथा ॥२६॥
त्यक्त्वा रत्नं यथा लोष्टं रत्नद्वीपाच्च संहरेत् ।
त्यक्त्वा नैःश्रेयसं धर्म्मं चिन्तयेदशुभं तथा ॥२७॥
हिमवन्तं यथा गत्वा विषं भुञ्जीत नौषधम् ।
मनुष्यत्वं तथा प्राप्य पापं सेवेत नो शुभम् ॥२८॥
तद्बुद्ध्वा प्रतिपक्षेण वितर्कं क्षेप्तुमर्हसि ।
सूक्ष्मेण प्रतिकीलेन कीलं दार्व्वन्तरादिव ॥२९॥
वृद्ध्यवृद्ध्योरथ भवेच्चिन्ता ज्ञातिजनं प्रति ।
स्वभावो जीवलोकस्य परीक्ष्यस्तन्निवृत्तये ॥३०॥

---

१ P. M. वाग्वक्तुमर्हसि T. २ P. M: नत्वेक० T.

संसारे कृष्यमाणानां सत्त्वानां स्वेन कर्म्मणा ।
को जनः सुजनः को वा मोहात्सको जने जनः ॥३१॥
अतीतेऽध्वनि संवृत्तः स्वजनो हि जनस्तव ।
अप्राप्ते चाध्वनि जनः स्वजनस्ते भविष्यति ॥३२॥
विहगानां यथा सायं तत्र तत्र समागमः ।
जातौ जातौ तथाश्लेषो जनस्य स्वजनस्य च ॥३३॥
प्रतिश्रयं बहुविधं संश्रयन्ति यथाध्वगाः ।
प्रतियान्ति पुनस्त्यक्त्वा तद्वत् ज्ञातिसमागमः ॥३४॥
लोके प्रकृतिभिन्नेऽस्मिन् न कश्चित् कस्यचित् प्रियः ।
कार्य्यकारणसंबद्धं बालुकामुष्टिवज्जगत् ॥३५॥
बिभर्त्ति हि सुतं माता धारयिष्यति मामिति ।
मातरं भजते पुत्रो गर्भेणाधत्त मामिति ॥३६॥
अनुकूलं प्रवर्त्तन्ते ज्ञातिषु ज्ञातयो यदा ।
तदा स्नेहं प्रकुर्व्वन्ति रिपुत्वं तु विपर्य्ययात् ॥३७॥
अहितो दृश्यते ज्ञातिरज्ञातिर्दृश्यते हितः ।
स्नेहं कार्य्यान्तराल्लोकश्छिनत्ति च करोति च ॥३८॥
स्वयमेव यथालिख्य रज्येच्चित्रकरः स्त्रियम् ।
तथा कृत्वा स्वयं स्नेहं सङ्गमेति जने जनः ॥३९॥
योऽभवत् बान्धवजनः परलोके प्रियस्तव ।
स ते कमर्थं कुरुते त्वं वा तस्मै करोषि कम् ॥४०॥
तस्मात् ज्ञातिवितर्केन मनो नावेष्टुमर्हसि ।
व्यवस्था नास्ति संसारे स्वजनस्य जनस्य च ॥४१॥

असौ क्षेमो जनपदः सुभिक्षोऽसावसौ शिवः ।
इत्येवमथ जायेत वितर्कस्तव कश्चन ॥४२॥
प्रहेयः स त्वया सौम्य नाधिवास्यः कथञ्चन ।
विदित्वा सर्व्वमादीप्तं तैस्तैर्दोषाग्निभिर्जगत् ॥४३॥
ऋतुचक्रविवर्त्ताच्च क्षुत्पिपासाक्लमादपि ।
सर्व्वत्र नियतं दुःखं न क्वचिद्विद्यते शिवम् ॥४४॥
क्वचित् शीतं क्वचिद्धर्मः क्वचिद्रोगो भयं क्वचित् ।
बाधतेऽभ्यधिकं लोके तस्मादशरणं जगत् ॥४५॥
जरा व्याधिश्च मृत्युश्च लोकस्यास्य महद्भयम् ।
नास्ति देशः स यत्रास्य तद्भयं[१] नोपपद्यते ॥४६॥
यत्र गच्छति कायोऽयं दुःखं तत्रानुगच्छति ।
नास्ति काचित् गतिर्लोके गतो यत्र न बाध्यते ॥४७॥
रमणीयोऽपि देशः सन् सुभिक्षः क्षेम एव च ।
कुदेश इति विज्ञेयो यत्र क्लेशैर्विदह्यते ॥४८॥
लोकस्याभ्याहतस्यास्य दुःखैः शारीरमानसैः ।
क्षेमः कश्चिन्न देशोऽस्ति स्वस्थो यत्र गतो भवेत् ॥४९॥
दुःखं सर्व्वत्र सर्व्वस्य वर्त्तते सर्व्वदा यदा ।
छन्दरागमतः सौम्य लोकचित्रेषु मा कृथाः ॥५०॥
यदा तस्मान्निवृत्तस्ते छन्दरागो भविष्यति ।
जीवलोकं तदा सर्व्वमादीप्तमिव मंस्यसे ॥५१॥

---

१ P. M. omits नास्ति देशः स यत्रास्य तद्भयं ।

अथ कश्चित् वितर्कस्ते भवेदमरणाश्रयः ।
यत्नेन स विहन्तव्यो व्याधिरात्मगतो यथा ॥५२॥
मुहूर्त्तमपि विश्रम्भः कार्य्यो न खलु जीविते ।
निलीन इव हि व्याघ्रः कालो विश्वस्तघातकः ॥५३॥
बलस्थोऽहं युवा वेति न ते भवितुमर्हति[१] ।
मृत्युः सर्व्वास्ववस्थासु हन्ति नावेक्षते वयः ॥५४॥
क्षेत्रभूतमनर्थानां शरीरं परिकर्षतः ।
स्वस्थाशा जीविताशा वा न दृष्टार्थस्य जायते ॥५५॥
निर्वृतः[२] को भवेत्कायं महाभूताश्रयं वहन् ।
परस्परविरुद्धानामहीनामिव भाजनम् ॥५६॥
प्रश्वसित्ययमन्वक्षं यदुच्छ्वसिति मानवः ।
अवगच्छ तदाश्चर्य्यमविश्वास्यं हि जीवितम् ॥५७॥
इदमाश्चर्य्यमपरं यत्सुप्तः प्रतिबुध्यते ।
स्वपित्युत्थाय वा भूयो बह्वमित्रा हि[३] देहिनः ॥५८॥
गर्भात् प्रभृति यो लोकं जिघांसुरनुगच्छति ।
कस्तस्मिन् विश्वसेन्मृत्यावुद्यतासावराविव ॥५९॥
प्रसूतः पुरुषो लोके श्रुतवान् बलवानपि ।
न जयत्यन्तकं कश्चिन्नाजयन्नापि जेष्यति ॥६०॥
साम्ना[४] दानेन भेदेन दण्डेन नियमेन वा ।
प्राप्तो हि रभसो मृत्युः प्रतिहन्तुं न शक्यते ॥६१॥

---

१ P. M. चेति न ते भवितुमर्हसि । २ P. M. निवृतः ।
३ P. L. M. lacuna, P. M. बह्वमित्रालि T. ४ P. M. साम्ना ।

तस्मान्नायुषि विश्वासं चञ्चले कर्त्तुमर्हसि ।
नित्यं[1] हरति कालो हि स्थाविर्य्यं न प्रतीक्षते ॥६२॥

निःशोच्यं पश्यतो लोकं तोयबुद्बुददुर्ब्बलम् ।
कस्यामरवितर्कों हि स्यादनुन्मत्तचेतसः ॥६३॥

तस्मादेषां वितर्काणां प्रहाणार्थं समासतः ।
आनापानस्मृतिं सौम्य विषयीकर्त्तुमर्हसि ॥६४॥

इत्यनेन प्रयोगेण काले सेवितुमर्हसि ।
प्रतिपक्षं वितर्काणां गदानामगदानिव ॥६५॥

सुवर्णहेतोरिव पांशुधावको
विहाय पांशून् बृहतो यथादितः ।
जहाति सूक्ष्मानपि तद्विशुद्धये
विशोध्य हेमावयवान्नियच्छति ॥६६॥

विमोक्षहेतोरपि युक्तमानसो
विहाय दोषान् बृहतस्तथादितः ।
जहाति सूक्ष्मानपि तद्विशुद्धये[2]
विशोध्य धर्म्मावयवान्नियच्छति ॥६७॥

क्रमेणाद्भिः शुद्धं कनकमिह पांशुव्यवहितम्
यथाग्नौ कर्म्मारः पचति भृशमावर्त्तयति च ।
तथा योगाचारो निपुणमिह दोषव्यवहितम्
विशोध्य क्लेशेभ्यः शमयति मनः संक्षिपति च ॥६८॥

---

१ P. M. नित्य T. २ P. M. द्विशुद्धये ।

यथा च स्वच्छन्दादुपनयति कर्माश्रयसुखं
सुवर्णं कर्मारो बहुविधमलंकारविधिषु ।
मनः शुद्धं भिक्षुर्वशगतमभिज्ञास्वपि तथा
यथेच्छं यत्रेच्छं शमयति मनः प्रेरयति च ॥६९॥

इति सौन्दरनन्दे महाकाव्ये वितर्कप्रहाणो नाम
पञ्चदशः सर्गः ।

## षोडशः सर्गः

एवं मनोधारणया क्रमेण व्यपोह्य किञ्चित् समुपोह्य किञ्चित् ।
ध्यानानि चत्वार्य्यधिगम्य योगी प्राप्नोत्यभिज्ञा[1] नियमेन पञ्च ॥१॥
ऋद्धिप्रवेकञ्च बहुप्रकारं परस्य चेतश्चरितावबोधम् ।
अतीतजन्मस्मरणञ्च दीर्घं दिव्ये[2] विशुद्धे श्रुतिचक्षुषी च ॥२॥
अतःपरं तत्त्वपरीक्षणेन मनो[3] दधात्यास्रवसंक्षयाय ।
ततो हि दुःखप्रभृतीनि सम्यक् चत्वारि सत्यानि पदान्यवैति ॥३॥
बाधात्मकं दुःखमिदं प्रसक्तं दुःखस्य हेतुः प्रभवात्मकोऽयम् ।
दुःखक्षयो निःशरणात्मकोऽयं त्राणात्मकोऽयं प्रशमाय मार्गः ॥४॥
इत्यार्य्यसत्यान्यवबुध्य बुद्ध्या चत्वारि सम्यक् प्रतिबुध्य चैव ।
सर्व्वास्रवान् भावनयाभिभूय न जायते शान्तिमवाप्य भूयः ॥५॥
अबोधतो ह्यप्रतिवेधतश्च तत्त्वात्मकस्यास्य चतुष्टयस्य ।
भवाद्भवं याति न शान्तिमेति संसारदोला[4]मधिरोह्य लोकः ॥६॥
तस्माज्जरादेर्व्यसनस्य मूलं समासतो दुःखमवेहि जन्म ।
सर्व्वौषधीनामिव भू[5]र्भवाय सर्व्वापदां क्षेत्रमिदं हि जन्म ॥७॥
यज्जन्म रूपस्य हि सेन्द्रियस्य दुःखस्य तन्नैकविधस्य जन्म ।
यः सम्भवश्चास्य समुच्छ्रयस्य मृत्योश्च रोगस्य च सम्भवः सः ॥८॥
सद्वाप्यसद्वा विषमिश्रमन्नं यथा विनाशाय न धारणाय ।
लोके तथा तिर्य्यगुपर्य्यधो वा दुःखाय सर्व्वं न सुखाय जन्म ॥९॥

---

१ P. M. drops त्य । २ P. M. drops ए in दिव्ये ।
३ P. M. ०रीक्षणे मम । ४ P. M. has दोलाधा ।
५ P. M. भुवर्भवाय ।

जरादयो नैकविधाः प्रजानां सत्यां प्रवृत्तौ प्रभवन्त्यनर्थाः ।
प्रवात्सु घोरेष्वपि मारुतेषु नह्यप्रसूतास्तरवश्चलन्ति ॥१०॥
आकाशयोनिः पवनो यथा हि यथा शमीगर्भशयो हुताशः ।
आपो यथान्तर्वसुधाशयाश्च दुःखं तथा चित्तशरीरयोनि ॥११॥
अपां द्रवत्वं कठिनत्वमुर्व्या वायोश्चलत्वं ध्रुवमौष्ण्यमग्नेः ।
यथा स्वभावो हि तथा स्वभावो दुःखं शरीरस्य च चेतसश्च ॥१२॥
काये सति व्याधिजरादि दुःखं क्षुत्तर्षवर्षोष्णहिमादि चैव ।
रूपाश्रिते चेतसि सानुबन्धे शोकारतिक्रोधभयादि दुःखम् ॥१३॥
प्रत्यक्षमालोक्य च जन्मदुःखं दुःखं तथातीतमपीति विद्धि ।
यथा च तद्दुःखमिदञ्च दुःखं दुःखं तथा नागतमप्यवेहि ॥१४॥
बीजस्वभावो हि यथेह दृष्टो भूतोपि भव्योपि तथानुमेयः ।
प्रत्यक्षतश्च ज्वलनो यथोष्णो भूतोऽपि भव्योपि तथोष्ण एव ॥१५॥
तन्नामरूपस्य गुणानुरूप यत्रैव निर्वृत्तिरुदारवृत्त ।
तत्रैव दुःखं न हि तद्विमुक्तं दुःखं भविष्यत्यभवद्भवेद्वा ॥१६॥

प्रवृत्तिदुःखस्य च तस्य लोके तृष्णादयो दोषगणा निमित्तम् ।
नैवेश्वरो न प्रकृतिर्न कालो नापि स्वभावो न विधिर्यदृच्छा ॥१७॥
ज्ञातव्यमेनेन च कारणेन लोकस्य दोषेभ्य इति प्रवृत्तिः ।
यस्माद् म्रियन्ते सरजस्तमस्का न जायते वीतरजस्तमस्कः ॥१८॥
इच्छाविशेषे सति तत्र तत्र यानासनादिर्भवति प्रयोगः ।
यस्मादतस्तर्षवशा[त्] तथैव जन्म प्रजानामिति वेदितव्यम् ॥१९॥
सत्त्वान्यभिष्वङ्गवशानि दृष्ट्वा स्वजातिषु प्रीतिपराण्यतीव ।
अभ्यासयोगादुपपादितानि तैरेव दो[षै]रिति तानि विद्धि ॥२०॥

क्रोधप्रहर्षादिभिराश्रयाणामुत्पद्यते चेह यथा विशेषः ।
तथैव जन्मस्वपि नैकरूपो निर्वर्त्तते क्लेशकृतो विशेषः ॥२१॥
दोषाधिके[१] जन्मनि तीव्रदोष उत्पद्यते रागिणि तीव्ररागः ।
मोहाधिके मोहबलाधिकस्य तदल्पदोषे च तदल्पदोषः ॥२२॥
फलं हि यादृक् समवैति साक्षात् तदागमो बीज[२]मवैत्यतीतम् ।
अवैत्य बीजप्रकृतिञ्च साक्षादनागतं तत्फलमभ्युपैति ॥२३॥
दोषक्षयो जातिषु यासु यस्य वैराग्यतस्तासु न जायते सः ।
दोषाशयस्तिष्ठति यस्य यत्र तस्योपपत्तिर्विवशस्य तत्र ॥२४॥
तज्जन्मनो नैकविधस्य सौम्य तृष्णादयो हेतव इत्यवेत्य ।
तांश्छिन्धि दुःखाद् यदि निर्मुमुक्षा कार्य्यक्षयः कारणसङ्क्षयाद्धि ॥२५॥
दुःखक्षयो हेतुपरिक्षयाच्च शान्तं शिवं साक्षिकुरुष्व धर्म्मम्[३] ।
तृष्णाविरागं लयनं निरोधं सनातनं त्राणमहार्य्यमार्य्यम् ॥२६॥
यस्मिन्न जाति र्न जरा न मृत्युर्न व्याधयो नाप्रियसम्प्रयोगः ।
नेच्छाविपन्न प्रियविप्रयोगः क्षमं पदं नैष्ठिकमच्युतं तत् ॥२७॥
दीपो यथा निर्वृतिमभ्युपेतो नैवावनिं गच्छति नान्तरिक्षम् ।
दिशं न काञ्चिद् विदिशं न काञ्चित् स्नेहक्षयात् केवलमेति शान्तिम् ॥२८॥
एवं कृती निर्वृतिमभ्युपेतो नैवावनिं गच्छति नान्तरिक्षम् ।
दिशं न काञ्चिद् विदिशं न काञ्चित् क्लेशक्षयात् केवलमेति शान्तिम् ॥२९॥

---

१ P. M. दोषा० T. २ P. M. बीजगं० । ३ P. M. धर्म्मं ।

अस्याभ्युपायोऽधिगमाय मार्गः प्रज्ञात्रिकल्पः प्रशमद्विकल्पः ।
स भावनीयो विधिवद् बुधेन[१] शीले शुचौ त्रिप्रमुखे स्थितेन ॥२०॥

वाक्कर्म सम्यक् सहकायकर्म यथावदाजीवनयश्च शुद्धः ।
इदं त्रयं वृत्तविधौ प्रवृत्तं शीलाश्रयं धर्मपरिग्रहाय ॥२१॥

सत्येषु दुःखादिषु दृष्टिरार्य्या सम्यग्वितर्कश्च पराक्रमश्च ।
इदं त्रयं ज्ञानविधौ प्रवृत्तं प्रज्ञाश्रयं क्लेशपरिक्षयाय ॥२२॥

न्यायेन सत्याभिगमाय युक्ता सम्यक् स्मृतिः सम्यगथो समाधिः ।
इदं द्वयं योगविधौ प्रवृत्तं शमाश्रयं चित्तपरिग्रहाय ॥२३॥

क्लेशाङ्कुरान्[२] प्रतनोति शीलं बीजाङ्कुरान् काल इवातिवृत्तः ।
शुचौ हि शीले पुरुषस्य दोषा मनः सलज्जा इव धर्षयन्ति ॥२४॥

क्लेशांस्तु विष्कम्भयते समाधिर्वेगानिवाद्रिर्महतो नदीनाम् ।
स्थिते समाधौ हि न धर्षयन्ति दोषा भुजङ्गा इव मन्त्रबद्धाः ॥२५॥

प्रज्ञा त्वशेषेण निहन्ति दोषांस्तीरद्रुमान् प्रावृषि निम्नगेव ।
दग्धा यया न प्रभवन्ति दोषा वज्राग्निनेवानुसृतेन वृक्षाः ॥२६॥

त्रिस्कन्धमेतं प्रविगाह्य मार्गं प्रस्पष्टमष्टाङ्गमहार्य्यमार्य्यम् ।
दुःखस्य हेतून् प्रजहाति दोषान् प्राप्नोति चात्यन्तशिवं पदं तत् ॥२७॥

अस्योपचारं धृतिरार्जवञ्च ह्रीरप्रमादः प्रविविक्तता च ।
अल्पेच्छता तुष्टिरसङ्गता च लोकप्रवृत्तावरतिः क्षमा च ॥२८॥

याथात्म्यतो विन्दति यो हि दुःखं तस्योद्भवं तस्य च यो निरोधम् ।
आर्य्येण मार्गेण स शान्तिमेति कल्याणमित्रैः सह वर्त्तमानः ॥२९॥

---

१ P. M. drops धे in बुधेन । २ P. M. ०ङ्कुरं ।

यो व्याधितो व्याधिमवैति सम्यग् व्याधेर्निदानञ्च तदौषधञ्च ।
आरोग्यमाप्नोति हि सोऽचिरेण[1] मित्रैरभिज्ञैरुपचर्य्यमाणः ॥४०॥

तद् व्याधिसंज्ञां कुरु दुःखसत्ये दोषेष्वपि व्याधिनिदानसंज्ञाम् ।
आरोग्यसंज्ञाञ्च निरोधसत्ये भैषज्य[2]संज्ञामपि मार्गसत्ये ॥४१॥

तस्मात् प्रवृत्तिं परिगच्छ दुःखं प्रवर्त्तकानप्यवगच्छ दोषान् ।
निवृत्तिमागच्छ च तन्निरोधं निवर्त्तकञ्चाप्यवगच्छ मार्गम् ॥४२॥

शिरस्यथो वाससि संप्रदीप्ते सत्यावबोधाय मतिर्विचार्य्या ।
दग्धं जगत् सत्यनयं ह्यदृष्ट्वा प्रदह्यते सम्प्रति धक्ष्यते[3] च ॥४३॥

यदैव यः पश्यति नामरूपं क्षयीति तद्दर्शनमस्य सम्यक् ।
सम्यक् च निर्वेदमुपैति पश्यन् नन्दीक्षयाच्च क्षयमेति रागः ॥४४॥

तयोश्च नन्दीरजसोः क्षयेण सम्यग् विमुक्तं प्रवदामि चेतः ।
सम्यग् विमुक्तिर्मनसश्च ताभ्यां न चास्य भूयः करणीयमस्ति ॥४५॥

यथास्वभावेन हि नामरूपं तद्धेतुमेवास्तगमं च तस्य ।
विजानतः पश्यत एव चाहं ब्रवीमि सम्यक् क्षयमास्रवाणाम् ॥४६॥

तस्मात् परं सौम्य विधाय वीर्य्यं शीघ्रं चकास्रवास्रवसंक्षयाय ।
दुःखाननित्यांश्च निरात्मकांश्च धातून् विशेषेण[4] परीक्षमाणः ॥४७॥

धातून् हि षड्भू[5]सलिलानलादीन् सामान्यतः स्वेन च लक्षणेन ।

---

१ P. M. चिरेन, P. L. M. अचिरेण which spoil the metre.

२ P. L. M. भैष्यज्य० ।

३ P. M. सम्प्रतिवक्ष्यते ।

४ P. M. धातुविशेषेण which spoils the metre.

५ P. M. धातुं हि षट्कं ।

अवैति यो नान्यमवैति तेभ्यः सोत्यन्तिकं मोक्षमवैति तेभ्यः ॥४८॥

क्लेशप्रहाणाय च निश्चितेन कारोऽभ्युपायश्च परीक्षितव्यः ।
योगोऽप्यकाले ह्यनुपायतश्च भवत्यनर्थाय न तद्गुणाय ॥४९॥
अजातवत्सा यदि गा दुहीत नैवाप्नुयात् क्षीरमकालदोही ।
कालेऽपि वा स्यान्न पयो लभेत मोहेन शृङ्गाद् यदि गा दुहीत॥५०॥
आर्द्राच्च काष्ठाज्ज्वलनाभिकामो नैव प्रयत्नादपि वह्निमृच्छेत् ।
काष्ठाच्च शुष्कादपि पातनेन नैवाग्निमाप्नोत्यनुपायपूर्व्वम् ॥५१॥
तद्देशकालौ विधिवत्परीक्ष्य योगस्य मात्रामपि चाभ्युपायम् ।
बलाबले चात्मनि संप्रधार्य्य कार्य्यः प्रयत्नो न तु तद्विरुद्धः ॥५२॥

प्रग्राहकं यत्तु निमित्तमुक्तमुद्धन्यमाने हृदि तन्न सेव्यम् ।
एवं हि चित्तं प्रशमं न याति [न] वह्निना वह्निरिवेर्य्यमाणः ॥५३॥
शमाय [य]त्स्यान्नियन्निमित्तं जातोद्धवे चेतसि तस्य कालः ।
एवं हि चित्तं प्रशमं नियच्छत्य[ु]दीर्य्यमाणोऽग्निरिवोदकेन ॥५४॥
शमावहं यत् [नियतं] निमित्तं सेव्यं न तच्चेतसि लीयमाने ।
एवं हि भूयो लयमेति चित्तमनीर्य्यमाणोऽग्निरिवाल्पसारः ॥५५॥
प्रग्राहकं यन्नियतं निमित्तं लयं गते चेतसि तस्य कालः ।
क्रियासमर्थं हि मनस्तदा स्यात् मन्दायमानोऽग्निरिवेन्धनेन ॥५६॥
औपेक्षिकं नापि निमित्तमिष्टं लयं गते चेतसि सोद्धवे वा ।
एवं हि तीव्रं जनयेदनर्थमुपेक्षितो व्याधिरिवातुरस्य ॥५७॥
यत्स्यादुपेक्षा नियतं निमित्तं साम्यं गते चेतसि तस्य कालः ।
एवं हि कृत्याय भवेत् प्रयोगो रथो विधेयाश्व इव प्रयातः ॥५८॥
रागोद्धतव्याकुलितेऽपि चित्ते मैत्रोपसंहारविधिर्न कार्य्यः ।

रागात्मको मुह्यति मैत्रया हि स्नेहं कफक्षोभ[१] इवोपयुज्य ॥५९॥

रागोद्भवे चेतसि धैर्य्यमेत्य निषेवितव्यं त्वशुभं निमित्तम् ।
रागात्मको ह्येवमुपैति शर्म्म कफात्मको रूक्षमिवोपयुज्य ॥६०॥

व्यापाद[२]दोषेण मनस्युदीर्णे न सेवितव्यं त्वशुभं निमित्तम् ।
द्वेषात्मकस्य ह्यशुभा वधाय पित्तात्मनस्तीक्ष्ण इवोपचारः ॥६१॥

व्यापाददोषक्षुभिते तु चित्ते सेव्या स्वपक्षोपनयेन मैत्री ।
द्वेषात्मनो हि प्रशमाय मैत्री पित्तात्मनः शीत इवोपचारः ॥६२॥

मोहानुबद्धे मनसः प्रचारे मैत्रा शुभा चैव भवत्ययोगः ।
ताभ्यां हि संमोहमुपैति भूयो वाय्वात्मको रूक्षमिवोपनीय ॥६३॥

मोहात्मिकायां मनसः प्रवृत्तौ सेव्यस्त्विदंप्रत्ययताविहारः ।
मूढे मनस्येष हि शान्तिमार्गो वाय्वात्मके स्निग्ध इवोपचारः ॥६४

उल्कामुखस्थं हि यथा सुवर्णं सुवर्णकारो धमतीह काले ।
काले परिप्रोक्षयते जलेन क्रमेण काले समुपेक्षते च ॥६५॥

दहेत्सुवर्णं हि धमन्न काले जले क्षिपन् संशमयेदकाले ।
न चापि सम्यक् परिपाकमेनं नयेदकाले समुपेक्षमाणः ॥६६॥

संप्रग्रहस्य प्रशमस्य चैव तथैव काले समुपेक्षणस्य ।
सम्यग् निमित्तं मनसा त्ववेक्ष्यं नाशो हि यत्नोऽप्यनुपायपूर्व्वः ॥६७

इत्येवमन्यायनिवर्त्तनञ्च न्यायञ्च तस्मै सुगतो बभाषे ।
भूयश्च तत्तच्चरितं विदित्वा वितर्कहानाय विधीनुवाच ॥६८॥

यथा भिषक् पित्तकफानिलानां य एव कोपं[३] समुपैति दोषः ।

---

१ P. L. M. ०क्षोभय । २ P. M. व्यापार० ।
३ P. M. कोषं ।

शमाय तस्यैव विधिं विधत्ते व्यधत्त दोषेषु तथैव बुद्धः ॥६९॥
एकेन कल्पेन स चेन्न हन्यात् स्वभ्यस्तभावादशुभान् वितर्कान् ।
ततो द्वितीयं क्रममारभेत नत्वेव हेयो गुणवान् प्रयोगः ॥७०॥
अनादिकालोपचितात्मकत्वात् बलीयसः क्लेशगणस्य चैव ।
सम्यक्प्रयोगस्य च दुष्करत्वात् छेत्तुं न शक्याः सहसा हि दोषाः ॥७१॥
अण्व्या यथाण्या विपुलाणिरन्या निर्वाह्यते तद्विदुषा नरेण ।
तद्वत् तदेवाकुशलं निमित्तं क्षिपेन् निमित्तान्तरसेवनेन ॥७२॥
तथाथवाध्यात्मनवग्रहत्वान्नैवोपशाम्येदशुभो वितर्कः ।
हेयः स तद्दोषपरीक्षणेन सश्वापदो मार्ग इवाध्वगेन ॥७३॥
यथा क्षुधार्त्तोपि विषेण पृक्तं जिजीविषुर्नेच्छति भोक्तुमन्नम् ।
तथैव दोषावहमित्यवेत्य जहाति विद्वानशुभं निमित्तम् ॥७४॥
न दोषतः पश्यति यो हि दोषं कस्तं ततो वारयितुं समर्थः ।
गुणं गुणे पश्यति यश्च यत्र स वार्य्यमाणोपि ततः प्रयाति ॥७५॥
व्यपत्रपन्ते हि कुलप्रसूता मनःप्रचारैरशुभैः प्रवृत्तैः ।
कण्ठे मनस्वीव युवा वपुष्मान् न चाक्षुषैरप्रयुतै विषक्तैः ॥७६॥
निर्धूयमाणास्त्वथ लोषतोपि तिष्ठेयुरेवाकुशला वितर्काः ।
कार्य्यान्तरैरध्ययनक्रियाद्यैः सेव्यो विधिर्विस्मरणाय तेषाम् ॥७७॥
स्वप्तव्यमप्येव विच[क्ष]णेन कायक्लमो वापि निषेवितव्यः ।
नत्वेव सञ्चिन्त्यमसन्निमित्तं यत्रावसक्तस्य भवेदनर्थः ॥७८॥
यथा हि भीतो निशि तस्करेभ्यो द्वार[ं] प्रियेभ्योऽपि न दातुमिच्छेत् ।
प्राज्ञस्तथा संहरति प्रयोगं समं शुभस्याप्यशुभस्य[1] दोषैः ॥७९॥

---

१ P. L. M. drops ०प्यशुभस्य ।

एवं प्रकारैरपि यद्युपायैर्निवार्य्यमाणा न पराङ्मुखाः स्युः ।
ततो यथास्थूलनिवर्हणेन सुवर्णदोषा इव ते प्रहेयाः ॥८०॥
द्रुतप्रयाणप्रभृ[तीं]श्च तीव्रणकामप्रयोगात् परिखिद्यमानः ।
यथा नरः संश्रयते तथैव प्राज्ञेन दोषेष्वपि वर्त्तितव्यम् ॥८१॥
ते चेदलब्धप्रतिपक्षभावा नैवोपशाम्येयुरसद्वितर्काः ।
मुहूर्त्तमप्यप्रतिबध्यमाना गृहे भुजङ्गा इव नाधिवास्याः ॥८२॥
दन्तेऽपि दन्तं[१] प्रणिधाय कामं ताल्वग्रमुत्पीड्य च जिह्वयापि ।
चित्तेन चित्तं परिगृह्य चापि कार्य्यः प्रयत्नो न तु तेऽनुवृत्ताः ॥८३॥
किमत्र चित्रं यदि वीतमोहो वनं गतः स्वस्थमना न मुह्येत् ।
आक्षिप्यमाणो हृदि तन्निमित्तै र्न क्षोभ्यते यः स कृती स धीरः ॥८४॥
तदार्य्यसत्याधिगमाय पूर्व्वं विशोधयानेन नयेन मार्गम् ।
यात्रागतः शत्रुविनिग्रहार्थं[२] राजेव लक्ष्मीमजितां जिगीषन् ॥८५॥
एतान्यरण्यान्यभितः शिवानि योगानुकूलान्यजनेरितानि ।
कायस्य कृत्वा प्रविवेकमात्रं क्लेशप्रहाणाय भजस्व मार्गम् ॥८६॥

कौण्डिन्य-नन्दक्रिमिलानिरुद्धाः तिष्योपसेनौ विमलोऽथ राधः[३] ।
बाष्पोत्तरौ धौतकि-मोहराजौ कात्यायनद्रव्यपिलिन्दवत्साः ॥८७॥
भद्दालि-भद्रायण-सर्पदास-सुभूति-गोदत्त-सुजात-वत्साः ।
संग्रामजिद् भद्रजिदश्वजिच्च श्रोणश्च शोणश्च स कोटिकर्णः ॥८८॥
क्षेमाजितो[४] नन्दकनन्दमाता वुपालि-वागीश-यशोयशोदाः ।
महाह्वयो वल्कलि-राष्ट्रपालौ सुदर्शन-स्वागत-मेघिकाश्च ॥८९॥

---

१ P. M. दत्तं । २ P. M. ०विनिर्व्वर्हार्थं ।
३ P. M. रूधः । ४ P. M. हमाजितो ।

स कप्फिनः काश्यपश्चोरुविल्वो महामहाकाश्यप-तिष्य-नन्दाः ।
पूर्णश्च पूर्णश्च स पूर्णकश्च शोणापरान्तश्च स पूर्ण एव ॥९०॥
शारद्वतीपुत्र-सुबाहु-चुन्दाः कोन्देय-काप्य-भृगु-कुण्ठधानाः ।
सशैवलौ रैवत-कौष्ठिलौ च मौद्गल्यगोत्रश्च गवांपतिश्च ॥९१॥
यं विक्रमं योगविधावकुर्व्वंस्तमेव शीघ्रं विधिवत् कुरुष्व ।
ततः पदं प्राप्स्यसि तैरवाप्तं संख्याञ्च ते स्वन्नियतं यशश्च ॥९२॥

द्रव्यं यथा स्यात् कटुकं रसेन तच्चोपयुक्तं मधुरं विपाके ।
तथैव वीर्य्यं[१] कटुकं श्रमेण तस्यार्थसिद्धौ मधुरो विपाकः ॥९३॥
वीर्य्यं परं कार्य्यकृतौ हि मूलं वीर्य्यादृते काचन नास्ति सिद्धिः ।
उदेति वीर्य्यादिह सर्वसम्पन्निर्वीर्य्यता चेत्सकलश्च पाप्मा ॥९४॥

अलब्धस्यालाभो नियतमुपलब्धस्य विगमः
तथैवात्मावज्ञा कृपणमधिकेभ्यः परिभवः ।
तमो निस्तेजस्त्वं श्रुतिनियमतुष्टिव्युपरमो
नृणां निर्वीर्य्याणां भवति विनिपातश्च भवति ॥९५॥

नयं श्रुत्वाशक्तो यदयमभिवृद्धिं न लभते
परं धर्म्मं ज्ञात्वा यदुपरि निवासं न लभते ।
गृहं त्यक्त्वा मुक्तौ यदयमुपशान्तिं न लभते
निमित्तं कौसीद्यं भवति पुरुषस्यान्तररिपुः ॥९६॥

अनिक्षिप्तोत्साहो यदि खनति गां वारि लभते
प्रसक्तं व्यामथ्नन् ज्वलनमरणिभ्यां जनयति ।

---

१ P. M. वीर्य्य० ।

प्रयुक्ता योगे तु ध्रुवमुपलभन्ते श्रमफलं
द्रुतं नित्यं यान्त्यो गिरिमपि हि भिन्दन्ति सरितः ॥९७॥

कृष्ट्वा गां परिपाल्य च श्रमशतैरश्नाति सस्यश्रियं
यत्नेन प्रविगाह्य सागरजलं रत्नश्रिया क्रीडति ।
शत्रूणामवधूय वीर्य्यमिषुभिर्भुङ्क्ते नरेन्द्रः श्रियं
तद्वीर्य्यं कुरु शान्तये विनियतं वीर्य्यं हि सर्वर्द्धये ॥९८॥

इति सौन्दरनन्दे महाकाव्ये आर्य्यसत्यव्याख्यानो
नाम षोडशः सर्गः ।

# सप्तदशः सर्गः

अथैवमादेशिततत्त्वमार्गो नन्दस्तदा प्राप्तविमोक्षमार्गः ।
सर्वेण भावेन गुरौ प्रणम्य क्लेशप्रहाणाय वनं जगाम ॥१॥
तत्रावकाशं[1] मृदुनीलशष्पं ददर्श शान्तं तरुषण्डवन्तम् ।
निःशब्दया निम्नगयोपगूढं वैदूर्य्यनीलोदकया वहन्त्या ॥२॥
स पादयोस्तत्र विधाय शौचं शुचौ शिवे श्रीमति वृक्षमूले ।
मोक्षाय बद्धा व्यवसायकक्षां पर्य्यङ्कमङ्कावहितं बबन्ध ॥३॥
राजन्[2] समग्रं प्रणिधाय कायं काये स्मृतिं चाभिमुखीं विधाय ।
सर्वेन्द्रियाण्यात्मनि सन्निधाय स तत्र योगं प्रयतः प्रपेदे ॥४॥
ततः स तत्त्वं निखिलं चिकीर्षु र्मोक्षानुकूलांश्च विधींश्चिकीर्षन् ।
ज्ञानेन लोक्येन शमेन चैव चचार चेतः परिकर्म्मभूमौ ॥५॥
संधाय धैर्य्यं प्रणिधाय वीर्य्यं[3] व्यपोह्य सक्तिं परिगृह्य शक्तिम् ।
प्रशान्तचेता नियमस्थचेताः स्वस्थस्ततो[भू]द्विषयेष्वनास्थः ॥६॥

आतप्तबुद्धेः प्रहितात्मनोऽपि स्वभ्यस्तभावादथ कामसंज्ञा ।
पर्य्याकुलं तस्य मनश्चकार प्रावृट्सु विद्युज्जलमागतेव ॥७॥
स पर्य्यवस्थानमवेत्य सद्यश्चिक्षेप तां धर्म्मविघात-कर्त्रीम् ।
प्रियामपि क्रोधपरीतचेता नारीमिवोद्वृत्तगुणां मनस्वी ॥८॥
आरब्धवीर्य्यस्य मनः शमाय भूयस्तु तस्याकुशलो वितर्कः ।
व्याधिप्रणाशाय निविष्ट[4]बुद्धेरुपद्रवो घोर इवाजगाम ॥९॥

---

१ P. M. तत्रावभासं । २ P. M. राज्यं ।
३ P. M. धैर्य्यं । ४ P. M. निरस्त० ।

स तद्विघाताय निमित्तमन्यद्योगानुकूलं कुशलं प्रपेदे ।
आर्त्तायनं क्षीणबलो बलस्थं निरस्यमानो बलिनारिणेव ॥१०॥

पुरं विधायानुविधाय दण्डं मित्राणि संगृह्य रिपून् विगृह्य ।
राजा यथाप्नोति हि गामपूर्व्वां नीतिर्मुमुक्षोरपि सैव योगे ॥११॥

विमोक्षकामस्य हि योगिनोपि मनः पुरं ज्ञानविधिश्च दण्डः ।
गुणाश्च मित्राण्यरयश्च दोषा भूमिर्विमुक्तिर्यतते यदर्थम् ॥१२॥

स दुःखजालान्महतो मुमुक्षुर्विमोक्षमार्गाधिगमे विविक्षुः ।
पन्थानमार्य्यं परमं दिदृक्षुः शमं ययौ किञ्चिदुपात्तचक्षुः[१] ॥१३॥

यः स्यान्निकेतस्तमसोऽनिकेतः श्रुत्वापि तत्त्वं स भवेत्प्रमत्तः ।
यस्मात्तु[२] मोक्षाय स पात्रभूतः तस्मान्मनः स्वात्मनि संजहार ॥१४॥

सम्भारतः प्रत्ययतः स्वभावादास्वादतो दोषविशेषतश्च ।
अथात्मवान् निःशरणात्मतश्च धर्म्मेषु चक्रे विधिवत् परीक्षाम् ॥१५॥

सरूपिणं कृत्स्नमरूपिणञ्च सारं दिदृक्षुर्विचिकाय कायम् ।
अथाशुचिं दुःखमनित्यमस्वं निरात्मकं चैव चिकाय कायम् ॥१६॥

अनित्यतस्तत्र हि शून्यतश्च निरात्मतो दुःखत एव चापि ।
मार्गप्रवेकेन स लौकिकेन क्लेशद्रुमं सञ्चलयाञ्चकार ॥१७॥

यस्मादभूत्वा भवतीह सर्व्वं भूत्वा च भूयो न भवत्यवश्यम् ।
सहेतुकञ्च क्षयिहेतुमच्च तस्मादनित्यं जगदित्यविन्दत् ॥१८॥

यतः प्रसूतस्य च कर्म्मयोगः प्रसज्यते बन्धविघातहेतुः ।
दुःखप्रतीकारविधौ सुखाख्यं ततो भवं दुःखमिति व्यपश्यत् ॥१९॥

---

१ P. M. उपान्त० । २ P. M. तस्मात् ।

यतश्च संस्कारगतं विविक्तं न कारकः कश्चन वेदको वा ।
सामग्र्यतः सम्भवति प्रवृत्तिः शून्यं ततो लोकमिमं ददर्श ॥२०॥
यस्मान्निरीहं जगदस्वतन्त्रं नैश्वर्य्यमेकः[1] कुरुते क्रियासु ।
तत्तत् प्रतीत्य प्रभवन्ति भावा निरात्मकं तेन विवेद लोकम् ॥२१॥

ततः स वातं व्यजनादिवोष्णे काष्ठाश्रितं निर्मथनादिवाग्निम् ।
अन्तःक्षितिस्थं खननादिवाम्भो लोकोत्तरं वर्त्म दुरापमाप ॥२२॥
सज्ज्ञान-चाप-स्मृति-वर्म्म बद्धा विशुद्धशीलव्रतवाहनस्थः ।
क्लेशारिभिश्चित्तरणाजिरस्थैः सार्द्धं युयुत्सु विजयाय तस्थौ ॥२३॥
ततः स बोध्यङ्गशिताात्तशस्त्रः सम्यक्प्रधानोत्तमवाहनस्थः ।
मार्गाङ्गमातङ्गवता बलेन शनैः शनैः क्लेशचमूं जगाहे ॥२४॥
स स्मृत्युपस्थानमयैः पृषत्कैः शत्रून् विपर्य्यासमयान् क्षणेन ।
दुःखस्य हेतूंश्चतुरश्चतुर्भिः स्वैः स्वैः प्रचारायतनैर्ददार ॥२५॥
आर्य्यैर्बलैः पञ्चभिरेव पञ्च चेतःखिलान्यप्रतिमैर्बभञ्ज ।
मिथ्याङ्गनागांश्च तथाङ्गनागैर्विनिर्दुधावाष्टभिरेव सोऽष्टौ ॥२६॥

अथात्मदृष्टिं सकलां विधूय चतुर्षु सत्येष्वकथंकथः सन् ।
विशुद्धशीलव्रतदृष्टधर्म्मा धर्म्मस्य पूर्व्वां फलभूमिमाप ॥२७॥
स दर्शनादार्य्यचतुष्टयस्य क्लेशैकदेशस्य च विप्रयोगात् ।
प्रत्यात्मिकाच्चापि विशेषलाभात् प्रत्यक्षतो ज्ञानसुखस्य चैव ॥२८॥
दार्ढ्यात् प्रसादस्य धृतेः स्थिरत्वात् सत्येष्वसंमूढतया चतुर्षु ।
शीलस्य चाच्छिद्रतमोत्तमस्य निःसंशयो धर्म्मविधौ बभूव ॥२९॥

---

१ P. M. एकं ।

कुदृष्टिजालेन स विप्रयुक्तो लोकं तथाभूतमवेक्षमाणः ।
ज्ञानाश्रयं प्रीतिमुपाजगाम भूयः प्रसादश्च गुरावियाय ॥२०॥
यो हि प्रवृत्तिर्न्नियतामवैति नैवान्यहेतोरिह नाप्यहेतोः ।
प्रतीत्य तत्तत्[१] समवैति तत्तत् स नैष्ठिकं पश्यति धर्म्ममार्य्यम् ॥२१॥
शान्तं शिवं निर्ज्जरसं विरागं निःश्रेयसं पश्यति यश्च धर्म्मं ।
तस्योपदेष्टारमथार्य्यवर्य्यं संप्रेक्षते बुद्धमवाप्तचक्षुः ॥२२॥
यथोपदेशेन शि[वे]न मुक्तो रोगादरोगो भिषजं कृतज्ञः ।
अनुस्मरन् पश्यति चित्तदृष्ट्या मैत्र्या च शास्त्रे ज्ञतया च तुष्टः ॥२३॥
आर्य्येण मार्गेण तथैव मुक्तस्तथागतं तत्त्वविदार्य्यतत्त्वः ।
अनुस्मरन् पश्यति कायसाक्षी मैत्र्या च सर्वज्ञतया च तुष्टः ॥२४॥
स नाशकैर्दृष्टिगतैर्विमुक्तः पर्य्य[न्त]मालोक्य पुनर्भवस्य ।
भक्त्वा घृणाक्लेशविजृम्भितेषोर्म्मृत्यो र्न तत्रास न दुर्गतिभ्यः ॥२५॥
त्वक्स्नायुमेदोरुधिरास्थिमांसकेशादिनाऽमेध्यगणेन पूर्णम् ।
ततः स कायं समवेक्षमाणः सारं विचिन्त्याण्वपि नोपलेभे ॥२६॥

स कामरागप्रतिघौ स्थिरात्मा तेनैव योगेन तनू चकार ।
कृत्वा महोरस्कतनुस्तनू तौ प्रापद्द्वितीयं फलमार्य्यधर्म्मे ॥२७॥
स लोभचापं परिकल्पबाणं रागं महावैरिणमल्पशेषम् ।
कायस्वभावाधिगतैर्बिभेद योगायुधास्त्रैरशुभापृषत्कैः ॥२८॥
द्वेषायुधं क्रोधविकीर्णबाणं व्यापादमन्तःप्रसवं सपत्नम् ।
मैत्रीपृषत्कै धृतितूणसंस्थैः क्षमाधनुर्ज्याविसृतै र्जघान ॥२९॥

---

१ P. M. drops तत्त० ।

मूलान्यथ त्रीण्यशुभस्य वीरस्त्रिभिर्विमोक्षायतनैश्चकर्त्त ।
चमूमुखस्थान् धृतकार्म्मुकांस्त्रीनरीनिवारिस्त्रिभिरायसाग्रैः ॥४०॥
स कामधातोः समतिक्रमाय पार्ष्णिग्रहांस्तानभिभूय शत्रून् ।
योगादनागामिफलं प्रपद्य द्वारीव निर्व्वाणपुरस्य तस्थौ ॥४१॥

कामैर्विविक्तं मलिनैश्च धर्म्मैः वितर्कवच्चापि विचारवच्च ।
विवेकजं प्रीतिसुखोपपन्नं ध्यानं ततः स प्रथमं प्रपेदे ॥४२॥
कामाग्निदाहेन स विप्रमुक्तो ह्लादं परं ध्यानसुखादवाप ।
सुखं विगाह्याप्स्विव घर्म्मखिन्नः प्राप्येव चार्थं विपुलं दरिद्रः ॥४३॥
तत्रापि तद्धर्म्मगतान् वितर्कान् गुणागुणे च प्रसृतान् विचारान् ।
बुद्ध्वा मनःक्षोभकरानशान्तांस्तद्विप्रयोगाय मतिश्चकार ॥४४॥
क्षोभं प्रकुर्व्वन्ति यथोर्म्मयो हि धीरप्रसन्नाम्बुवहस्य सिन्धोः ।
एकाग्रभूतस्य तथोर्म्मिभूताश्चिन्ताम्भसः क्षोभकरा वितर्काः ॥४५॥
खिन्नस्य सुप्तस्य च निर्वृतस्य बाधां यथा संजनयन्ति शब्दाः ।
अध्यात्ममेकाग्र्यमुपागतस्य भवन्ति बाधाय तथा वितर्काः ॥४६॥

अथावितर्कं क्रमशोऽविचारमेकाग्रभावान्मनसः प्रसन्नम् ।
समाधिजं प्रीतिसुखं द्वितीयं ध्यानं तदाध्यात्मशिवं स दध्यौ ॥४७॥
तद्ध्यानमागम्य च चित्तमौनं लेभे परां प्रीतिमलब्धपूर्व्वाम् ।
प्रीतौ तु तत्रापि स दोषदर्शी यथा वितर्केष्वभवत्तथैव ॥४८॥
प्रीति[ः] परा वस्तुनि यत्र यस्य विपर्य्ययात्तस्य हि तत्र दुःखम् ।
प्रीतेरतः[१] प्रेक्ष्य स तत्र दोषान् प्रीतिक्षये योगमुपारुरोह ॥४९॥

---

१ P. M. प्रीतौवतः T.

प्रीते र्विरागात् सुखमार्य्यजुष्टं कायेन विन्दन्नथ संप्रजानन् ।
उपेक्षकः स स्मृतिमान् व्यहार्षीत् ध्यानं तृतीयं प्रतिलभ्य धीरः ॥५०॥

यस्मात् परं तत्र सुखं सुखेभ्यस्ततः परं नास्ति सुखप्रवृत्तिः ।
तस्माद् बभाषे शुभकृत्स्नभूमिं परापरज्ञः परमेति मैत्र्या ॥५१॥

ध्यानेऽपि तत्राथ ददर्श दोषं मेने परं शान्तिमनिञ्जमेव ।
आभोगतोऽपीञ्जयति स्म तस्य चित्तं प्रवृत्तं सुखमित्यजस्रम् ॥५२॥

यत्रेञ्जितं स्पन्दितमस्ति तत्र यत्रास्ति च स्पन्दितमस्ति दुःखम् ।
यस्मादतस्तत्सुखमिञ्जकत्वात् प्रशान्तिकामा यतयस्त्यजन्ति ॥५३॥

अथ प्रहाणात् सुखदुःखयोश्च मनोविकारस्य च पूर्व्वमेव ।
दध्यावुपेक्षास्मृतिमद्विशुद्धं ध्यानं तथाऽदुःखसुखं चतुर्थम् ॥५४॥

यस्मात्तु तस्मिन् न सुखं न दुःखं ज्ञानं च तत्रास्ति तदर्थचारि ।
तस्मादुपेक्षा स्मृतिपारिशुद्धि[१] र्निरुच्यते ध्यानविधौ चतुर्थे ॥५५॥

ध्यानं स निःश्रित्य ततश्चतुर्थमर्हत्वलाभाय मतिं चकार ।
सन्धाय मित्रं बलवन्तमार्य्यं राजेव देशानजितान् जिगीषुः ॥५६॥

चिच्छेद कार्त्स्न्येन ततः स पञ्च प्रज्ञासिना भावनयेरितेन ।
ऊर्द्धंगमान्युत्तमबन्धनानि संयोजनान्युत्तमबन्धनानि ॥५७॥

बोध्यङ्गनागैरपि सप्तभिः स सप्तैव चित्तानुशयान् ममर्द्द ।
द्वीपानिवोपस्थितविप्रणाशान् कालो ग्रहैः सप्तभिरेव सप्त ॥५८॥

अग्निद्रुमाज्याम्बुषु या हि वृत्तिः कबन्धवाय्वग्निदिवाकराणाम् ।
दोषेषु तां वृत्तिमियाय नन्दो निर्व्वापणोत्पाटनदाहशोषैः ॥५९॥

---

१ P. M. पारिशुद्धं ।

इति त्रिवेगं त्रिझषं त्रिवीचमेकाम्भसं पञ्चरयं द्विकूलम् ।
द्विग्राहमष्टाङ्गवता प्लवेन दुःखार्णवं दुस्तरमुत्ततार ॥६०॥

अर्हत्त्वमासाद्य स सत्क्रियार्हो निरुत्सुको निष्प्रणयो निराशः ।
बिभीर्विशुग्वीतमदो विरागः स एव धृत्यान्य इवावभासे ॥६१॥
भ्रातुश्च शास्तुश्च तयानुशिष्ट्या नन्दस्ततः स्वेन च विक्रमेण ।
प्रशान्तचेताः परिपूर्णकार्यो वाणीमिमामात्मगतां जगाद ॥६२॥

नमोऽस्तु तस्मै सुगताय येन हितैषिणा मे करुणात्मकेन ।
बहूनि दुःखान्यपवर्त्तितानि सुखानि भूयांस्युपसंहृतानि ॥६३॥
अहं ह्यनार्य्येण शरीरजेन दुःखात्मके वर्त्मनि कृष्यमाणः ।
निवर्त्तितस्तद्वचनाङ्कुशेन दर्पान्वितो नाग इवाङ्कुशेन ॥६४॥
तस्याज्ञया कारुणिकस्य शास्तुः हृदिस्थमुत्पाट्य हि रागशल्यम् ।
अद्यैव तावत् सुमहत्सुखं मे सर्व्वक्षये किं बत निर्वृतस्य ॥६५॥
निर्व्वाप्य कामाग्निमहं हि दीप्तं धृत्यम्बुना पावकमम्बुनेव ।
ह्लादं परं साम्प्रतमागतोऽस्मि शीतं ह्रदं घर्म्म इवावतीर्णः ॥६६॥
न मे प्रियं किञ्चन नाप्रियं मे न मेऽनुरोधोऽस्ति कुतो विरोधः ।
तयोरभावात्सुखितोऽस्मि सद्यो हिमातपाभ्यामिव विप्रमुक्तः ॥६७॥
महाभयात् क्षेममिवोपलभ्य महावरोधादिव विप्रमोक्षम् ।
महार्णवात् पारमिवाप्लवः सन् भीमान्धकारादिव च प्रकाशम् ॥६८॥
रोगादिवारोग्यमसह्यरूपादृणादिवानृण्यमनन्तसंख्यात् ।
द्विषत्सकाशादिव चापयानं दुर्भिक्षयोगाच्च यथा सुभिक्षम् ॥६९॥
तद्वत् परां शान्तिमुपागतोऽहं यस्यानुभावेन विनायकस्य ।
करोमि भूयः पुनरुक्तमस्मै नमो नमोऽर्हाय तथागताय ॥७०॥

येनाहं गिरिमुपनीय रुक्मशृङ्गं
स्वर्गञ्च प्लवगवधूनिदर्शनेन ।
कामात्मा त्रिदिवचरीभिरङ्गनाभि-
र्निष्कृष्टो युवतिमये कलौ निमग्नः ॥७१॥

तस्माच्च व्यसनपरादनर्थपङ्कात्
उत्कृष्य क्रमशिथिलः करीव पङ्कात् ।
शान्तेऽस्मिन् विरजसि विज्वरे विशोके
सद्धर्मे वितमसि नैष्ठिके विमुक्तः ॥७२॥

तं वन्दे परमनुकंपकं[1] महर्षिं
मूर्द्धाहं प्रकृतिगुणज्ञमाशयज्ञम् ।
संबुद्धं दशबलिनं भिषक्प्रधानं
त्रातारं पुनरपि चास्मि सन्नतस्तम् ॥७३

आर्य्याश्वघोषकृतौ महाकाव्ये सौन्दरनन्दे
अमृताधिगमो नाम सप्तदशः सर्गः ।

---

१ P. M. drops ०पकं ।

# अष्टादशः सर्गः

अथ द्विजो बाल इवाप्तवेदः क्षिप्रं वणिक् प्राप्त इवाप्तलाभः ।
जित्वा च राजन्य इवारिसैन्यं नन्दः कृतार्थो गुरुमभ्यगच्छत् ॥१॥
द्रष्टुं सुखं ज्ञानसमाधि[१]काले गुरुर्हि शिष्यस्य गुरोश्च शिष्यः ।
परिश्रमस्ते [स]फलो मयीति यतो दिदृक्षास्य मुनौ बभूव ॥२॥
यतो हि येनाधिगतो विशेषस्तस्योत्तमां सोऽर्हति कर्त्तुमीड्याम् ।
आर्य्यः सरागोपि कृतज्ञभावात् प्रक्षीणमानः किमु वीतरागः ॥३॥
यस्याथ कामप्रभवा हि भक्तिः स्वतोऽस्य[२] सा तिष्ठति रूढमूला ।
धर्म्मान्वयो यस्य तु भक्तिरागस्तस्य प्रसादो हृदयावगाढः ॥४॥
काषायवासाः कनकावदातस्ततः स मूर्द्ध्ना गुरवे प्रणेमे ।
वातेरितः पल्लवताम्ररागः पुष्पोज्ज्वलश्रीरिव कर्णिकारः ॥५॥
अथात्मनः शिष्यगुणस्य चैव महामुनेः शास्तृगुणस्य चैव ।
सन्दर्शनार्थं स न मानहेतोस्स्वां कार्य्यसिद्धिं कथयाम्बभूव ॥६॥
यो दृष्टिशल्यो हृदयावगाढः प्रभो भृशं मामतुदत्सुतीक्ष्णः ।
त्वद्वाक्यसंदंशमुखेन मे स समुद्धृतः शल्यहृतेव शल्यः ॥७॥
कथंकथीभावगतोऽस्मि येन छिन्नः स निःसंशय संशयो मे ।
त्वच्छासनात् सत्पथमागतोऽस्मि सुदेशिकस्येव पथि प्रनष्टः ॥८॥
यत्पीतमास्वादवशेन्द्रियेण दर्पेण कन्दर्पविषं मयासीत् ।
तन्मे हतं त्वद्वचनागदेन विषं विनाशीव महागदेन ॥९॥
क्षयं गतं जन्म निरस्तजन्म सद्धर्म्मचर्य्यामुषितोऽस्मि सम्यक् ।

---

१ P. M. समाप्त ।

२ P. M. सुतस्य P. L. M. lacuna T.

कृत्स्नं कृतं मे कृतकार्य्य कार्य्यं लोके प्रभूतोऽस्मि न लोकधर्म्मा ॥१०॥

मैत्रीस्तनीं व्यञ्जनचारुसास्नां सद्धर्मदुग्धां प्रतिभानशृङ्गाम् ।
तवास्मि गां साधु निपीय तृप्तस्तृषेव गामुत्तमवत्सवर्णः ॥११॥

यत्पश्यतश्चाधिगमो ममायं तन्मे समासेन मुने निबोध ।
सर्वज्ञ कामं विदितं तवैतत् स्वन्तूपचारं प्रविवक्षुरस्मि ॥१२॥

अन्येऽपि सन्तो विमुमुक्षवो हि श्रुत्वा विमोक्षाय नयं परस्य ।
मुक्तस्य रोगादिव रोगवन्तस्तेनैव मार्गेण सुखं घटन्ते ॥१३॥

द्रव्यादिकान् जन्मनि वेद्मि धातून् नात्मानमुर्व्यादिषु तेषु किञ्चित् ।
यस्मादतस्तेषु न मेऽस्ति सक्तिर्बहिश्च कायेन समा मतिर्मे ॥१४॥

स्कन्धांश्च रूपप्रभृतीन् दशार्द्धान् पश्यामि यस्माच्चपलानसारान् ।
अनात्मकांश्चैव वधात्मकांश्च तस्माद्विमुक्तोऽस्म्यशिवेभ्य एभ्यः ॥१५॥

यस्माच्च पश्याम्युदयञ्च सत्त्वां[1] सर्वास्ववस्थास्वहमिन्द्रियाणाम् ।
तस्मादनित्येषु निरात्मकेषु दुःखेषु मे तेष्वपि नास्ति सङ्गः ॥१६॥

यतश्च लोकं समजन्मनिष्ठं पश्यामि निःसारमसच्च सर्वम् ।
अतो धिया मे मनसा विबद्धमस्मीति मे नेञ्जितमस्ति येन ॥१७॥

चतुर्विधे नैकविधप्रसङ्गे यतोऽहमाहारविधावसक्तः[2] ।
अमूर्च्छितश्चाग्रथितश्च तत्र त्रिभ्यो विमुक्तोऽस्मि ततो भवेभ्यः ॥१८॥

अनिःश्रितश्चाप्रतिबद्धचित्तो दृष्टश्रुतादौ व्यवहारधर्म्मे ।
यस्मात् समात्मानुगतश्च तत्र तस्माद्विसंयोगगतोऽस्मि मुक्तः ॥१९॥

इत्येवमुक्त्वा गुरुबाहुमान्यात् सर्वेण कायेन स गां निपन्नः ।
प्रवेरितो लोहितचन्दनाक्तो हैमो महास्तम्भ[१] इवावभासे ॥२०॥

ततः प्रमादात् प्रसृतस्य पूर्वं श्रुत्वा धृतिं व्याकरणञ्च तस्य ।
धर्म्मान्वयं चानुगतं प्रसादं मेघस्वरस्तं मुनिराबभाषे ॥२१॥

उत्तिष्ठ धर्म्मे स्थित शिष्यजुष्टे किं पादयोर्मे पतितोऽसि मूर्द्ध्ना ।
अभ्यर्च्चनं मे न तथा प्रणामो धर्म्मे यथैषा प्रतिपत्तिरेव ॥२२॥

अद्यासि सुप्रव्रजितो जितात्मन्नैश्वर्य्यमप्यात्मनि येन लब्धम् ।
जितात्मनः प्रव्रजनं हि साधु चलात्मनो न त्वजितेन्द्रियस्य ॥२३॥

अद्यासि शौचेन परेण युक्तो वाक्कायचेतांसि शुचीनि यत्ते ।
अतः पुनश्चाप्रयतामसौम्यां यत् सौम्य नो वेक्ष्यसि गर्भशय्याम् ॥२४॥

अद्यार्य्यवृत्त श्रुतवच्छ्रुतं तच्छ्रुतानुरूपं प्रतिपद्य धर्म्मम् ।
कृतश्रुतो विप्रतिपद्यमानो निन्द्यो हि निर्व्वीर्य्य इवात्तशस्त्रः ॥२५॥

अहो धृतिस्ते विषयात्मकस्य यत्त्वं मतिं मोक्षविधावकार्षीः ।
यास्यामि निष्ठामिति बालिशो हि जन्मक्षयात् त्रासमिहाभ्युपैति॥२६॥

[२]दिष्ट्या दुरापः क्षणसन्निपातो नायं कृतो मोहवशेन मोघः ।
उदेति दुःखेन गतो ह्यधस्तात् कूर्म्मो युगच्छिद्र इवार्णवस्थः ॥२७॥

निर्ज्जित्य मारं युधि दुर्निवारमद्यासि लोके रणशा[स्त्र]शूरः ।
शूरोऽप्यशूरः स हि वेदितव्यो दोषैरमित्रैरिव हन्यते यः ॥२८॥

निर्व्वाप्य रागाग्निमुदीर्णमद्य दिष्ट्या सुखं स्वप्स्यसि वीतदाहः ।
दुःखं हि शेते शयनेऽप्युदारे क्लेशाग्निना चेतसि दह्यमानः ॥२९॥

---

१ P. M. ०शुम्भः ।

२ P. M. has अतोवियामे before verse 27.

अभ्युच्छ्रितो द्रव्यमदेन पूर्व्वमद्यास्मि तृष्णोपरमात् समृद्धः ।
यावत् सतर्षः पुरुषो हि लोके तावत्समृद्धोऽपि सदा दरिद्रः ॥३०॥
अद्योपदेष्टुं तव युक्तरूपं शुद्धोदनो मे नृपतिः पितेति ।
भ्रष्टस्य धर्म्मात् पितृभिर्निपातादश्लाघनीयो हि कुलोपदेशः ॥३१॥
दिष्ट्यास्मि शान्तिं परमामुपेतो निस्तीर्णकान्तार इवाप्तसारः ।
सर्व्वो हि संसारगतो भयार्त्तो यथैव कान्तारगतस्तथैव ॥३२॥
आरण्यकं भैक्षचरं विनीतं द्रक्ष्यामि नन्दं निभृतं कदेति ।
आसीत् पुरस्तात् त्वयि मे दिदृक्षा तथास्मि दिष्ट्या मम दर्शनीयः॥३३॥
भवत्यरूपोपि हि दर्शनीयस्स्वलंकृतः श्रेष्ठतमैर्गुणैः स्वैः ।
दोषैः परीतो मलिनीकरैस्तु सुदर्शनीयोऽपि विरूप एव ॥३४॥
अद्य प्रकृष्टा तव बुद्धिमत्ता कृत्स्नं यया ते कृतमात्मकार्य्यम् ।
श्रुतोन्नतस्यापि हि नास्ति बुद्धिर्नोत्पद्यते श्रेयसि यस्य बुद्धिः॥३५॥
उन्मीलितस्यापि जनस्य मध्ये निमीलितस्यापि तथैव चक्षुः ।
प्रज्ञामयं यस्य हि नास्ति चक्षुश्चक्षुर्न तस्यास्ति सचक्षुषोपि ॥३६॥
दुःखप्रतीकारनिमित्तमार्त्तः कृष्यादिभिः खेदमुपैति लोकः ।
अजस्रमागच्छति तच्च भूयो ज्ञानेन यस्याद्य कृतस्त्वयान्तः ॥३७॥
दुःखं न मे स्यात् सुखमेव मे स्यादिति प्रवृत्तः सततं हि लोकः ।
न वेत्ति तच्चैव तथा यथा स्यात् प्राप्तं त्वयाद्यासुलभं यथावत् ॥३८।
इत्येवमादि स्थिरबुद्धिचित्तस्तथागतेनाभिहितो हिताय ।
स्तवेषु निन्दासु च निर्व्यपेक्षः कृताञ्जलिर्वाक्यमुवाच नन्दः ॥३९॥
अहो विशेषेण विशेषदर्शिंस्त्वयानुकम्पा मयि दर्शितेयम् ।
यत्कामपङ्के भगवन्निमग्नस्त्र[ा]तोऽस्मि संसारभयादकामः ॥४०॥

भ्राचा त्वया श्रेयसि दैशिकेन पित्रा फलस्थेन तथैव मात्रा ।
हतोऽभविष्यं यदि न व्यमोक्ष्यं सार्थात् परिभ्रष्ट इवाकृतार्थः ॥ ४१ ॥
शान्तस्य तुष्टस्य सुखो विवेको विज्ञाततत्त्वस्य परीक्षकस्य ।
प्रहीणमानस्य च निर्मदस्य सुखं विरागत्वमसक्तबुद्धेः ॥ ४२ ॥
अ[थो] हि तत्वं परिगम्य सम्यग्निर्धूय दोषानधिगम्य शान्तिम् ।
स्वं नाश्रमं सम्प्रति चिन्तयामि न तं जनं नाप्सरसो न देवान् ॥ ४३ ॥
इदं हि भुक्त्वा शुचि शामिकं सुखं न मे मनः कांक्षति कामजं सुखम् ।
महार्हमप्यन्नमदैवताहृतं दिवौकसो भुक्तवतः सुधामिव ॥ ४४ ॥
अहोऽन्धविज्ञाननिमीलितं जगत् पटान्तरे पश्यति नोत्तमं सुखम् ।
स्वाधीनमध्यात्मसुखं व्यपास्य हि श्रमं तथा कामसुखार्थमृच्छति ॥ ४५ ॥
यथा हि रत्नाकरमेत्य दुर्मतिर्विहाय रत्नान्यसतो मणीन् हरेत् ।
अपास्य सम्बोधिसुखं यथोत्तमं श्रमं व्रजेत् कामसुखोपलब्धये ॥ ४६ ॥
अहो हि सत्त्वेष्वतिमैत्रचेतसस्तथागतस्यानुजिघृक्षुता परा ।
अपास्य यद्ध्यानसुखं मुने परं परस्य दुःखोपरमाय खिद्यसे ॥ ४७ ॥
मया नु शक्यं प्रतिकर्त्तुमद्य किं गुरौ हितैषिण्यनुकम्पके त्वयि ।
समुद्धृतो येन भवार्णवादहं महार्णवाच्चूर्णितनौरिवोर्म्मिभिः ॥ ४८ ॥
ततो मुनिस्तस्य निशम्य हेतुमत् प्रहीणसर्व्वास्रवसूचकं वचः ।
इदं बभाषे वदतामनुत्तमो यदर्हति श्रीघन एवं भाषितुम् ॥ ४९ ॥
इदं कृतार्थः परमार्थवित् कृती त्वमेव धीमन्नभिधातुमर्हसि ।
अतीत्य कान्तारमवाप्तसाधनः सुदैशिकस्येव कृतं महावणिक् ॥ ५० ॥
अवैति बुद्धं नरदम्य[1]सारथिं कृती यथार्हन्नुपशान्तमानसम् ।

---

१ P. M. ०दत्त० ।

न दृष्टसत्योपि तथाच बुध्यते पृथग्जनः किं बत बुद्धिमानपि ॥५१॥
रजस्तमोभ्यां परिमुक्तचेतसस्तवैव वेयं सदृशी कृतज्ञता ।
रजःप्रकर्षेण जगत्यवस्थिते कृतज्ञभावो हि कृतज्ञ दुर्लभः ॥५२॥
सधर्म्म धर्म्मान्वयतो यतश्च ते मयि प्रसादोऽधिगमेन कौशलम् ।
अतोऽस्ति भूयस्त्वयि मे विवक्षितं नतो हि भक्तश्चभियोगमर्हसि ॥५३।

अवाप्तकार्य्योसि परां गतिं गतो न तेऽस्ति किञ्चित्करणीय-
मण्वपि
अतःपरं सौम्य चरानुकम्पया विमोचयन् कृच्छ्रगतान् परानपि ॥५४।
इहार्थमेवारभते नरोऽधमो विमध्यमस्तूभयलौकिकीं क्रियाम् ।
क्रियाममुत्रैव फलाय मध्यमा विशिष्टधर्म्मा पुनरप्रवृत्तये ॥५५॥
इहोत्तमेभ्योपि मतः सुभूमो य उत्तमं धर्ममवाप्य नैष्ठिकम् ।
अचिन्तयित्वा सुगतं परिश्रमं शमं परेभ्योऽप्युपदेष्टुमिच्छति ॥५६॥
विहाय तस्मादिह कार्य्यमात्मनः कुरु स्थिरात्मन् परकार्य्यमप्यथो ।
भ्रमत्सु सत्त्वेषु तमोवृतात्मसु श्रुतप्रदीपो निशि धार्य्यतामयम् ॥५७।
ब्रवीतु तावत्पुरि विस्मितो जनः त्वयि स्थिते कुर्व्वति धर्मदेशनाः ।
अहोवताश्चर्य्यमिदं विमुक्तये करोति रागी यदयं कथामिति ॥५८।

ध्रुवं हि संश्रुत्य तव स्थिरं [म]नो
निवृत्तनानाविषयैर्मनोरथैः ।
वधूर्गृहे सापि तवानुकुर्व्वती
करिष्यते स्त्रीषु विरागिणीः कथाः ॥५९॥
त्वयि परमधृतौ निविष्टतत्त्वे
भवनगता न हि रंस्यते ध्रुवं सा ।

मनसि शमदमात्मके विविक्ते
मतिरिव कामसुखैः परीक्षकस्य ॥६०॥

इत्यर्हतः परमकारुणिकस्य शास्तुः
मूर्ध्ना वचश्च चरणौ च समं गृहीत्वा ।
स्वस्थः प्रशान्तहृदयो विनिवृत्तकार्य्यः
पार्श्वान्मुनेः प्रतिययौ विमदः करीव ॥६१॥

भिक्षार्थं समये विवेश च पुरीं दृष्टीर्जनस्याक्षिपन्
लाभालाभसुखासुखादिषु समः स्वस्थेन्द्रियो निस्पृहः ।
निर्मोक्षाय चकार तत्र च कथां काले जनायार्थिने
नैवोन्मार्गगतान् [जनान्] परिभवन्नात्मानमुत्कर्षयन्[1] ॥६२॥

सौन्दरनन्दे महाकाव्ये आज्ञाव्याकरणं
नामाष्टादशमः सर्गः ॥

---

१ P. M. उत्कर्षति ।

इत्येषा व्युपशान्तये न रतये मोक्षार्थगर्भाकृतिः
श्रोतृणां ग्रहणार्थमन्यमनसां काव्योपचारात्कृता ।
यन्मोक्षात्कृतमन्यदत्र हि मया तत्काव्यधर्म्मात् कृतम्
पातुं तिक्तमिवौषधं मधुयुतं हृद्यं कथं स्यादिति ॥६३॥

प्रायेणालोक्य लोकं विषयरतिपरं मोक्षात् प्रतिहतं
काव्यव्याजेन तत्त्वं कथितमिह मया मोक्षपरमिति ।
तद्बुद्ध्वा शामिकं यत् तदवहितमितो ग्राह्यं न ललितम्
पांशुभ्यो धातुजेभ्यो नियतमुपकरं चामीकरमिति ॥६४॥

आर्य्यसुवर्णाक्षीपुत्रस्य साकेतकस्य[1] भिक्षो-[2]
राचार्य्य-भदन्ताश्वघोषस्य महाकवेर्महावादिनः कृतिरियम् ॥

---

१ P. M. साङ्केतकस्य । २ P. L. भिक्षोः श्री ।

# APPENDIX

## Notes on the Readings of the Text

I. 2. सुश्रियाय is not classical Sanskrit. P.L.M. lacuna.

I. 3. अधोत्तत् is wrong in grammar, so it has been changed into अधुत्तत्. P.L.M. lacuna.

I. 7. P.L.M. lacuna. स्कैकटे: in P.M. The modern Nepalese scribes change very frequently ष्ठ into स्त and स्त into ष्ठ. So it has been changed into सैकतैः.

P.M. केसरास्तरपाण्डुभिः. The reading of P.L.M. केशरास्तरपाण्डुभिः, which has been adopted.

I. 25. P.M. मनिमद्वं कुमारस्य. P.L.M. the lower parts of सु, नि and ड are gone. But there is sufficient indication to show that the subscript उ in सु was there. द्वं is almost entire with an anusvāra at the top. But as the anusvāra cannot be construed, it has been changed into visarga.

I. 28. तेषां वृद्धिचिकीर्षया. P.M. has तेषां वृ प्रिय चिकीर्षया. P.L.M. has a long lacuna. But the anusvāra in तेषां is clearly visible. वृ is altogether gone. And after that, the upper part of द्धि, that is दि, is visible. There is room only for two letters after तेषां. So I have made it वृद्धिचिकीर्षया. The word वृद्धि in the sense of prosperity is well known in the Hindu ritualistic works, as in the term वृद्धिश्राद्ध. It is also used in the same sense in this work (I. 39 and 44).

I. 33. निर्म्मिमीध्वं. P.L.M. lacuna. P.M. निर्म्मिताध्वं which has been changed into the correct grammatical form of निर्म्मिमीध्वं.

I. 44. P.M. has विदुषस्तस्य पथ्यत्सु कर्म्मसु. In P.L.M. the upper parts of the letters from वि to क are corroded. There is the subscript त, subscript षु, and the lower curve of प or ष or य, then the lower part of subscript ष, and then the lower part of the subscript सु. From this I have made तस्युपष्षट्सु कर्म्मसु or तस्युषः षट्सु कर्म्मसु।

I. 46. P.M. has evidently यत्रं. P.L.M. has the upper portions above the mātrā corroded. The subscript below त is also corroded. The first letter प has a long nose, from which it may be either यत्र or यत्. I prefer the reading of P.M., because P.L.M. is so indistinct.

I. 54. P.M. has आल्लानां वाहुसालिनाम् P.L.M. आलानां वाहुशान्दिनां. Both the readings are obscure. But as the word आलानं is well-known and gives a clear meaning, I have ventured to change the first word into आलानं.

I. Col. P.L.M. invariably calls the work सौन्दरनन्द, but P.M. सौन्दरानन्द. I have preferred the reading of P.L.M. as more ancient.

II. 13. Very corrupt. P.M. has नश्चबान्धाबुरतः सत्यान्मुहूर्त्तमपि जीवितं. P.L.M. has नश्च distinct. The lower parts of the next two letters are, to a certain extent, visible. These may be the lower part of क and the lower part of च. The next two letters are absolutely gone. Then faint traces of सत्या. Then the lower part of न्मु. The whole of हूर्त्तं. The greater part of the lower section मपि जावत. I suggest नश्चकाञ्चीश्चुरतः सत्यान्मुहूर्त्तमपि जीवितं as in the text.

II. 18. P.L.M. complete lacuna. P.M. has संत्वमर्पवत् which gives no meaning. I suggest स स्वमर्पवत्. (He gave wealth to good purpose.)

II. 30. P.L.M. मपप्रथत्. P.M. अवतपत् which has been neglected.

II. 31. Both MSS. read कालमस्य मसूसवत्. I cannot make any meaning out of this with grammatical consistency. I suggest कालं स स्वमसूषवत् (that is, he made time produce wealth).

II. 41. P.L.M. तेनाधिरपि. P.M. तेनारपि. I have suggested तेनारिरपि.

II. 53. According to classical Sanskrit वर्ष is masculine as a word formed by the suffix अल्, and so in the body of the book I restored a visarga. But I find that Aśvaghoṣa often uses an अलन्त word in neuter, both in this poem and Buddhacarita. And so in the errata I have corrected the restoration into anusvāra instead of visarga [corrected in the *text* in this edition]. In P.L.M. I find a slight trace of anusvāra too.

III. 3. P.M. has तथेन्द्रकं which is evidently wrong as this teacher is known in Buddhist traditions as रुद्रकः रामपुत्रः or उद्रक. P.L.M. has तथोर्द्रकः. But the scribe of this MS. is in the habit of adding a superscript र whenever there is a subscript र.

III. 4. P.M. has हन्तमागमम् । निश्चयमनवगतः in which हन्त is absolutely unmeaning, as there is no necessity for खेद here. I have accepted the reading of P.L.M.

III. 18. P.M. has अपरिग्रहस्य. But the sixth case-ending cannot be construed. The P.L.M. has only the left-hand half of स, and there is a faint trace of the tip of the nose of the subscript स. So I have ventured to make it अपरिग्रहः सः.

III. 20. P.M. वर्ण॰ P.L.M. has only the lower subscripts visible, the first subscript is ऊ and the second subscript र्ण. I take it to be तूर्ण.

III. 22. P.M. निश्चलमतिरस्वयिषु पुनर्नं बहुधाभवत् पुनरभूत्त-

धैकधा. P.L.M. after a long lacuna has धु पुनर्न्नर्बहुधा०. I make it as in the text. असयिषु is ungrammatical, and so I make it शिश्रयिषुः After पुनः I drop न.

III. 28. Both P.L.M. and P.M. प्रषन० which destroys the metre. I make it प्रषन्न.

III. 34. P.M. ग्ट corrected into व; and ह्व P.L.M. ग्टह्व. I have taken the corrected reading of P.M.

P.M. नृप इव P.L.M. तृप्र इव. The latter reading has been accepted.

IV. I. P.M. मनोत्रुवाणे P.L.M. has the upper part of म and the superscript of औ, from which I make it सुनौ.

IV. 12. P.L.M. has a long lacuna. P.M. पइयांस. The letter resembling इ has been found several times in P.M. as an ornament. I have ventured to make it प्रियां सः

IV. 17. P.M. योक्तिताभ्यां. P.L.M. has lower part of यो, lower part of न्त्र, lower part of त, and lower part of भ्यां. I take the right-hand vertical line of यो to be the vertical remain of left-hand ि of न्त्रि. So the reading would be योन्त्रिताभ्यां. I suggest यन्त्रिताभ्यां. It may also be योक्त्रकाभ्यां, as the word योक्त्रक has been used in VI. 3. The त in P.L.M. is however distinct enough not to be क.

IV. 34. P.M. धर्म्मपीड़ां. P.L.M. धर्म्मयाच्ञां. This shews that P.M. is a copy of a manuscript other than our P.L.M.

V. 31. P.L.M. सविद्यो. P.M. स वैद्यो. The latter has been preferred because he has medicine in his hand.

VI. 16. Both the MSS. read यद्विश्रिष्टा. मद्विशिष्टा would give a better meaning.

VII. 6. P.L.M. absolute lacuna. I have changed

प्रियं भूः in P.M. into प्रियङ्गुं ; and प्रियं सप्रसवावदातां in the same into प्रियङ्गुप्रसवावदातां . As the verse stands in P.M., it gives no meaning. प्रियङ्गु, a flowering tree, is a great favourite with Sanskrit poets. It is a delicate plant and well deserves the epithets प्रतनुं and भीतामिव निष्पतन्तीं .

VII. 9. P.M. पुष्पोत्कुभरगा . In P.L.M. the whole line is a lacuna, with the exception of a cape-like projection containing the lower parts of रा and ला and the letters अ, पि and ना almost entire. Before रा there is a slight trace with a letter with an ākāra. It may be रा. So I take it to have been (पुष्पै) राराला . But as the letter रा with an ākāra interferes with metre, I have made it पुष्पैरराला, bending down with flowers.

In the same verse P.M. reads दन्तैः समुङ्गैः . It is not difficult to change ङ्ग into द्ग for a scribe who transcribes an old Newari MS. into modern Newari. I am tempted to make it समुद्ग, as the flowers of the Nāga or the Nāgakeśara tree look like a flowerpot made of ivory. Inside the flower it is yellow. Therefore the flowers of Nāgakeśara answers to the description दान्तैः समुद्गैरिव हेमगर्भैः .

VII. 11. P.M. reading is evidently the better one here. It shews also that it was copied from a MS. other than our P.L.M.

VII. 14. P.L.M. तान्तव and P.M. आश्मर . I do not know which reading to prefer. Along with wooden and iron chain, one would be tempted to prefer a chain made of stone. But I have preferred the P.L.M. reading, as that MS. is, as a rule, a surer guide than the P.M.

VII. 26. P:L.M. long lacuna. P.M. यतो which gives no meaning. I have ventured to change it into रतो .

VII. 30. P.L.M. lacuna. P.M. वेश्मवर्या. This is वेश्मवध्वा as वेश्मवधू is a word often met with in contemporary literature. In Buddhacarita it is used in this very connection. See 4. 16.

VII. 38. P.M. has नकाश्रशाङ्कस्य. P.L.M. has न almost entire, and of the next letter the subscript त is entirely visible with a convex curve and an आकार. I take it to be नप्ता. I am justified by the fact that Buddha's son was the grandson of the moon god as well as the explicit statement in Buddhacarita. See XIII. 12.

VII. 40. P.M. गङ्गाजलेनांग० P.L.M. गङ्गाजलेनङ्ग० which gives exactly the meaning wanted.

VIII. 5. P.L.M. long lacuna. P.M. रजस्तमसत्त्व. सत्त्व with a guru श्र in स spoils the metre. I have changed it into रजस्तमःसतां. It saves the metre. But सत् as a substitute for सत्त्व is unusual. There is something like a dot in the centre of the vertical line of र. But I am sure it cannot be read as. रु. It is a very doubtful passage.

VIII. 34. P.L.M. lacuna. P.M. कुराजा which spoils metre, sense and grammar. I have ventured to suggest सुजनाः which saves all the three.

VIII. 38. P.L.M. complete lacuna. P.M. वखिता वनितेव चञ्चला तदितरेष्विवनावद्यते. The fourth pāda has a letter less, and as it stands, it gives no sense. I have changed it as in the text. वद्यते has been changed into विद्यते and a न has been placed before विद्यते to supply the shortage of letters wanted in the metre. ष्वि has been changed into षु and ना into ने. These suggested changes have at least one recommendation. It gives a good sense. In the third pāda I was almost tempted to change वखिता into वनिता. But P.M. is against it.

VIII. 40. P.M. सूतवत् which is nonsense. P.L.M. has the lower parts of the two letters before वत्. The subscript र in the second letter is distinctly visible with a faint trace of उकार, which has suggested श्रु and the first letter has turned out to be the lower part of श.

VIII. 42. Of this verse P.L.M. has only न वहन्ति सोऽहं fully and distinctly visible. In P.M. this portion has been written in a very bad hand by one who knew no Sanskrit. The first half of the verse as it stands in P.M. runs thus:—प्रविशत्यपि हि स्त्रियश्चितामवधन्त्यपि मत्कृजीविताः। प्रविशति is certainly wrong as स्त्रियः, the subject, is in plural. So I read प्रविशन्ति. अवधन्ति is wrong. I have suggested अनुबध्नन्ति as a correct Sanskrit plural verbal form consistent with metre. मत्कृ has been changed into मुक्त.

VIII. 44. Covered by a long lacuna in P.L.M. P.M. has श्वपचं किलशो जिसुता, which has been made शक्रजिसुता; and प्रमदानाच गति न्न विद्य which has been changed into प्रमदानामगतिर्न विद्यते.

VIII. 45. P.L.M. has श्च गोतमः समवापूर्वनितोद्धतं रजः. A little before this we have subscript उ at the end of a vertical line with a concave curve faintly visible. This I take to be सु. After this letter, there is a vertical line representing the lower part of medial इ and the lower part of न. Then the lower part of र with a medial उ hanging from the middle of its vertical line; and after that there is a subscript र. Next to this there is a subscript त. I have made the last two letters द्भ्रान्त. Then there are three vertical strokes of मना. The whole would read रुद्भ्रान्त मना. P.M. reads मुनिरखंतवाच गोतमः. One would be tempted to read मुनिरभ्रान्तमनाश्च. But I could not accept this reading, as there is a medial उ after र and the ākāra in भ्रान्त would come down vertically to the foot of the line. But it is not so. In the P.L.M., the 'Ā' stroke in भ्रा need not come down so low. It generally comes down from the mātrā to a little above the subscript म.

VIII. 47. In P.L.M. भ्रय is visible, the lowest parts of सूक्ष्म are traceable. Then after a short complete lacuna the lowest parts of श्र and य are visible. Before श्र, the very lowest part of a vertical stroke is traceable. In P.M. the reading is भ्रय शुक्ष्ममतीह्वयांश्र घृक्. But it is not justified by the traces in P.L.M. So I have made it सूक्ष्ममतिः प्रियाश्रया. In the next line I have changed व्रतं or त्रतं in P.M. into चरितं, thus saving the metre. Anyone having some experience of modern Newari manuscript, will, I believe, sympathize with me.

IX. 18. P.L.M. तुरंग० and P.M. तरंग०. Both readings are equally acceptable. But I have preferred तरङ्गराजस्य, as I know of a fight between Śrīkṛṣṇa and Samudra, but I know of no fight between a horse and Śrīkṛṣṇa.

IX. 23. P.M. ०द्विपानरान्. From which I made it ०द्विपान्नरान्. But P.L.M. has a better reading, द्विपानरीन् [which is incorporated in the text].

IX. 36. P.L.M. complete lacuna. P.M. ०शरीरे न यशोऽस्ति. I have made it शरीरं न यशोऽस्ति.

IX. 45. Both the MSS. have चमं. So I have kept it. But चयं would give a better meaning, specially when read with the next line.

X. 9. P.L.M. covered by a long lacuna. P.M. तापीकृताश्रो. This has been changed into पीतीकृताङ्गो. For, the lion covered with मनःशिला, etc., is compared to golden leaves.

X. 26. P.M. °विराजनाजायते, from which I have made विराजन् प्रजायते. But on a closer inspection of P.L.M. it turns out to be विराजन् राजायते. Corrected in the erratum. [Corrected in the *text* in the present edition.]

X. 56. Both P.L.M. and P.M. बोढ्रेन. This is in the 7th case-ending which is ungrammatical. I think it is the 6th case-ending of वोढु, a great Sāṃkhya teacher of antiquity. His name is sometimes written as बोढ्रुन.

X. 57. यामी in both MSS. But यामी is very unusual. I have changed it into यायी with future णिन्, having in view लब्धा in the next line, which is in future तृन्.

XI. 15. Both MSS. read सचते. But as it cannot be construed, it has been changed into सचतां.

XI. 20. Both MSS. read तद्रुजः. But in connection with औषध, रुजः as in the text seems to me to be a better reading. In P.M. in the middle of the vertical line of र there is a dot which is not, however, a medial उ..

XI. 29. P.L.M. मघ्येव and P.M. मभ्येव. Both are unmeaning. A slight alteration in P.L.M. would make it मध्वेव which gives a better sense; as the honey-seeker in hilly tracts looks upwards for honey-combs, and thus fails to notice precipices.

XIII. 53. P.L.M. lacuna. P.M. संयोगः which destroys the metre. I have made it सङ्गः, which improves the metre as well as the sense.

XIII. 55. This is a peculiar metre. The first line contains 15 syllables, the odds being *guru* and the evens *laghu*. The second line contains 16 syllables with the odds *laghu* and the evens *guru*. The third corresponds to the first and the fourth to the second. On this principle I had to add a क at the end of the second line. It was जिक्रै: in P.M. Both being *guru* I have added a क and made जिक्रकै: . The fourth line in P.M. has only 14 syllables. I had to restore a इ both for the sense and the metre and to change चिकित्सेत् into चिकित्सयेत् for the sake of the metre. P.L.M. complete lacuna.

XIII. 56. P.M. मास्मिन्नवेत्तणेमपि which gives no sense. I have adopted the P.L.M. reading.

XIV. 47. P.M. त्तण्यते . P.L.M. has only the superscript ए of ते.

XV. 16. P.M. स्वमनोद्रुश्ठ चेतसः . P.L.M. has in a projection in a long lacuna, only three letters, superscript स with anusvāra, म and नो . I have rendered it स्वं मनो दुष्टचेतसः .

XV. 18. P.M. नति . Following the use of classical Sanskrit I have made it रति . But नति in the sense of परिणति is often used in Buddhist Sanskrit.

XV. 22. P.M. नत्वेककुशलं, which does not come in quite correctly at a place when अकुशलकर्म्म is the subject of teaching. I have changed it into नत्वेवाकुशलं .

XV. 25. P.M. म्द्वतोगर्तः खनन्निव . I have changed ओकार in तो of म्द्वतो, into ईकार .

XV. 50. P.M. लोके चित्रेषु मा कृथाः P.L.M. लोकचित्रेषु which gives better sense.

XVI. 6. Both MSS. अप्रतिवेधतः . But अप्रतिबोधतः would give a better meaning. The use of अवबुद्ध्य and प्रतिबुध्य in the previous verse justifies my observation. But it is difficult to go against both the MSS.

XVI. 11. Both the manuscripts read शरीरयोनिः . But I believe it to be the adjective of दुःखं . So I have made it neuter.

XVI. 14. Both the MSS. अवेहि which is wrong in classical Sanskrit.

XVI. 23. P.L.M. lacuna. P.M. अवेत्य which I have adopted in the text, though it is wrong in grammar.

XVI. 26. P.L.M. धर्म्मं and P.M. धर्म्म. Both may be correct, as the author uses both the vaidika form of धर्म्मन् and the classical form of धर्म्म.

XVI. 27. Both MSS. व्याधियोः. I have made it classical Sanskrit व्याधयो.

XVI. 41. P.L.M. अपि मार्गसत्ये P.M. अभिमार्गसत्ये. I prefer the reading of P.L.M., as a cumulative conjunction is necessary here.

XVI. 74. P.M. मूर्च्छति. P.L.M. the upper part of a न with रेफ and एकार, the top of a letter, then ति almost entire. I have, therefore, adopted the P.L.M. reading नैच्छति.

XVI. 76. In P.L.M. nearly the whole of the two pādas are a lacuna. P.M. कण्ठे which gives no meaning. But कपवे and कण्ठे in P.M. handwriting are so near that I have made it कपवे, which means पापे and which fits with the context.

XVI. 83. P.M. दन्तेऽपि दत्तं which gives no meaning. P.L.M. the upper part absolutely gone; the lower parts of the 2nd and the 5th letters are the same. So I have made it दन्तेऽपि दन्तं.

XVI. 87. Both the MSS. ०क्रमिल० which spoils the metre. I have therefore made it ०क्रिमिल०.

XVI. 90. Both MSS. कफिणः which spoils the metre. I have made it कफ्फिनः, as that appears to be the name (Mitra—*Sans. Buddh. Lit. of Nep.*, p. 38). It is also justified by the name of a work entitled कफ्फिणाभ्युदय discovered in Madras and Uḍiṣyā. [This probably refers to the *Kapphaṇābhyudaya* of Śiva-svāmin—Keith, *Hist. Sans. Lit.*, pp. 133-4.]

XVII. 43. Both MSS. कामाग्निदेहेन. But would not ०दाहेन be preferable ?

XVIII. 31. P.M. शुद्धोदनोमनृपति. P.L.M. has a long lacuna here with a cape-like projection in which are distinctly visible नृपतिः पितेति. I change म into मे and read शुद्धोदनो मे नृपतिः पितेति.

XVIII. 62. I have restored जनान् for the metre.

XVIII. 63. मोषात् I have changed into मोच्छात् as scribes in Nepal for many centuries freely interchange क्ष. च्छ and ष.

# EMENDATIONS

## I

1a गौतमः H, J
2a यस्ततं (?) H
यः सततम् P
०यद्यः स० J
प्रततं (?) Jn
c समियाय H
अभिश्राय (?) P
3a हविःषु J
हवींषि Japp
b ०मधुच्चुत् J, G2
०मभौच्चौत् H
5d ०माश्रमो G2, P
7a ०स्सैव तैः (?) Jn
c असंकीर्णैः or असंकीर्णाः P
10c तपोवृद्धैः H
तपोमृगैः G2
तपोभृद्भिः J
11d यत्र J, G2
13a क्रूरमृगाः (?) G2
14a ०प्यपुन० J
16b सुबुद्धयः H
19d श्रियास्व (?) P
21b नाभिषेहिरे or
नाभिपेदिरे Jn
c गुरुगोत्रादतः J
24d शाक्या इव भुवि स्मृताः Nandargikar (referred to in G2).
25c मुनिरूर्वैः H
मुनिरूर्द्ध्वं J
मुनिरौर्वैः Jn
27c शान्तं गुप्तं च G
28a ०कलषं H, P, J
29a या पतेत् H, J
30d शीघ्रवाहान० H, P
31c सदाश्रम० (?) G
तां तु G, H
तदाश्रममहीपांसुम् (?) P
०ही प्रान्तं J
32b सरलीकृत H
c तानुवाच H, P
35a बद्धगोधाङ्गुलित्राणाः G2
b धृतविस्तृतकार्मुकाः G2
हस्तविष्ठित० J
c शराध्मातमहातूणा H, B, J
d व्यायताविद्धवाससः G
०बद्धवाससः J
37b क्रुद्धान् G

| | | |
|---|---|---|
| 38b | स्मून्यचैतसैः (?) | P |
| 39b | ०बुद्धयः | G2 |
| 45c | प्रभावेन for प्रभावेण | Jmp |
| d | भृत्यदण्डान् | J |
| 46c | अतिष्ठिपन् यत्र | H, P, J |
| | अतिष्ठिपन् | P |
| 47a | यत्र ते० or यस्मिंस्ते० | G2 |
| d | सचिवान् स्वान् | G2 |
| | सचिवांश्च (?) or सचिवांस्तु (?) | Jn |
| 50c | अत्ययाः | H |
| | G does not support the emendation of Hultzsch. | |
| 52c | ०र्थिविभव० | J |
| d | ०ज्ञात्यगौरवम् | Jn |
| 54d | आस्थानं | Gu |
| 56b | ०चीकरन् | H, J, P |
| 60a | ०रपि राजपुत्रै० | H |
| | तन्नाथत्वैरपि | J |
| c | दीप्यमानम् | G2 |

## II

| | | |
|---|---|---|
| 1b | कुलक्रमात् | B, J |
| 2a | ससञ्जे | B, P |
| | ससज्ञे | H, J |
| 6d | ०तान्वगम० | J |
| 8d | यस्य | G, J |
| d | ०मेयिवान् | J |
| 10d | ०हास्थितान् | B, J |
| | स्थितान् probably correct | P |
| 11ab | यस्य यच्छीलम् | G3 |
| 12d | नापैष्ट | H |
| | न व्यैष्ट | J |
| 13a | इत्यावाप्तीत् | G, J |
| | अराप्तीत् | P |
| c | न ह्यवाङ्क्षीच्चुरतः | H, J |
| 16c | अजैषीत् (?) | G2 |
| 17a | अम्लासीत् or अग्लासीत् | G |
| c | यष्टो लोभात् | B |
| 18b | मित्रेषु | G2 |
| d | स्वार्थम् | G2 |
| | स स्वम० | Happ |
| | स्वं स्वम् | J |
| 19d | चौरतर्षेण | J |
| 20a | बलिं | G, J |
| | नास्पृक्षत् (?) | G2 |
| 21c | नाधुक्ष० | J |
| 22d | इवोरगम् | G |
| 23a | नाक्रुक्ष० | G, S, H2, J |
| | नाक्षप्सत् | P |
| | नाक्षक्ष० | Jn |
| 24c | अदर्षीत् | G, J |
| 28b | अबीभवत् | G2 |
| d | अवापिपत् | H |
| | रात्रिचरसान् | Gu |

| | | |
|---|---|---|
| 29b | अबीभवत् | G2 |
| b-d | अवापिपत् | H |
| 30a | अतीटपत् | H |
| | अपप्रथत् supported by | G2 |
| 31b | सामं for सोमं | Jmp |
| d | सस्यम् | G, S, J |
| | कालं सस्यम् | H2 |
| | स स्वम॰ | Happ |
| 32ab | ॰मचकथन्न कथाम॰ | H |
| 33a | बलेर्न | H, S |
| 34a | अदीदिपत् | H |
| c | ॰तीतपत् or ॰पीपिडत् | H |
| 37b | अवापिपत् | G3 |
| | अवीवसत् | J |
| d | अवीवहत् | G2 |
| | अवीविशत् | H |
| | अवीवसत् | J |
| 38a | श्लक्ताम् | G3 |
| | ॰क्तत्येषु | G3 |
| 39b | अदीदहत् | G |
| | अबीभयत् | H |
| 42a | मार्यादा for मर्यादा | Jmp |
| 43d | विक्रिया | G |
| | निक्रियाः | J |
| 45b | वभूवासुलभैर्गुणैः | H, J |
| c | अशक्यशक्र॰ | G |
| | अशक्यशक्त॰ | H |
| c | अशक्यः | Japp |
| 46d | ॰चर्यां | P |
| | ॰चर्यां (?) | Jn |
| 49c | वीतक्रोधतमोमाया | H, J, P |
| 53b | पुष्पवर्षं | J |
| 54c | ॰भ्यधिकं | H, J |
| 55a | चैव | G |
| c | सद्धर्म॰ | H, P, J |
| | सद्धर्म (?) | S |
| 56a | यशःकेतुः | G |
| b | ॰केतुधरः | Jn |
| 61b | भवाय तौ | J |
| 62d | ॰पारियात्र॰ | H |
| 64b | ॰हृत्वाः | H |
| | ॰च्चित्तः | J |
| c | ॰जात॰ | G |
| | हृदयगतपरदृष्णौ | J |
| d | ॰भयमभितो | H, J |
| 65b | ॰ङ्नास्वनास्थः | P, Japp |

## III

| | | |
|---|---|---|
| 2a | ॰स्तपसि तांश्च | H, Ja, J |
| | ॰स्तपसितांश्च | S, P |
| b | प्रेक्ष्य placed at the end of the first line whereas it should begin the second | S, J, H, P |

| | | |
|---|---|---|
| 3b | तथोद्र्कं | J |
| d | तप इति | P, H, J |
| | °द्र्कम् | J |
| 5a | नैष मार्गं | H |
| c | ध्यानविषयम् | P, J |
| d | वराङ्गम् | G, S, H2, J |
| 6a | °पीत | G3 |
| 10d | वराणसा° | P, H |
| | वराणसी° | J |
| 11b | नेमिवत् | H |
| 13c-d | °मतिर्विनिनाय | H |
| | °मृषिर्विनिनाय | J |
| 14c | °तरङ्गचलं | H, S, J, P |
| d | चात्यतारयत् | P |
| | चोदतारयत् | G3 |
| | च व्यतारयत् | J |
| 15d | जिहृत्तया | H |
| 16d | विजघान (?) | Jn |
| 17c | वस्तु | J |
| d | निःस्पृहतया | H, J |
| 18b | नियतमतिः | G3, P, J |
| d | इव | H |
| | स्वदेशवदमित्रवास्तुषु | Ja |
| | स्वजन स्वदेश[⏑ ⏑] | P |
| | स्वजनस्वदेशजनमित्र-वस्तुषु | J |
| 19d | दुःखसुखयोश्च | H, J, P |
| 21a | अवेक्ष्य | G, P, J |
| b | °मानसम् | H |
| | °माशया | J |
| c | शेषमपि च | H, P, J |
| 22c | °गतिरशयिष्ट | G2 |
| | °मतिरशयिष्ट | H, J |
| 23d | पुनरुज्ज्वलन्नव | Ja, J |
| 26c | तत्प्रसवे | H |
| | तत्प्रसवम् (?) | P |
| | तत्प्रवणम् | J |
| 27b | °सिद्धये | G3, P, Japp |
| d | ततो (?) | G3 |
| | स सुतो (?) | P |
| 29c | नियमविधिमा मरणात् | H |
| d | दध्यिरे | H |
| | दध्रिरे | Ja, P, J |
| 30d | °रुपासकः (?) | P, Jn |
| | °रुपासकः | Japp |
| 31a | कृश° | S, H, P, J |
| d | हि विव्यथे | G, J |
| 32d | परमा हि ता | H |
| | परमं हि ता | J |
| | °माहिता (? ?) | P |
| 33c | च न | H |
| | श्लक्ष्णमपि च न | P, J |
| 34b | गृद्धमानसः | G2, J |
| 35b | सद्गुणो | H, J |
| | सद्गुणोऽप्यचिन्तयत् (?) | P |
| 37c | गुणोऽपि | J |
| 39a | अकथंकथा गृहिणा | H, P, J |

| | | |
|---|---|---|
| d | पुरे | G2 |
| 40a | विषयेषु | S, P, H2 |
| 41c | तत्र च सुसुख॰ | P, J |
| d | कृतयुगे मनोरिव | H, S, P, J |
| 42b | ॰पूरुपुरोपमं | H, P, J |
| c | अभवदभय॰ | H, P, J |
| d | वीतरागे | H, P, J |

## IV

| | | |
|---|---|---|
| 2c | वैश्रवणम् | G2, P |
| d | कुत एव धर्मं | J |
| 3b | भामिनीति | G2 |
| c | भामेन | Gu |
| | भासेन (?) or भावेन (?) | Jn |
| | मानिनीति | G2 |
| d | यातो | J |
| 4b | ॰त्युन्नत॰ | J |
| c | ॰सुकुलो॰ | H |
| | सकलो॰ | Gu |
| 5d | पुरुषस्तु | G2 |
| | ॰श्रीः पुरुषस्तु (?) | P |
| | स्त्रीषु नरेषु | J |
| 8b | ॰नन्द्यो॰ | Japp |
| d | तद् अन्धभूतम् | Jn |
| 9b | परस्परव्याहृत॰ | H, J |
| 10c | ॰स्वाभि॰ | J |
| 11c | ॰ऽन्योन्यविनोदनेन | J |
| | ॰बलाहरेण or ॰विनोदनेन | Jn |
| 14a | निरूपयन्ती | H |
| | निरूपयाणा | S |
| | निरीक्षमाणा | J |
| b | सापि | G2, J |
| c | ॰बाष्पेण | Gu |
| d | किञ्चिच्छुचित्वं नि॰ | Gu |
| 15c | भूत्वा च (?) | G |
| d | भ्रकुटिं | J |
| 16c | पचाञ्जलिं | Gu |
| 17a | ॰योक्त्रिताभ्यां | J |
| | ॰योक्त्रकाभ्यां | Happ |
| b | ॰वरा (?) | G2 |
| 20d | समापयामास | H, J |
| 21b | ॰धरौष्ठं | J |
| 22b | तद् आमण्डनसाक्षि-भूतम् | G |
| | तद् आमण्डनसाचि-भूतम् | H, J |
| 23a | तत्कुण्डलोदस्त॰ | H |
| | ॰लादष्ट॰ | J |
| 26a | ॰ङ्गविलेपनं | H, J |
| | ॰नुविलेपनं | Japp |
| c | अयोजयन् | Jn |
| 27b | ललितं | J |
| 33a | परिसस्वजे for परिषस्वजे | Jmp |
| 35d | चालपेयम् | G, J, Ja |

| | | |
|---|---|---|
| 36b | मय्येष्यसि | G, Ja, J |
| d | विभूषितेन (?) | G |
| | निर्भूषणो॰ | J |
| 37b | ॰सवर्णांस्तनया | J |
| | जगाद | G, P, J |
| | चखड़े | Japp |
| 38a | ततः स्तनो॰ | P, H, J |
| | सत्कार॰ | J |
| d | तत्कार्यं (?) | Jn |
| 39b | ॰स्थिर॰ | G2 |
| c | ॰स्थिरो॰ | G2 |
| 41a | क्षातो॰ | J |
| b | रूच्च | H |
| 42d | तुरंस्त॰ | J |
| 43a | अदर्शनीभूय | G, H |
| | गते च तस्मिन् | G |
| | तूपगत॰ | P, J |
| | आदर्शीभूय गत॰ | S |
| b | सावततार | G |
| 44c | निवर्त्यमानः | G2 |
| | निवर्तमानः | G3 |
| 45b | ॰र्दितः | G3 |

## V

| | | |
|---|---|---|
| 2d | कृताञ्जलिं | P |
| 3a | बुद्धस्ततस्तत्र | H, P |
| | बुद्धस्तुभं (? ?), | |
| | बुद्धस्तु तत् तत्र | G |
| 5a | निर्मुमुक्षुं (?) | Jn |
| 7b | पटावृतांसो | H, J |
| 8d | कच्यामवृतो or | |
| | कच्चामवृतो | G |
| | कच्यामवृतो | J |
| 10a | प्रणातेन | G, J |
| d | नाद्याग्रकालं | G2 |
| 11d | पुष्करपत्त्र॰ for | |
| | पुष्करपत्र॰ | Jmp |
| 13a | ॰स्वस्त्वन्य॰ | J |
| 15b | म्रदु | J |
| c | स पश्च | G |
| | गतं च | H |
| | ॰नुकूलान् विषयान् | |
| | सितश्च (?) | P |
| | ॰कूलं विषयात्मकं | J |
| 18d | तं स्नेह॰ | G2 |
| d | संक्लेशपच्चान् (?) | P |
| | तं स्नेहपङ्कान् | J |
| 22c | ॰वस्थासु हि (?) | Jn |
| 24d | विद्यारति॰ | J |
| d | माऽरतिभ्यः | P |
| 25c | क्रियाभ्यः | G, P, J |
| d | ॰मिन्द्रियाणा॰ | J |
| 27a | जरासमा | H, S |
| 30b | नो शान्ति॰ | Ja |
| | नो त्वान्ति | J |
| | निष्क्रान्ति (or नैष्क्रम्य) | |
| | विशास्य हि or | |
| | विशा इह (?) | Jn |
| 31a | स वैद्यो | G2 |

| | | |
|---|---|---|
| | सविद्यो | H, P, J |
| c | ०नपेक्षोज्झित० or ०नपेक्षाजित० | G |
| | ०नपेक्षो० | P, J |
| 37a | ०तेऽजिता० | J |
| d | किं ते | G |
| 39b | तत्त्यागक्षतं | H, J |
| d | मुमुक्षो० or देहं मुमूर्षो० | G |
| 41d | प्रसन्नः (?) | G |
| 44d | यदा | Japp |
| 45b | क्षिप्रम् | S, P, J, H |
| 46a | अमिष्टम् | G |
| 47a | विनिगर्ह्य (?) | G2 |
| b | ०त्यास्यपुट० | G, Ja, J |
| 48b | विगर्ह्य (?) | G2 |
| 49a | एवम् (?) or एष (?) | Jn |
| 51d | केशाश्रिया (?) | G2 |
| 52a | अधोद्दतं | Ja |
| | अधो नतम् | G, J |
| b | प्रवाप्यमाणेषु | H |
| 53a | तनु० | P |
| | ०स्तनस्तट०, ०विरक्त० | J |

## VI

| | | |
|---|---|---|
| 5d | सपादुकैकार्ध० | G, J |
| 6a | सबाष्पा | G |
| b | ०मभीप्समाना | H |
| d | व्रजन्ती | G2 |
| 7c | प्रसह्यैव | G2 |
| | प्रसक्तैव | J |
| | प्रीत्यां | Japp |
| 9c | चैव or चारु (?) | G3 |
| 10c | ०मुपोपविष्टा | J |
| 12b | ०विमुखे | G |
| 15c | तथैव | G |
| 16a | भावेन च मद्विप्रिष्टा | H, P, J |
| | मद्विप्रिष्टा | Happ |
| c | सोऽद्य सान्त्वम् (?) | Jn |
| 17b | सोपदेशः | J |
| | सोऽपदेशः | Jn |
| d | ननु मद् (?) | G |
| | अन्तताद् | G2, J |
| 18a | सेवार्थम् | G, J |
| 19a | एतं | G2 |
| d | जनवत्सलेन (? ?) | P |
| 20d | तां स्त्री | J |
| 21d | ०पश्यसि | H |
| | त्वमन्यथा यस्यसि कातराम्मिन् | S |
| | यास्यतिका० | J |
| 22a | दोषतो गाः | G, J |
| 26c | इव should not be missing | G2 |
| | पतिता चलाक्षी | H |
| | पतितेव लक्ष्मीः | J |
| 27c | ०श्रीं निहितां | H |

| | | |
|---|---|---|
| | ०श्रीर्निहिते | J |
| 31a | रुक्माङ्कपादे (?) | Jn |
| 32b | प्रभृतींश्च लीलाः | J |
| d | गौः ससाद | G2 |
| 33b | दरी गुहे० | Japp |
| 34b | दध्यौ | S, H2, J |
| 36d | तामनु दह्यमाना | H, J |
| 38c | पृष्ठतः | P, J |
| d | वचोऽभ्युवाच (?) | Jn |
| 43b | स्वस्थोऽपां० | Gu |
| d | विक्लवे | G |
| | विक्लवा | H |
| 49b | हतहृदया | H |
| c | ०मुखी | H, J |

## VII

| | | |
|---|---|---|
| 1a | स्वास्य or स्वात्म (?) | G |
| | ततः शास्त्रविधि० | Ja |
| | ततः शास्तृविधि० | P, J |
| | लिङ्गं ततश्शास्त्रविधि-प्रदिष्टम् | S |
| d | जेक्रीयमाणो | H, J |
| | क्रीयमाणो | P |
| 3c-d | Obscure | G |
| 4a | सायक | G |
| | पीतकच्चोद० | J |
| | च्चोभम्, च्चेपम्, पातम् (?) | G |
| c | निश्वस्वास | P |
| d | इवावबद्धः | G, J |
| 7d | स्युक्तांस्युकिट्टा० | J |
| 8c | कदैवं | G2, Japp |
| d | ०भवन्मास० | J |
| | ०भवेन्मास० | Japp |
| 9a | पुष्पोत्कमाला | J |
| | पुष्पैः कमाला | Japp |
| 10a | वसन्तोऽपि च गन्धपर्णा | J |
| b | ०वेश्या | J |
| 11a | कण्ठेश्च विनील० | J |
| 13a | व्यथैव्य० | G |
| 16b | गैच्यम् | G |
| 17b | द्विर्गुरुणा | H, J |
| | वै गुरुणा | P |
| | बद्धामनः | P |
| 20a | पर्वतनिर्झर० | G2, J |
| c | सक्तः | H, P, Gu |
| 22d | चङ्क्रम्यमाणाय | G, J |
| 23a | ०माणाय | J |
| b | वनं सपुष्पम् (?) | P |
| | फुल्लं | J |
| c | धैर्यं | G3, J |
| 26a | सूर्यः सरण्यूं | H, J |
| | स संज्ञां | Ja |
| b | तष्ट | Ja, J |
| d | यतो | H, P, J |
| 28b | वशिष्ठश्च | P |
| | सहरिष्ठः | J |
| | सद्द्वसिष्ठः (?) | Jn |
| 29c | सुतोऽस्य | G, J |

30b वेश्यवध्वा J
32c स्रुचम् P, J
34b शान्तोऽपि (?) Jn
37a प्रमदरायां H, J
c-d सर्पान्स्त्रीयं H
सर्पान् प्रियं G, Ja, J
सर्वान् दृढं or दीर्घं Ja
सर्वान् दृढं S
सर्पान् क्रियं न
रोषे न P, Japp
41a नृपस्य J
b साल J
d शान्तनु॰ J
42d ॰भिन्नमर्मा H
॰भिन्नवर्मा J
चित्तोद्भव॰ (?) P
43d आत्तसेनः P, J
44a शान्तनौ J
45a ॰र्दमनेन Jn
d विममर्श H
॰दसेव्यसेवी J
46c सन् G, S, H2, J
50d गृहारण्यभीयुः H, S
51b रामोऽन्ध J

## VIII

2b भ्रमम् H, P
तमः J
4b तूर्णमनून॰ Ja, J
5c ॰स्तमस्खतो॰ G2
॰स्तमस्विनो॰ J
6d मदा॰ J
7a चोदित॰ J
c करे करेण तं H, P, J
9c ॰वाग्विशदाय J
10a सदृशं खलु or बत G2
सदृशं हृदि (?) P
11b क्षमवादिनि H, J
25d न रतं न विद्यते G
न रतिर्न P, J
27a प्रहितस्य (?) Jn
30d प्रियां J
श्रियं Jn
32c च याः G2
33c ॰विचक्षणाशयाः H
॰विचक्षणाः शठाः J
34a कुलजाः H, J
स्वजनाः P
d ॰मङ्गनाः P, H, J
रभसात्तत्र G, P, J
35a वल्गुना H, G2, S, Gu, J
करोन्ति वर्णनाम् P
वर्णिना (?) F. W. Thomas in JRAS, 1911, p. 1125.
d हृदि हालाहलमेव केवलम् H
38a न चादरं (?) Jn
b क्वचित् H, J

| | | |
|---|---|---|
| c | बनिता | Happ |
| c-d | कलिता वनितैव चञ्चला तदिहारिष्विव नावलम्ब्यते | J |
| 39d | दृमतराश्च | G3, P |
| 40a | शत्रुवत् | G3 |
| b | भर्त्तृवत् | G3 |
| | पुत्रवत् | J |
| 41b | वने हि | G2 |
| 42b | अनुबध्नन्त्य॰ or अनुगच्छन्त्य॰ | G2 |
| | मुक्तजीवितान् (?) | G2 |
| c | चैव | G |
| | चैव यन्त्रणाम् | P |
| 44a | शोकजित्॰ | H |
| | सेनजित्॰ | J |
| b | चकमे मीन॰ | H, J |
| | वक [—] मीनरिपुम् | P |
| 45c | मुनिरुग्रतपाश्च | G3, J |
| | मुनिरश्रान्तमनाश्च | Happ |
| | मुनिरुत्कमनाश्च | H |
| 47a | ॰मतिप्रियाग्नयाल्॰ | P |
| b | ॰मति दयाग्निवं | J |
| | अतिदयाग्निवं | Jn |
| | लघु तासां | P, S, H, J |
| d | चलितम् | P |
| | ॰मस्तुर्चिं | J |
| | ॰ज्वलनं or ॰चपलं | G |
| 48a | प्रसाधने॰ | G |
| d | तमस्मावृतेच्छगाः | G3 |
| 49a | अम्बुभां | H |
| b | ननु | G3 |
| 52a | स्रवतीं | G2 |
| b | मध्वगो | J |
| | मद्दगो | Japp |
| 55c | भवनोत्सुकं | G2, J |
| 59b | भैक्ष्यं | P, J |

## IX

| | | |
|---|---|---|
| 1d | विमंशवदनः | H, J |
| | विमङ्क॰ (?) | P |
| 5c | इदं तत् | P |
| d | तथावबुद्ध्यमे | G, J |
| | यथावबुध्ये | G3, Japp |
| 6a | इमं (?) | G2 |
| b | नदीतटाशोकक॰ | P, H, J |
| 7a | ॰सम॰ | P, G2, J |
| 8b | ॰रूपमीयते | G, J |
| | ॰रूपनीयते | Japp |
| | ॰रूपपीड्यते | H2 |
| d | व्रजन् | S, H2, J |
| 9d | हि मन्यसे or विकत्थसे (?) | G |
| 12b | विरुद्धा | G, H2, P, S, J |
| | सद्भावरुद्धा (?) | Jn |
| d | ॰विधो | J |
| 13c | कदा च | G |
| | कदापि | G2 |
| | क्वचिच्च | J |

| | | |
|---|---|---|
| 14a | शय्यासन० | G2, P, J |
| 16c | ०स्वान्त० | S, H2 |
| 18b | तुरंगराजस्य | H, J |
| c | जराः | P |
| 22a | ते च | G |
| | वा न मन्यसे | J |
| d | न ते | G2 |
| 24d | शाम्बस्य | Japp |
| 28d | नृणां | G, J |
| 30b | निशाविवासे सुचिराद् | G3 |
| 31a | ०रत्यन्तरसप्रपीडितो० | J |
| 32a | ०पत्रमीरितम् | S, H2, J |
| 33b | वाच्छ्रुति० | J |
| 34a | दैविकम् | P |
| | विधिवत् स्वदैहिकं | G |
| | निधनस्य | J |
| c | बलवान् | S, G, P, H2, Gu, J |
| 35a | रक्तचेतसः | P, Jn |
| b | तव यः | S, H2, J |
| | शरीरसंज्ञे तव यः | P |
| | शरीरसंज्ञा तव यः | J |
| | शरीरसंज्ञस्तव | Jn |
| c | भयाद् | P |
| | शाम्यता भवेद् | J |
| d | चर्हति | S, G2 |
| | चार्हति | J |
| | चार्च्हसि | Jn |
| 36a | शरीरे न वशोऽस्ति | |
| | कस्यचिन्० | P, J |
| b | निरस्यमाने | P, J |
| 37c | ०स्रुचौ | J |
| 38a | बलिं | G |
| | बलीन् | J |
| c | वसनादि | J |
| 39a | तृणान्य० | H, P, J |
| 40a | ०मार्तं | J |
| 41c | तथानपेक्ष्य | P, J |
| 42b | ०नावगच्छसि | J |
| d | निगृह्यतां | G3, J |
| | सस्यलालसा | Japp |
| 44b | प्रधर्षणेनैव | G2 |
| | प्रतापनान्नैव | J |
| | प्रतापयन्नैव | Japp |
| 45b | तत्त्वयं | Happ |
| 46d | विषमा | G, J |
| 49b | ०धर्माभ्युप० (?) | G |
| | ०धर्मेऽभ्युप० | P, G2 |
| | ०धर्माद्युप० | J |
| 50c | ०ययौ न शर्म | H, J |
| 51b | गृहसुखेऽभिमुखं | G2 |

## X

| | | |
|---|---|---|
| 1b | भार्यां | H, P, S, J |
| 2c | स्त्रीविगतो | G |
| | स्त्रीविनतो | G2, J |
| 3d | मणिं | J |
| | मर्म | Gu |

| | | |
|---|---|---|
| | मौनं...मद्गु० | Jn |
| 4d | सरःप्रतीर्णा or सरोवतीर्णा | G3 |
| 5c | काञ्चनधातुमन्तं | H, J |
| 6c | आगम्य | J |
| 9b | पीताक्तांसो | J |
| d | रूप्याङ्गदं | H, J |
| | ०म्बिकस्य | J |
| 10b | कृतापसव्यः | H, J |
| d | ०म्योऽम्भ० | P, H, J |
| 11d | कुलोद्भूतां | G, J |
| 12b | मयूरपत्रो० | J |
| | ०लेखाः | J |
| | मयूरपित्तो० | Japp |
| 13d | पुष्पोत्काचानाम् | J |
| 14c | येभ्यः | G2 |
| 15a | अलसायमानां | Jn, Japp |
| 15c, 16c | सुषितैक० | G2 |
| 24a | वैडूर्य० | J |
| 25a | यत्रा० | H, J |
| b | सुषिरान् | J |
| d | ०याश्लिद० | J |
| 26d | राजायते | P, J |
| 27a | ०पीलहलै० | J |
| 28c | प्रावेश्व | J |
| | प्रयावेश्व | Jn |
| 29a | तथान्ये | G, P, J |
| | तथास्यैः | H |
| d | मनःस्रोत्र० | H, J |
| 31b | ०वर्गा ज्वलितै० | J |
| 32b | निगार्तयो | G |
| | Verse 33 occurs as 37 in J | |
| 38d | काड्गडव० | J |
| 39a | ताः निस्त्ता | J |
| 41b | ०धिष्ठितविस्फावास्यः | G3 |
| d | धृतिं चकार | J |
| 42a | मनुष्यो | H, J |
| b | ०कर्गोन्ति | P |
| 43a | ०ज्जिघांसु० | Jn |
| 44a | यथा प्रभाते | P |
| | यथान्धकारे | J |
| 45c | च मद्दौं | J |
| 48b | ब्रूहि यथार्थतत्त्वम् | H, J |
| | यथातथं त्वम् | S |
| c | एतावरं | G3 |
| 49a | ०प्सरस्त्वेव | G3 |
| | ०प्सरःस्वेव | P, J |
| 51c | तस्यां ततः | J |
| 53d | सदृत्ताग्रम् | H, J |
| | सदृत्त० | P |
| 54a | मा मुने | J |
| c | विमुक्तमानम | G |
| | विमोच्यामि | H, P, J |
| 56a | मदनाह्निना हि मा | H, S, J |
| c | वोढोर्हि | Happ, H, G |
| | ०र्थ्यपक्षात्मनो | G, J |

c बोध्यो० J
पाण्डो० Ja
57b यायां G
यामीह वसन्० J
c लब्ध्वा H, S, J
59b श्रुतचेतसी J
60a शक्यं हरितुं H
शक्या J
61d न चाप्य० P, J
62b कदाचिद्धि लभेत P, G, S, H2, J
63b चरस्व (?) G
यतस्व G3
यतस्व (?) Jn

XI

2a ०नैष्क्रम्य० J
5a स वृत्तेन P
6a स्वभावदर्शनीयो० J
7a प्रस्तरेष्वपि भार्यायां J
c इव तस्थौ or less probably इवाबभौ G
इवोत्तस्थौ J
13a साध्वनार्येण P, G, Ja, J
15b मन्तव्य० S, Ja
नावगन्तव्य० Jn
18a त्वा J
c विवक्षामि H
d यतो H, G, J

यत्ते Jn
यत्त्वाम् P
नार्हस्यु० H, G
20d तद्व्रजः P, J
21b सोऽभिहित० Ja
25a दुष्टो G
दृप्तो(?) P
स्तृप्तो J
27b कार्षकः J
d ०स्त्यक्तवानसि H, P, J
32c कामैः सतृष्णस्य G2, P, J
35c यत्र तत्र० G, J
36d तृष्णा चास्ति G, J
40a यदा H, J
41d किमास्वादं करिष्यति (? ?) G2
43c गते J
45a तथैवेलिविलो० J
46b ते ते चान्ये G2
ते चान्ये च J
d अत्यजन् H, P, J
49b ०स्य त्रिविक्रमः J
०स्येन्द्रविक्रमः Jn
51b ०मिह तावन्मु० G2, Gu, J
d ०देवत्व० G
०देवात्त० Gu
०देवानां (?) P
०देवान्ते J

| | | |
|---|---|---|
| 52a | ग्टह्णन्ति | J |
| d | मतिर्भवति नाशिनी | G |
| | घृतिः, नाशने | P |
| | नासने | J |
| 53c | अरिष्टानि | G2 |
| d | अनिष्टानि | G2 |
| 54c | यच्च | G, P, J |
| d | ०व विशिष्यते | J |
| 56-57 | Omitted in J as spurious (see Jn) | |
| 60c | ०नियमध्यानादिभिः | P, H |
| | ०नियमैर्ध्यानादिभिः | J |
| 61b | न रोधजनितं | H, J |
| | ०ऽजानन्तो | P |
| c | दिवि स्थायिनो | P |
| 62b | भ्राम्यमाणां | G, J |
| c | शिवममरजरं | H, J |

## XII

| | | |
|---|---|---|
| 3b | परिहासत्तमो (?) | P |
| | परिहाससहो | Gu |
| 4c | द्वेषाणुं | J |
| d | ०मेयिवान् | J |
| 6c | मिष्टाद० | Ja |
| 7c | तथानित्य० | H, S, P, J |
| 9c | वृद्धि० | G |
| | धातोरर्थं इवाख्याते | H |
| | धातुरेधिरिवा० | J |
| 10a | कामात्मनः | J |
| c | स्वस्थेषु | H |
| 16b | सुचलाचलम् (?) | Jn |
| 20a | ०विहृतो | G, J |
| | ०निहृतो | Jn |
| 21d | नैष्क्राम्या० | J |
| 24c | कामादिषु | Ja, J |
| 26a | अनर्हं सं० | G |
| | अनर्हसं० | J |
| d | ०स्व परा० | G, P, J |
| 27b | दुष्टुराहृतिः | H2, S, P |
| | दुष्करा घृतिः | J |
| d | पार्श्येनेव | G, Jn |
| | पथिनेव | J |
| 28b | विरुद्धा | P |
| 34b | अद्ध्यात्तं | J |
| 36b | श्रद्धा विशेषतः | G |
| d | इव स्वतः or इवाश्रितः | Jn |
| 39b | यतः | H, P |
| | ०त्यदा | J |
| 43d | ०त्त्यस्य (?) | P |

## XIII

| | | |
|---|---|---|
| 7c | मन्तुकाले | J |
| 13a | शुद्धः | P |
| 14a | दोषानां for दोषाणां | Jmp |
| 15a | प्राणाघात० | G, Jn |
| c | भेत्ता० | P, J |
| 17a | तथा (?) | G |

| | | |
|---|---|---|
| | दृष्टात् | J |
| 18d | परेष्वायत्त० | P, Japp |
| 19d | न गृहस्थता | G, J |
| 22c | संवेदः | H, Gu, J |
| 24a | प्रस्रब्धिः or प्रश्रब्धिः | H |
| | प्रश्रब्धिः | J |
| | कायमनसोः | G |
| 26a | अहृल्लेखस्य | Ja, J |
| | अविलेखस्य | Japp |
| 27b | शीलनं | H, P, J |
| c | सेवनं त० | H, P, J |
| d | निर्देशस्व | J |
| 29c | स्थानमथान्येषु | P |
| 31b | ०र्नाम्ने० | G, S |
| | शचीर्नाखो० | H |
| | शचीर्नाम्ने० | J |
| 33c | यत्र | P |
| | नित्यं तु (?), तत्रनिम्नस्तु, निम्नंस्तु | Jn |
| 36d | तैक्ष्णाग्रतः (?) | Jn |
| 41a | गोचरे स्वे स्वे | G2, J |
| | गोचरैः स्वैः स्वैः | Jn |
| b | ०हैन्द्रियैः | Jn |
| 48b | ०र्दितम् | P |
| 52b | रुज्यते | G |
| | प्रदुष्यति | J |
| 53d | योगो | Jn |
| 55 | Spurious | J |
| 56c | भव ह्वि (?) | P |
| | भव वि० | J |

## XIV

| | | |
|---|---|---|
| 1a | ०कवाटेन | J |
| 7a | अत्याक्रान्तो | J |
| 10c | अभिजाते | Jn |
| 12b | ०भ्युच्यते | G |
| | ०भ्यज्ञते | P |
| | ०भ्यज्यते | J |
| 13a | समतिक्रमणार्थ० | P, J |
| 16d | महौघस्य ति | P |
| 17d | ०स्योत्तितीर्षया | Jn |
| 20d | ०मयैः | J |
| 21a | हृदि यत्संज्ञिनः | P, J |
| c | ०संज्ञिन् तां | P |
| 32a | पूर्वं | J |
| b | ०णातिनाम्य तु | J |
| d | ०र्थं स्वतन्त्रिणा | J |
| | ०तन्त्रिणा | Jn |
| 33c | हृदये | H, J |
| d | शान्तमानसः | H, J |
| 34c | मनःशुद्धौ | G |
| 35ab | अथासनगतस्थानप्रेक्षित-व्याहृतादिषु | G, S, P, H2, J |
| a | आसनगतस्थान० | P |
| b | ०प्रेक्षितव्याहृतादिषु | P |
| 39d | विषमेषु | G2, P, J |
| | विषयेषु | Jn |
| 45b | तस्थिवान् | G |

| | | |
|---|---|---|
| | तिष्ठति (?) | P |
| | धिष्ठितः | J |
| c | कार्येषु (?) | Jn |
| 48d | पुष्टोदरा (?) | G2 |
| | क्वष्टोद्गता | Gu |
| | क्रुष्टादको | J |
| 50d | परेषां | J |
| | पराभ्यस्तं | [परायत्तं (?)] |
| | सङ्गं | Jn |

## XV

| | | |
|---|---|---|
| 8a | मोहधर्म्माणो | G2 |
| | मोषधर्माणो | J |
| d | बद्ध्यां | J |
| | वध्या | Japp |
| 14d | स स्नात | J |
| 15d | ध्यातुम् | G |
| 16d | स्वं मनः | Happ, J |
| 17b | मैत्रीं | H, P, J |
| 18d | नति॰ | P, J |
| 21c | पात्रीभावोपघातात्तु | P, J |
| 22a | ॰कर्मस्वविक्षेप॰ | J |
| b | वाभ्यस्तु॰ | G |
| | वास्वस्तु॰ | S, H2 |
| | स्वस्तु॰ | P |
| | चाभ्यस्तु॰ | J |
| 23c | तं (?) or तद् | Jn |
| 24b | चात्मनः | J |
| 25d | म्टद्गतो गां | J |
| 26b | ॰गुरु काष्ठवत् | S, H, J |
| 27a | लोष्टं | J |
| 31c | स्वजनः | H, S, P, J |
| 39b | रज्येत् | G2, J |
| 44a | ॰निवर्तांश्च | J |
| 45c | लोकं (?) | G3, Jn |
| | लोकं | Japp |
| 48a | ॰तत्त्वेन | J |
| 54d | अपेक्षते | P |
| 55c | स्वास्थ्यप्राप्ता | G, J |
| 63a | निःशौचं | P |
| | निःसारं | J |
| 65c | ॰पश्चात् | G2, J |
| 66a | ॰हेतोरपि | J |
| 69c | मनःशुद्धौ (?) | G |
| | मनःशुद्धो | J |
| | तमःशुद्धं (?) | Jn |

## XVI

| | | |
|---|---|---|
| 4c | निःसरणा॰ | G |
| | निःसरणा॰ | P |
| 5b | प्रतिवेध्य | P |
| 5b | प्रतिविध्य | J |
| 6a | ॰प्रतिबोधत॰ | Happ |
| d | ॰धिरुह्य | J |
| 7b | अवेहि | P, Japp |
| 10 | 'This looks like two verses telescoped into one' | Jn |

| | | |
|---|---|---|
| 12b | उष्णाम् | G |
| 14d | तथानागतम् | G |
| | ०प्यवेहि | P, J |
| 16a | ०नुरूपं | J |
| | ०नुरूपा | Jn |
| 18a | एतेन | G, J |
| 19b | यानासनादि० | G, J |
| 20b | स्वज्ञातिषु (?) | Jn |
| 21a | आघ्रायानाम् (?) | Jn |
| 22a | रोषाधिके, तीव्ररोष | G2 |
| 23b | तदागमाद् | G2, J |
| | तदागमे | H |
| c | अवेत्य | H, P, J |
| 27d | क्षेमं | P, H, J |
| 31d | कर्म० | J |
| 33a | सत्याधिगमाय | G, J |
| | सत्याभिगमाय | Japp |
| 34d | वर्जयन्ति | G |
| 35c | स्थितम् | G2 |
| 38a | अस्योपचारो | G |
| | ०पचारे | J |
| d | लोकप्रवृत्तावरतिः (?) | P |
| | लोकप्रवृत्तावरतिः | Gu, J |
| 44d, 45a | नान्दी० | G |
| 47a | धैर्यं (?) | Jn |
| b | चरस्व or यतस्व (?) | G |
| | घटस्वास्व० | J |
| 49b | कालो | S, P, H, J |

| | | |
|---|---|---|
| 50a | वत्सा गा | J |
| d | गा | J |
| 53a | यन्नियतं निमित्तम् | P |
| d | वायुना वह्निः (?) | P |
| | * * * ना वह्निः | J |
| 54a | नियतं नि० | P, H, J |
| c | निगच्छ० | G2 |
| | नियच्छेत् | J |
| d | प्रदीप्यमानोऽग्निरिवो० | J |
| 56c | मनस्तथा | J |
| 59a | रागोद्भव० | G, J |
| 60a | रागोद्भते | J |
| 62c | मैत्रा (?) | Jn |
| 63b | मैत्रास्युभा | S, H2, J |
| 66a | धमन्नकाले | P, J |
| b | जलं क्षिपन् | G |
| 69 | To be omitted | Jn |
| 70a | हन्याः | Jn |
| c | आरभेथा | Jn |
| d | न त्वेव | J |
| 72d | क्षिपेद्० | Jn |
| 73a | तथाप्यथाध्यात्म० | G2, J |
| | तवाथवा० | Jn |
| 76c | कण्ठे मनस्वीव | P, J |
| | युव | P |
| | युवा | J |
| d | अचाद्रुसै० | P |
| | अचाद्रुधैरप्रयतै० | J |
| 77a | रोषतोऽपि | S, G2 |

लेशतोऽपि H, J
दोषतो P
80b पराङ्मखाः for पराङ्मुखाः Jmp
81a ॰प्रभृतीनि G3, Japp
तीक्ष्णान् J
82a भावान्नैवो (?) Jn
82c प्रतिवध्यमाना for प्रतिबध्यमाना Jmp
85c याचागतः G2, P, J
86c प्रविवेकमत्र G
87a ॰क्रमिल J
॰क्रमिश्र Jn
c ॰वाष्पो॰ Japp
89ab ॰नन्दमाते उपालि॰ Japp
॰माता उपालि॰ T2
90a काश्यप औरुविल्वो H, J
91b ॰काप्यौ, ॰कुण्ठधानौ G
कौन्देय (?) T1
c ॰कौष्ठिलौ J
92d तां तन्नियतम् or तेषां नियतं G
सुखावृतैस्त्वं J
93d ॰सिद्धौ G
॰सिद्धा Japp
95c ततो S, H2
d ॰स्याच न J
98a व्याप्नोति G, J
c नरेन्द्रश्रियं G, J
d सर्वर्धयः J

## XVII

2d ॰दकमाव॰ G3
4a ऋजुं समग्रं S, P, H2, J
5a च्चिकीर्षु॰ J
तितीर्षु॰ Gu
c शीलेन शमेन G
d चेतःपरिकर्मभूमौ H, S, J
7c पर्याविलं Jn
9a मनःशमाय H, P, J
15c निःसरणात्मको (?) G
निःसरणात्मल॰ J
निःसरणात्मक॰ Japp
निःसरणा॰ P
16a स रूपिणां G, P, J
18c व्यहेतुकं P
19c सुखाख्या or सुखाख्ये G
सुखाख्या G2
सुखाख्ये J
21b एकं G
नैश्वर्य॰ H, P, J
22b निर्मथना॰ H, J
23a सज्ज्ञानपापः H, J
24d क्लेशास्त्र॰ Japp
26c सदृक्॰ G
28c प्रत्यात्मका॰ G

| | | |
|---|---|---|
| d | ज्ञानमुखस्य (?) | P |
| 30b | यथाभूत० | P |
| c | ज्ञानाश्रयां | G, P, J |
| 32b | धर्मम् | H, J |
| d | स प्रेच्छते | J |
| 33c | चित्तदृष्ट्या | H, J |
| d | शास्त्रज्ञतया | H, P, J |
| 34b | आर्यतत्त्वम् | G |
| 35c | वस्त्राद् | G |
| | भक्त्वा | J |
| | भक्त्वा or कृत्वा | Jn |
| | घृणां क्लेशविजृम्भितेषु | J |
| 36a | त्वक्स्नायु० | P, J |
| 37d | प्राप द्वि० | G2, J |
| | आर्यधर्म्यम् (?) | Jn |
| 38d | योगायुधास्त्रैः | P, J |
| 43a | कामाग्निदाहेन | Happ, P, J |
| 45d | चित्ताम्भसः | P, G2, J |
| 46b | बाधं | G, J |
| 49c | प्रीतावतः | G2, J |
| 51d | मैत्राम् or मैत्रीम् | G2 |
| 52a | सुखेऽपि | P |
| b | शान्तम् | G, J |
| | परां | P |
| 56a | निश्रित्य | P, J |
| c | सहायमित्वा, ०मिरुं, ०मिच्छन्, ०मिच्छेत्, ०मत्र (?) | G2 |
| | सन्धाय मैत्रं | J |
| 62c | ०कार्यो | J |
| 68c | पारमिवाज्ञवाकात् (?) | P |

## XVIII

| | | |
|---|---|---|
| 2a | सुखं | G, J |
| | क्षमं (?) | G |
| 2a | ०समाप्ति० | G, H2, P, S, J |
| | Four pādas missing between 2b and 2c | P |
| 3b | ०त्तमाङ्गे० | J |
| | इड्याम् | J |
| | ईडाम् | Jn |
| | इज्याम् | Japp |
| 4a | यस्यार्थे० | J |
| b | न तस्य or तस्यापि | G2 |
| 7a | या दृष्टि० | J |
| 8a | ०कथाभाव० | J |
| 10a | ०जन्मन् | G2, J |
| d | प्रसूतो० | G |
| | ०षु भूतो० | J |
| 11d | ०वर्णाम् | G |
| | उत्तम वत्सवर्णैः | Japp |
| 12a | ममायं | H, J |
| 14a | उर्व्यादिकान् | P, J |
| b | कश्चित् | G, P |
| c | सक्ति० | G2, P, J |
| d | काये च | Japp |
| 16a | उदयं व्ययश्च (?) | P |
| | उदयं व्ययश्च | J |
| | व्ययश्च or क्षयश्च | Jn |
| | सान्तं | S, H2 |

17b निःसारमसत्त्ववन्तम् (?) P
c विरुद्धम् G, P
19a अनिश्रित° P, J
20c °चन्दनाक्तो S, P, H, J
22a श्लिष्ट° P
25a अद्यार्थवत्ते J
27d कूर्मो युगच्छित् स G
28b रणाग्रीरुडस्थूरः P
रणाग्रीर्षस्थूरः H2, S, J
31a अद्यापदेष्टुं J
d कुलापदेशाः J
34a तु H
a-b दर्शनीयः स्वलंकृतः S, H, J
b स्वलंकृतः (?) P
36a मन्ये Gu
b निमीलितं वास्ति (?) तवैव G
निमीलितं चास्ति (?) तवैव G
43a अतो हि J
अहं हि Jn
c न श्रमम् G2
नाश्रयं H2, S, J
44b °देवता° (?) P
45c स्वधीतम् G
सुधीरम् J
'स्वाधीनम् gloss on विधेयम् ? ?' G2
46c तथोत्तमं J
47c मुनेः (?) Jn
50d सुदेशिकस्येव H, P
सुदैशिकस्येव J
51b °मानसः G, P, J
c तथावबुध्यसे G, J
तथावबुध्यते P
52b चेयम् P, J
53b प्रमादाधिगमेन H2, P, S
प्रमादोऽधिगमे च J
d न तर्हि भक्तावभि° (?) P
भक्तास्व नियोग° J
55c मध्यमो P, H, J
56a स तूत्तमो G, J
स भूतले H
स उत्तमो P, S
c स्वगतं H, P
°त्वमगतं J
सुगतः S
57b अव्यथः Jn
58c इमां G
62a स पुरं J
d °परान् G2, J
63a मोक्षार्थगर्भा कृतिः H, J
64b मोक्षे परम् P, H
मोक्षः पर° J
d चामीकरमिव H

| Size. | Contents. | Per unit of 96 or 100 pages. |
|---|---|---|
| Demy octavo .. | Oriental text only .. .. | Rs. 0-12-0 |
| | Text and translation, English notes, etc., mixed; or translation only .. .. | ,, 1-0-0 |
| Royal octavo .. | Oriental text only .. .. | ,, 1-0-0 |
| | Text and translation, English notes, etc., mixed; or translation only .. .. | ,, 1-4-0 |
| Quarto .. | Oriental text only .. .. | ,, 2-0-0 |
| | Text and translation, English notes, etc., mixed; or translation only .. .. | ,, 2-8-0 |

There are some exceptions to this scale, which in each case will be indicated in the price-lists. For the calculation of prices, each part of a unit in excess of the 96 or 100 pages counts again as a full unit.

Single issues may be bought separately, but three years after the completion of a work no complete sets are broken for the sale of loose component parts.

Each issue bears, besides its issue number, a fascicle number indicating its place in the work and volume to which it belongs.

**With the issue of this Notice all previous prices and price-lists are cancelled.**

CALCUTTA,
1st *January*, 1939.

The publications or information about them are obtainable from the Royal Asiatic Society of Bengal, No. 1, Park Street, Calcutta, or from the Society's Agents:—

MESSRS. LUZAC & CO., 46, Great Russell Street, London, W.C.

M. PAUL GEUTHNER, 13, Rue Jacob, Paris, VIe.

BUCHHANDLUNG OTTO HARRASSOWITZ, 14, Querstrasse, Leipzig.

MESSRS. THACKER, SPINK & CO., LD., 3, Esplanade, East, Calcutta.

*Residents of Europe should order from the Agents.*

When ordering direct from the Society the following rules should be observed:—

Orders should be addressed to the Royal Asiatic Society of Bengal and not to any Official by name or title.

All Cheques, Money Orders, etc., should be made payable to the "Treasurer, Royal Asiatic Society of Bengal".

Orders for books should be accompanied by a full name and address, legibly written, and should be sent on a separate sheet of paper containing no other communication.

In India, books are supplied by V.-P.P.

*Published by*

**Facsimile Publisher**
Ashok Vihar, Delhi-110052 (India)
Website: www.facsimilepublishers.com

*Distributed by*

**Gyan Books Pvt. Ltd.**
5, Ansari Road, Daryaganj, New Delhi-110002 (India)
E-mail: books@gyanbooks.com, Website: www.gyanbooks.com

9 789333 632324